2002

Beowulf

and the

MEDIEVAL PROVERB TRADITION

MEDIEVAL & RENAISSANCE

TEXTS & STUDIES

VOLUME 155

Beowulf

and the

MEDIEVAL PROVERB TRADITION

Susan E. Deskis

ᗰᗴᗞᎥᗴᐯᗩᒪ & ᖇᗴᑎᗩᎥᔕᔕᗩᑎᑕᗴ ᴛᗴxᴛᔕ & ᔕᴛᘎᗞᎥᗴᔕ
Tempe, Arizona
1996

Library of Congress Cataloging-in-Publication Data

Deskis, Susan E.
    Beowulf and the medieval proverb tradition / Susan E. Deskis.
    p.   cm. — (Medieval & Renaissance texts & studies ; v. 155)
    Includes bibliographical references and index.
    ISBN 0-86698-195-0
    1. Beowulf. 2. Proverbs—History and Criticism. 3. Gnomic poetry,
English (Old)—History and criticism. 4. Epic poetry, English (Old)—History
and criticism. 5. Literature and folklore—England—History. 6. Proverbs,
English—History and criticism. 7. Aphorisms and apothegms in literature.
8. Literature, Medieval—Themes, motives. I. Title. II. Series.
PR1587.P75D47 1996
829'.3—dc20   95-26147
                                                              CIP

∞

This book was produced by MRTS
at SUNY Binghamton.
This book has been made to last.
It is set in Garamond typeface,
smyth-sewn and printed on acid-free paper
to library specifications

Printed in the United States of America

Contents

FOR MY PARENTS

Preface

I am proud to thank Joseph Harris, director of the Harvard dissertation (1991) that formed the basis of this study, for his generous encouragement, learned suggestions, and friendly counsel. I am also grateful to Jan Ziolkowski, reader of the thesis, for his kind support and scholarly assistance. Whatever value is to be found in this book can be attributed to the direction given me by these two scholars; its faults I have managed on my own.

Thomas D. Hill provided a great deal of help during the course of my work on this project; I thank him especially for his hospitality during the summer of 1992, when I completed some necessary research at Cornell University. That trip was made possible by a summer research grant from the Graduate School of Northern Illinois University. I am also grateful to Joseph B. Trahern, Jr., of the University of Tennessee, whose perceptive commentary allowed me to clarify and substantiate numerous points.

All translations in this volume are my own (except where otherwise indicated), and are intended as a convenience for the reader; therefore, I have attempted to render passages as literally as possible in order to point up similarities of word and phrase. The reader should note that I have usually translated sentences and phrases only at their first occurrence, and that I have not translated Middle English or any modern language. Corrections to some of my translations have been made by Professors Harris, Ziolkowski, and Hill, and also by Professors Philip Dust (Northern Illinois Univ.) and Eckehard Simon (Harvard); I am very grateful for their suggestions, and of course reserve to myself the responsibility for any remaining errors.

Finally, my greatest debt is to Mark and Hooter, who provided patient and good-natured support through several years of compulsive sententiousness.

Abbreviations

CCCM	Corpus Christianorum, Continuatio Mediaeualis
CCSL	Corpus Christianorum, Series Latina
CSEL	Corpus Scriptorum Ecclesiasticorum Latinorum
EETS	Early English Text Society
MGH	Monumenta Germaniae Historica
PL	Patrologiae Cursus Completus, Series Latina, ed. by J.-P. Migne, 221 vols. (Paris, 1844–64)

Beowulf

and the

MEDIEVAL PROVERB TRADITION

1

Introduction

The study of sources and analogues of *Beowulf* has a long and venerable history encompassing everything from biblical apocrypha to reconstructed folktales, and including an almost unlimited number of intermediate proposals. One might reasonably suppose that by this time every passage, even every line of *Beowulf*, had been fully documented and accounted for; however, such is not the case. At least one important facet of the poem remains to be integrated into its proper network of sources and parallels: that facet is the corpus of proverbial, sentential, or gnomic passages in *Beowulf*.

Several scholars have treated the sentential passages of *Beowulf*,[1] but they have all chosen to examine the sentences only as they function within the narrative, thematic, or stylistic structures of the text.

---

[1] See Kemp Malone, "Words of Wisdom in *Beowulf*," in *Humaniora: Essays in Literature, Folklore, Bibliography, honoring Archer Taylor* (Locust Valley, N.Y.: J. J. Augustin, 1960), 180–94; Robert Burlin, "Gnomic Indirection in *Beowulf*," in *Anglo-Saxon Poetry* (John C. McGalliard festschrift), ed. L. E. Nicholson and D. W. Frese (Notre Dame: Univ. of Notre Dame Press, 1975), 41–49; T. A. Shippey, "Maxims in Old English Narrative: Literary Art or Traditional Wisdom?" in *Oral Tradition/Literary Tradition: A Symposium*, ed. Hans Bekker-Nielsen (Odense: Odense Univ. Press, 1977), 28–46; and Catherine Karkov and Robert Farrell, "The Gnomic Passages of *Beowulf*," *Neuphilologische Mitteilungen* 91 (1990): 295–310. Also addressing the subject are Elaine Tuttle Hansen, *The Solomon Complex: Reading Wisdom in Old English Poetry*, McMaster Old English Studies and Texts 5 (Toronto: Univ. of Toronto Press, 1988); and Ursula Schaefer, *Vokalität: Altenglische Dichtung zwischen Mündlichkeit und Schriftlichkeit*, ScriptOralia 39 (Tübingen: Gunter Narr Verlag, 1992). Schaefer's book came to my attention too late for her findings to be addressed in this study.

Strangely enough, no one has attempted, at least in print, to identify the full range of possible analogues for these *Beowulf*ian proverbs. Several explanations may account for this scholarly vacuum. The first possibility might be that no sources or analogues *can* be traced for the passages that scholars have classed as "traditional" in nature, but the results of this study should eliminate such pessimism. Furthermore, a description of cognate sayings would seem to be required before one is entitled to attach the label "traditional" to any utterance. Perhaps more influential for *Beowulf*-studies has been the ambivalence with which scholars have addressed the gnomic passages of the poem.[2] Unsubtle pronouncements like "All men must die" have been considered unworthy of the *Beowulf*-poet, and hence ignored.

A third factor is the perception of proverb studies as falling within the domain of the folklorist. Consequently, literary scholars accustomed to tracing sources in Latin exegetical and homiletic writings tend to overlook both Latin and vernacular proverb collections, while folklorists often show a marked preference for the vernacular (and demonstrably oral), and a disinclination to consider Latin materials (or latterly, any historical topic at all). Thus, the huge corpus of Latin proverbs has been underutilized by students of Old English and paroemiology alike.[3] A related impediment to the study of medieval proverbs has

---

[2] Shippey ("Maxims in Old English Narrative," 42–46) discusses such attitudes and the cultural assumptions from which they stem. Non-narrative sapiential literature (i.e., gnomic poetry) has attracted similarly sporadic, but less ambivalent interest; see esp. Blanche Colton Williams, ed., *Gnomic Poetry in Anglo-Saxon* (New York: Columbia Univ. Press, 1914), (Williams treats *Beowulf* mainly on pp. 29–42); and Morton W. Bloomfield, "Understanding Old English Poetry," *Annuale Mediaevale* 9 (1968): 5–25, repr. in his *Essays and Explorations: Studies in Ideas, Language, and Literature* (Cambridge, Mass.: Harvard Univ. Press, 1970), 58–80.

[3] There are some notable exceptions to this trend: Latin and vernacular *sententiae* are treated together by Samuel Singer, *Sprichwörter des Mittelalters*, 3 parts (Bern: Peter Lang, 1944–47), and Joseph Harris makes extensive use of Latin proverbs in his " 'Deor' and its Refrain: Preliminaries to an Interpretation," *Traditio* 43 (1987): 23–53. A less speculative reason for the incomplete investigation of proverbial matter is the lack, until fairly recently, of research tools. Only the last quarter-century has seen the publication of Bartlett Jere Whiting's *Proverbs, Sentences, and Proverbial Phrases from English Writings Mainly before 1500*, with Helen W. Whiting (Cambridge, Mass.: Harvard Univ. Press, 1968), and that vast, though often intractable collection of Latin *sententiae* edited by Hans Walther and Paul Gerhard Schmidt (*Proverbia sententiaeque latinitatis medii aevi*, Carmina Medii Aevi Posterioris Latina, part 2 [Göttingen: Vandenhoeck & Ruprecht, 1963–69]). These tools, and others in various medieval European vernaculars, are indispensable for the study of the proverb tradition.

been the perceived distinction between learned and popular lore. Some students of the proverb have implied or insisted that the proverb is a popular genre, or a product of the people. Medieval Latin can by no stretch of the imagination be considered the language of the people, so it would follow that medieval Latin proverbs are not popular, and hence, not proverbs at all. Of course, not every scholar has taken this stance: Archer Taylor discusses some paradigms for the origin of a proverb, and notes that "learned" proverbs are merely "those with a long literary history," and that their origins are ultimately the same as for popular products. He concludes that "the distinction between 'learned' and 'popular' is meaningless and is concerned merely with the accidents of history."[4] More recently, Jan Ziolkowski has described the results of "cultural diglossia" in the European Middle Ages and its implications for an exchange between Latin and vernacular (especially oral) literature.[5]

One drawback to the existing studies of sententious statements in *Beowulf* has been the failure of their authors to describe those features that mark a sentence or phrase as "gnomic." As a result, each study has addressed a different corpus. Medieval proverbs and *sententiae*, particularly those embedded in a literary context, present special problems of interpretation; as no modern scholar can hope to attain the linguistic and cultural competence of a native speaker of Old English and participant in Anglo-Saxon culture, even the recognition of proverbs becomes a technical and methodological concern. Interpretation depends upon recognition.

Unfortunately, we have no authoritative definition of the proverb genre to guide us. Nearly every writer on proverbs has offered his or her own formulation, but none has been accepted as entirely adequate, and a thorough recapitulation of past pronouncements is unnecessary in a study such as this, in which such a definition is only an enabling condition.[6] Instead, I will discuss only those approaches which seem

---

[4] Archer Taylor, *The Proverb* (Cambridge, Mass.: Harvard Univ. Press, 1931), 4–5.

[5] Jan Ziolkowski, "Cultural Diglossia and the Nature of Medieval Latin Literature," in *The Ballad and Oral Literature*, ed. Joseph Harris, Harvard English Studies 17 (Cambridge, Mass.: Harvard Univ. Press, 1991), 193–213.

[6] For a concise review of paroemiological scholarship on definitions, see Carol R. Fontaine, *Traditional Sayings in the Old Testament: A Contextual Study*, Bible and Literature Series 5 (Sheffield: The Almond Press, 1982), 32–34; for a sampling of ancient and medieval definitions, see B. J. Whiting, "The Nature of the Proverb," *Harvard Studies and Notes in Philology and Literature* 14 (1932): 273–307.

most helpful in determining whether certain lines of *Beowulf* may
indeed be proverbial, and if so, how those passages may be further characterized within the context of the medieval proverb tradition.

For example, B. J. Whiting makes a useful, and oft-repeated, distinction among what he terms proverbs, proverbial phrases, and sententious remarks. According to Whiting, "A proverb is an expression
which, owing its birth to the people, testifies to its origin in form and
phrase. It expresses what is apparently a fundamental truth—that is, a
truism,—in homely language, often adorned, however, with alliteration
and rhyme." A proverbial phrase, on the other hand, is usually a simple comparison—as big as a house, not worth a plug nickel, etc. Finally,
Whiting describes an example of his third category, the sententious
remark, as "a piece of wisdom which has not crystallized into a specific
current form" and "a truism which everyone feels perfectly free to
rephrase to suit himself."[7] Although I would take issue with Whiting's
assumption that proverbs need show a popular origin, rather than
merely widespread currency, his three-fold division of subgenres can be
useful for the study of medieval proverbs. For example, the gnomic passages of *Beowulf* can, following this definition, be classified in some
cases as true proverbs, and in others as sententious remarks. We find
that proverbial phrases of the comparative type are rare in Old English
poetry, and that none appear in *Beowulf*. Whiting rightly makes no distinction between metaphorical and non-metaphorical proverbs; the former may present special problems of interpretation, and thus tend to be
more frequently treated in paroemiological scholarship, but the presence or absence of metaphor does not affect the proverbial status of a
saying.

Other approaches to the study of proverbs have included structural-
ist descriptions, and classifications of proverbial content,[8] but for purposes of recognition the most salient features are formal markers and
contextual characteristics. As lexical or grammatical markers, Shirley
Arora notes the use of repetition, departure from ordinary word order,
ellipsis of the verb, the appearance of meter, rhyme, and alliteration (in
a prose context), and the use of archaic language.[9] Arvo Krikmann
remarks that the usual lists of formal elements also include relational

---

[7] Whiting, "The Nature of the Proverb," 273.
[8] Studies of structure and content are reviewed by Fontaine, *Traditional Sayings in the Old Testament*, 34–43.
[9] Shirley L. Arora, "The Perception of Proverbiality," *Proverbium* 1 (1984): 11–14.

words (every, all, sometimes, never), words marking modalities (good, bad, must, cannot), interrogatives, and syntactic formulas (if x then y, where a then b, better c than d).[10] In the same article Krikmann rejects (but does not refute) this standard approach in order to highlight his own argument about how proverbs carry meaning and are interpreted; his revised list of proverb characteristics is based on the relation of a statement to its context, and the poetic qualities of a proverbial utterance. Krikmann's description of proverb markers is as follows:

1) "The text does not fit in with the situative and/or verbal context: it has an incorrect 'quantifier' (of generality) and its literal content is incompatible with the context."

2) The statement seems "too self-evident or trivial in its literal sense."

3) The literal statement seems incorrect, or the literal prescription seems unreasonable.

4) The text is literally nonsensical.

5) The text is "too regular and ornamental."[11]

Krikmann's criteria are especially helpful for the literary scholar, because he defines proverbs with reference to their context (and in literary studies a context always exists), and because his simple, easily recognized criteria more closely correspond to a literary audience's recognition factors. Finally, Krikmann's proverbial criteria function well in the case of non-metaphorical proverbs, which are the most common type in Old English, but in which few other paroemiologists are interested. Returning to *Beowulf*, it appears that Krikmann's first and second items—an incongruous level of generality and a literally ineffective self-evidence—are most relevant to the proverbs found there. For example, Beowulf's response to Hrothgar's lament over the death of Æschere does not refer directly to the king, but generalizes:

Selre bið æghwæm,
þæt he his freond wrece, þonne he fela murne.
(lines 1384b–85)[12]

---

[10] Arvo Krikmann, "On Denotative Indefiniteness of Proverbs," *Proverbium* 1 (1984): 59.

[11] Krikmann, "On Denotative Indefiniteness of Proverbs," 66. For other contextual studies, see Fontaine, *Traditional Sayings in the Old Testament*, 43–53.

[12] All quotations of *Beowulf*, unless otherwise noted, are from *Beowulf and the Fight at Finnsburg*, ed. Fr. Klaeber, 3rd ed. (Boston: D. C. Heath & Co., 1950).

[It is better for every man to avenge his friend than to mourn greatly.]

Likewise, the poet's expression of divine power may be described as "ineffectively self-evident":

> Metod eallum weold
> gumena cynnes,   swa he nu git deð.
>
> (lines 1057b–58)

[God ruled all of mankind, as He still does now.]

Krikmann's other proverbial characteristics are not relevant to *Beowulf*, as unreasonable and nonsensical statements do not appear in that text, and the presence of excessive regularity or ornamentation is difficult to establish.

It seems, then, that if we take the formal elements remarked upon by Arora and her predecessors, along with the contextual qualities described by Krikmann, we will possess sufficient tools for establishing the proverbiality of a statement. Then it will be possible to examine such a statement with relation to the proverb tradition, to elucidate its sources and influences, and hence to interpret it in its context. Although this author will not be so foolhardy as to offer her own defintion of "the proverb," it may help the reader to set forth some principles of terminology. In general, I have used the term *sententia* or sentence to refer to any statement that assumes sentential form as described above, and proverb to mean any such saying that seems to have circulated in a relatively fixed form, or to refer to the whole genre itself (i.e., proverbs, sentences, and proverbial comparisons). In the interests of simplicity, I have avoided the use of "maxim" or "gnome," except when the latter term refers to the established Old English genre of "gnomic poetry."

One *caveat* remains. A passage may bear every hallmark of proverbial form and function, but we are reminded by Archer Taylor that "The most convincing evidence [of proverbiality] is, of course, the actual proverbial use elsewhere of the doubtful passage, and above all, its use in contexts where it cannot easily be a quotation from the passage under examination."[13] That is, the presence or absence of analogues can be pivotal in determining the generic background of a questionable line. The composer of *Beowulf* was perfectly capable of inventing new *sententiae* along prover-

---

[13] Taylor, *The Proverb*, 7.

bial lines, so the collection of relevant analogues helps to establish the traditional background (or lack of such) for any gnomic statement in the poem. Furthermore, it is of general interest to know the background materials with which the *Beowulf*-poet was probably familiar, and to examine his reworking of those materials in the composition of the poem. As Dorothy Whitelock states the case: "we cannot guess at the effect the poet was hoping to obtain unless we know something of the meaning and associations his hints and allusions carried to those for whom he composed his poem."[14] The poet's proverbial background forms part of this matrix of "hints and allusions."

Of course, the recognition of analogues poses its own difficulties. There are two ways to trace and compare proverbs: the first is by their wording, and the second by their sense. When one is dealing with true proverbs—those often metaphorical utterances for which the wording is fixed—one can note verbal parallels with a fair amount of facility and ease. In these cases, the wording is actually more important than the meaning, which depends heavily upon context. Sententious remarks, on the other hand, cannot usually be compared with respect to their wording. Because their expression is more fluid, with only short phrases recurring, sentences must be traced via their literal sense or meaning. Luckily, sententious remarks are less metaphoric and more straightforward than true proverbs, so an unambiguous literal meaning is usually perceptible. The parallels may not share the exact meaning in context—proverbs and sentences rarely do—but their isolated literal sense will be similar.

The reader will notice that many of the analogues adduced in the following chapters postdate *Beowulf* by a century or two. The explanation for this relative lateness is, unfortunately, historical. Proverbs circulated in medieval Europe in three ways: that is, in oral discourse, in literature, and in deliberately compiled collections. The contents of oral communication are, of course, lost to us, and literature has preserved proverbs only unsystematically and accidentally, though one may occasionally be lucky in locating multiple versions of the same sentence. Written collections of proverbs are a Latin, rather than vernacular, genre which did not really blossom until the eleventh century;[15] fur-

---

[14] Dorothy Whitelock, *The Audience of Beowulf*, 2nd ed. (Oxford: Clarendon Press, 1958), 2.

[15] For a description of several early collections, and their probable uses, see Friedrich Seiler, *Deutsche Sprichwörterkunde* (Munich: Beck, 1967), 68–78.

thermore, their preservation and transmission were subject to the same vagaries of fate affecting all medieval texts. Thus, our knowledge of the medieval proverb tradition is less complete than is to be desired. Still, the material that is available should be used to its best advantage. Although most proverbial analogues to *Beowulf*, like its legendary and narrative analogues, are later than any accepted dating for the poem, the distribution of these analogues can provide information about the earlier period. That is, the appearance of a proverb or sentence in England, France, and Germany by the twelfth century presupposes a somewhat earlier origin for that proverb. We cannot pinpoint that origin, but neither should we discount it.

The relevance of Latin analogues to *Beowulf* is another question. The Latin language would have been the most effective means for dissemination of proverbs in the Middle Ages, and Latin texts form the bulk of our preserved corpus. The oral circulation of Latin proverbs is a possibility, though this seems somewhat less likely than in the case of the vernacular. However, florilegia and collectanea are not unknown in Anglo-Saxon England, and proverbs also appear in poetry, sermons, and various prose sources.[16] Finally, Hans Walther has argued for the circulation of Latin proverbs through grammars, vocabularies, and other school exercises. He suggests that proverbs sufficiently permeated the system of instruction so as to ensure familiarity with them by any educated person.[17] Such collections as that of Freidank and the Durham Proverbs provided a locus for the interchange of proverbs between the Latin and vernacular traditions. These avenues of dispersion deserve further study.

The proverbial or sentential passages of *Beowulf*, thirty-one by my count, have been grouped thematically for the purposes of this study. Seven of the passages take God as their subject, three fate, and eight death; three passages treat the essential dichotomy of joy and sorrow, while ten offer some form of warning or advice. The most important feature of these proverbs and sentences is that they convey a sense of generalization. This generality may appear with respect to time (one encounters the words *oft, æfre, a, seldan*) or to subject (*guma, se þe, eorl, drihtguma, man, gumcynnes gehwa*). In their contexts, the lines in ques-

---

[16] Twelfth- to fifteenth-century products of such transmission are examined by Arpad Steiner, "The Vernacular Proverb in Mediaeval Latin Prose," *American Journal of Philology* 65 (1944): 37–68.

[17] Walther, *Proverbia*, 1:xiii.

tion are "incorrectly quantified." Their general applicability characterizes the sentences as potentially free-standing units, used by the poet to enhance the thematic import of the narrative. I have included a few phrases which refer directly to characters in the poem, but these—dealing primarily with God and fate—meet other criteria for sential utterances.

Another device that appears in these *sententiae* is the use of comparison, sometimes in the syntactic formula "a is better than b" (*selre ... þonne ...*). As one would expect, these comparative phrases occur most often within the framework of "advice-giving."

The third distinguishing feature of these *sententiae* is the use of a modal verb carrying a consuetudinal or imperative connotation (*sceal, moste, mæg*). These verbs, along with their implications of positivism and inevitability, convey a sense of universality that well befits a traditional sentence. The modal may appear as part of a formula like "So should a man do," but often, the imperative sense is more straightforward: "Gæð a wyrd swa hio scel" (455b) [Fate always happens as it must].

A more slippery characteristic of these thirty-one passages is that they are concise, or at least reducible to some pithier form. A statement like "Fate always happens as it must" is recognizable as a potential proverb as it stands in the text, but other passages must be open to paraphrase and reduction. This point is of particular interest with respect to the sentences dealing with God, as several of them can be reduced to the truism "The divine will rules all." The amorphous quality of these passages characterizes them, according to Whiting's classification, as sententious remarks rather than proverbs proper.

My application of proverbial analogues and methods to the *sententiae* of *Beowulf* is designed, first, to give some idea of the proverbial and sentential matter that would have been available to the poet; second, to suggest, wherever possible, the form a sentence may have had before it was adapted for use in the poem; and finally, to analyze the use of these passages as proverbs or *sententiae* within the poem. I have tried to restrict myself to presenting such analogues as might actually be relevant to the composition of the poem: that is, analogues found in the Bible, in other Germanic literatures, and in those classical and patristic authors most frequently encountered in medieval florilegia. It is important to bear in mind throughout that few, if any, of the *Beowulf*ian *sententiae* appear exactly as they would have circulated, as the exigencies of sense and meter require accommodation of a sentence to its specific poetic context. My findings, as detailed in the following chapters, indicate that the inclusion of sentential material in *Beowulf* fits established medieval patterns in both style and substance. For some *Beowulf*ian *sententiae* I have been able to locate close analogues that move freely across linguistic boundaries; others seem to circulate in a more limited sphere, and a few probably represent individual inventions by the poet himself. However, even these last cases illustrate the importance of sentential discourse in the *Beowulf*-poet's world.

2

The Rule of God

The Christian quality and resituated paganism of *Beowulf* has long been a vexed issue,[1] one which is unlikely to be resolved by a simple re-examination of the textual evidence. However, the passage of time has reduced the intensity of the argument from a rolling boil to a slow simmer, so that one may at least consider the deistic passages of the poem in relative safety from scathing attacks by proponents of either camp. Most current criticism recognizes these passages as portraying a Judeo-Christian, or "Old Testament" God, and that is the interpretative stance I will adopt here, particularly as this picture of a generalized deity is strengthened by its prevalence in Christian Latin proverbial analogues to the poem. Classical literature offers little in the way of enlightening parallels, nor do references to pagan gods in the related vernacular literatures provide substantial analogues. Although

---

[1] Participants in this debate are too numerous to list in full, but include F. A. Blackburn, "The Christian Coloring in the *Beowulf*," *PMLA* 12 (1897): 205–25, repr. in *An Anthology of Beowulf Criticism*, ed. Lewis E. Nicholson (Notre Dame: Univ. of Notre Dame Press, 1963), 1–21; Fr. Klaeber, "Die christliche Elemente im *Beowulf*," *Anglia* 35 (1911–12): 111–36, 249–70, 453–82; and continued in *Anglia* 36 (1912): 169–99; Marie P. Hamilton, "The Religious Principle in *Beowulf*," *PMLA* 61 (1946): 309–31, repr. in Nicholson, 105–35; Larry D. Benson, "The Pagan Coloring of *Beowulf*," in *Old English Poetry: Fifteen Essays*, ed. R. P. Creed (Providence: Brown Univ. Press, 1967), 192–213; and Margaret E. Goldsmith, *The Mode and Meaning of 'Beowulf'* (London: The Athlone Press of the Univ. of London, 1970). More recent criticism has focused on specific passages, such as the "heathen practices" described in lines 175–88.

one might expect the coiners of Christian *sententiae* to have adopted or adapted generalized deistic proverbs from classical sources, such seems rarely to have been the case, at least for those sentences associated with *Beowulf*. This separatism might be attributed to Christian writers' frequent ambivalence toward classical literature, a discomfort that would be intensified in matters of religion. Similarly, the Germanic form of paganism was too fiercely denounced by Anglo-Saxon homilists and other Christian polemicists to allow adoption of its deistic sayings.

The seven deistic sentences of *Beowulf* can be grouped under four thematic headings or paraphrases: God rules mankind, God works wonders, No plan or action avails against the will of God, and He whom God helps none can harm. God also plays a role in the distribution of joy and sorrow, but that aspect of the poem will be treated in a later chapter, as will the relation between God and fate. The passages relevant to our present purposes are as follows:

God rules mankind

A.   Soð is gecyþed,
þæt mihtig God   manna cynnes
weold wideferhð   (lines 700b–702a)

[The truth is known, that the mighty God always ruled mankind]

B.   Metod eallum weold
gumena cynnes,   swa he nu git deð (lines 1057b–58)

[God ruled all of mankind, as He still does now]

C. wolde dom Godes   dædum rædan
gumena gehwylcum,   swa he nu gen deð
                                   (lines 2858–59)

[The judgment of God was wont to rule over deeds, over every man, as it still does now]

God works wonders

D.   a mæg God wyrcan
wunder æfter wundre,   wuldres Hyrde
                              (lines 930b–31)

[God, the guardian of heaven, can always perform wonder after wonder]

No plan (action) avails against the will of God

E.   þæt wæs yldum cuþ,
þæt hie ne moste,   þa Metod nolde,
se scynscaða   under sceadu bregdan   (lines 705b–7)

[It was known to men that if God did not will it, the hostile demon could not draw them into the darkness]

F. ic hine ne mihte,   þa Metod nolde,
ganges getwæman   (lines 967–68a)

[As God did not will it, I could not restrain him from leaving]

He whom God helps none can harm

G. Swa mæg unfæge   eaðe gedigan
wean ond wræcsið,   se ðe Waldendes
hyldo gehealdeþ   (lines 2291–93a)

[So may the undoomed easily endure woe and exile, he who holds the favor of the Lord].

Before examining these passages in detail, some general observations are in order. First, the vocabulary for God tends towards the generalized in these passages: *god* occurs three times, *metod* twice, *waldend* and *hyrde* once each, whereas other possibilities such as Jesus, Christ, or Savior are avoided. This pattern is consonant with the vocabulary of *Beowulf* as a whole, as F. A. Blackburn has counted thirty occurrences of *god*, eight of *metod*, ten of *waldend*, and one use of *hyrde* with reference to the deity. Other divine epithets noted by Blackburn are *drihten* (ten times), *frea* (thrice), *fæder* or *cyning* (twice each), and *rædend* (once). *Drihten* stands alone as a name for God only twice, but in its other eight appearances is qualified by an adjective, a genitive noun, or a compounded word.[2] The slightly larger deistic vocabulary in the poem as a whole compared to that of our sentential passages, particularly the distribution of *drihten*, may perhaps be explained by reference to the Latin proverbial tradition.

The same principle of divine characterization obtains to a certain degree in the Latin proverbial corpus as in *Beowulf*—Hans Walther's

---

[2] Blackburn, 11–12. I have combined Blackburn's total numbers for simple and compound epithets.

index lists over one thousand texts using *Deus*, but only eleven mentioning *Jesus*, 111 naming *Christus*, 151 referring to *Dominus*, and fifty-nine using *Pater*;[3] of these latter two terms, most describe a terrestrial, rather than deistic, figure.[4] Thus, the distribution of *drihten* as a divine epithet in the sentential passages of *Beowulf* may follow the proverbial usage illustrated by *Dominus* in Walther's collection, that is, most often as an earthly lord. The constraint does not seem to apply to the non-proverbial passages of the Old English poem. The absence of *frea*, *fæder*, and *cyning* in our passages is explained the same way, as the proverbial tradition seems to favor words for God devoid of any distinguishing or descriptive connotations.[5]

Another aspect common to the passages here designated as D, E, and F is the discretionary nature of God's activity. We find that God *can* work wonders (D), not that He *does* perform miracles, and the verb *nolde* is used twice (E and F) with reference to the possibility of divine intervention. As will be demonstrated below, this uncertainty regarding the will of God is more frequent in vernacular than Latin proverbs.

God rules mankind

A. (lines 700b–702a):

> Soð is gecyþed,
> þæt mihtig God   manna cynnes
> weold wideferhð.

The form of this passage is strongly proverbial, particularly with respect to Krikmann's factor of excessive self-evidence:[6] one hardly expects God's reign to be anything but eternal. The passage is also over-generalized in its context, as at this point in the poem the audience is concerned not so much with the fate of "mankind" as with the outcome of Beowulf's upcoming contest with Grendel. Furthermore, the

---

[3] See Walther, vol. 6.

[4] See, for example, Walther, nos. 1768, 2208.b, 2392, 2626, etc.

[5] Goldsmith (148–60) proposes that the *Beowulf*-poet avoided "purely ecclesiastical words" and "precise words for religious concepts, so as to give an effect of intuitive rather than inculcated knowledge," but she also suggests that the poet's conception of humanity without Christ was based on Job (through Augustine and Gregory) and on the Psalms (through Gregory). A stronger case could be made for the appearance of intuitive (or at least non-patristic) knowledge by accepting that the poet's deistic vocabulary reflects a well-established proverbial tradition.

[6] Krikmann, "On Denotative Indefiniteness," 66.

phrase "Soð is gecyþed" introduces the sentence as a piece of conventional wisdom. The main verb, however, employs the past tense, as opposed to the present or consuetudinal that give nearly all proverbs their generalized flavor. This passage (like those below) employs a different means of indicating temporal continuity—in this case, the adverb *wideferhð*, which may be translated as "always" or "for a long time."[7] The tense of *weold* links the sentence to the preceding narrative (conducted in the past tense), while *wideferhð* provides for the inclusion of present and future time in the connotation of the phrase.

A similar invocation of eternity is made in *Maxims I*:

> Woden worhte weos,   wuldor alwalda,
> rume roderas;   þæt is rice god,
> sylf soðcyning,   sawla nergend,
> se us eal forgeaf   þæt we on lifgaþ,
> ond eft æt þam ende   eallum wealdeð
> monna cynne.   Þæt is meotud sylfa.   (132–37)[8]

> [Woden made idols, the almighty (made) heaven, the spacious skies; that is the mighty God, the true king Himself, the savior of souls, He gave us everything by which we live, and then at the end will rule all of mankind. That is God Himself.]

The juxtaposition of the past tense *forgeaf* with the present/future tense *wealdeð* creates the same effect as in passage A. The description of God's activity as *wealdan* is common to *Maxims I* along with passages A and B, so it may be considered a consistent element of the Old English sentential tradition. *Maxims I* (137a) also shares with A the phrase *monna cynnes*, of which the *gumena cynnes* of B is only a slight variant. The proliferation of divine names in *Maxims I* (*alwalda*, *god*, *soðcyning*, *nergend*, *meotud*) seems to be a stylistic, rather than sentential feature, as it detracts from the economy of the passage in a way that contrasts sharply with proverbial style. The names do, of course, help to define the Christian God in contrast to Woden.

---

[7] See Johannes Hoops, *Kommentar zum Beowulf* (Heidelberg: Carl Winter, 1932), 90.

[8] *Maxims I*, lines 132–37, in *The Exeter Book*, ed. George Philip Krapp and Eliott Van Kirk Dobbie, Anglo-Saxon Poetic Records, vol. 3 (New York: Columbia Univ. Press, 1936), 161. Subsequent references to the ASPR will be cited by volume and page number.

The function of God as eternal ruler had obtained proverbial status in Latin literature at least as early as the eleventh century, when Otloh included the first phrase of Psalms 144.13 in his *Libellus proverbiorum*: "Regnvm tuum, Domine, regnum omnium saeculorum"[9] [Your kingdom, Lord, is a kingdom for all the ages]. Although the psalms were popular and well-known texts for reading, Otloh's inclusion of verses (or parts of verses) from the Book of Psalms is nevertheless intriguing. He intended his *Libellus proverbiorum* as a primer for young boys, a function, he tells us, that previously had been served by the distichs of Cato or the "fabulosa ... dicta" of Avian.[10] Otloh, however, considered sacred Scripture to constitute a more salutary reading matter for young minds than the sayings of pagans, and it is this concern with the content, and not merely the form of pedagogical exercises, which allies his *Libellus* more closely to the genre of instructional literature (exemplified in Old English by *Maxims I* and *II* and *Precepts*) than to the use of Cato or the psalter as the source of simple texts.[11] Otloh does not entirely scorn to include material from pagan writers (most notably Publilius Syrus), but the first third of each of his chapters is taken up by Scriptural quotations, of which psalmic verses constitute the largest block (nearly one-fourth) and verses from Proverbs the next largest (about one-fifth).[12] As Otloh does not provide source designations for his *proverbia*, the net impression of each chapter is that of sacred proverbs followed by miscellaneous prose proverbs, and finally proverbs in verse, with the second and third divisions deriving from varied sources.

We might now consider the function of passage A within the narrative structure of the poem. Beowulf has announced his intention to battle Grendel without benefit of weaponry, and the Geats have bedded down with slim hopes of ever returning to their homeland. But, we are told, God granted *frofor ond fultum* to the Geats such that they all overcame their enemy through the might of one man. "Soð is gecyþed ..." concludes this revelation, and the description of Grendel's approach follows our passage. The functions of sentence A are clear: it

---

[9] Otloh, *Libellus proverbiorum*, ed. Gulielmus Carolus Korfmacher (Chicago: Loyola Univ. Press, 1936), no. 1 (p. 72).

[10] Otloh, *Lib. prov.*, ed. Korfmacher, Prologue, p. 2.

[11] For recent work on the genre of instructional literature, see Elaine Tuttle Hansen, "*Precepts*: An Old English Instruction," *Speculum* 56 (1981): 1–16; this article was later incorporated into Hansen's book, *The Solomon Complex*.

[12] On the arrangement of Otloh's collection, see Korfmacher's edition, pp. xxxi–xxxiii.

provides the grounds (however self-evident) for divine assistance to the
Geats, it explains the outcome of the combat, and its generality sums
up the preceding observations.[13] The two last-mentioned functions
provide a sense of closure which allows the audience to concentrate on
the descriptive details of the fight rather than the possibility of loss and
disaster for the Geats. The poetic form of expression switches from
monologue to description to sentence, after which the scene shifts to
outside the hall.

B. (lines 1057b–58):

> Metod eallum weold
> gumena cynnes,   swa he nu git deð.

This passage resembles A in its proverbial form: a brief, past-tense
declaration of God's rule over mankind, followed by an expression of
temporal continuity. The latter is effected by the comparative phrase
"swa he nu git deð," in which *swa* links the past tense of *weold* with
the *nu* of *deð*; *git* reinforces the connection. The same phrase (lacking
only the pronoun *he*) is used to similar effect in the Finnsburh episode,
as Hengest awaits the good weather he needs to travel home. Winter
has kept the seas impassable,

> oþ ðæt oþer com
> gear in geardas,—   swa nu gyt deð,
> þa ðe syngales   sele bewitiað,
> wuldortorhtan weder.   (1133b–36a)

[Until the next season came among the dwellings—as it
still does now—the gloriously bright weather that always observes the seasons.]

Like the reign of God, the changing of the seasons is eternal, and creates a link between the action of the poem and the world experienced
by the audience; the link is particularly effective in this case, as nearly
any listener could empathize with Hengest's impatience for the end of
winter.

---

[13] For the proverbial function of "summing up," see Archer Taylor, "The
Wisdom of Many and the Wit of One," *Swarthmore College Bulletin* 54 (1962): 4–7;
repr. in *The Wisdom of Many: Essays on the Proverb*, ed. Wolfgang Mieder and Alan
Dundes, Garland Folklore Casebooks 1 (New York and London: Garland Publishing, Inc., 1981), 1–6.

One further use of this phrase to evoke continuation over time can be seen in a slightly different context, that of Hrothgar's blessing of Beowulf after the victory over Grendel:

> Alwalda þec
> gode forgylde,   swa he nu gyt dyde!   (955b–56)

[May the Almighty repay you with good, as He has now already done!]

Whereas in passages B and C the final half-line completes a transition from the past tense to a present/future connotation, the process is here reversed, and the link made between future subjunctive ("forgylde") and present/past ("nu . . . dyde"). Thus, this multi-purpose formula can be made either to "contemporize the past,"[14] in the words of Stanley Greenfield, or to archaize the future, as its base purpose remains the expression of temporal continuity.

Passage B differs lexically from A in that here God rules not just humanity, but *all* ("eallum") of mankind. This variant is also found in *Maxims I* (136b–37a, cited above), and in the fifteenth-century *Proverbia communia*:

> God es bouen al
> Est super omne deus rex dominusque meus[15]

[God is above all; God, my king and lord, is above all].

Here, the spatial metaphor of God's superiority is stressed, so He is positioned above not just humanity, but all of creation. However, the connotation of the proverbs—the omnipotence of God—remains the same in all cases. The unspecified use of "all" as the object of God's rule occurs elsewhere in *Beowulf*, as in a half-line tag in Hrothgar's sermon: "he ah ealra geweald" (1727b) [He has dominion over all].

Passage B occupies an interesting place in the poem, initiating a short string of sentential pronouncements. After Hrothgar makes monetary reparations for the warrior killed by Grendel, we are told that Grendel would have killed even more men had not God and the

---

[14] Stanley B. Greenfield, "The Authenticating Voice in *Beowulf*," *Anglo-Saxon England* 5 (1976): 51–72; repr. in *Hero and Exile: The Art of Old English Poetry*, ed. George H. Brown (London and Ronceverte: The Hambledon Press, 1989), 49.

[15] *Proverbia communia*, ed. R. Jente, Indiana University Publications, Folklore Series, no. 4 (Bloomington: Univ. of Indiana Press, 1947), 70.

courage of Beowulf prevented him. The evocation of God's power in this specific case allows the poet to continue the theme in a more generalized fashion, hence passage B follows. Having entered a proverbial mode of discourse, the poet adds two more *sententiae* which are less apparently relevant to the situation at hand in that they are not immediately applicable to the scene in Heorot. Their inclusion is initially justified only by the proverbial form of B, but they use that form to address the audience directly in terms of advice ("Understanding is best") and prophecy ("A long life brings good and bad experiences"). Considered as a whole, the sententious passage (1057b–62) serves a structural function similar to that of A: it provides a sense of closure to the scene of Hrothgar's gift-giving, after which the poet shifts his focus to the scop and his relation of the Finn episode.

C. (lines 2858–59):

> wolde dom Godes   dædum rædan
> gumena gehwylcum,   swa he nu gen deð.

The translation of this sentence is of some interest, although its complexities have received little attention. Translators have consistently (and without comment) taken "dædum ... gumena gehwylcum" to mean something like "the deeds of every man," while ignoring the morphological impossibility of that reading. To cite just a few examples, Michael Alexander reverses subject and predicate, producing "every man's action was under the sway of God's judgement, just as it is now."[16] Howell Chickering renders the sense of the line more closely, but makes the same error (along with mistaking the antecedent of "he"): "The judgment of God then ruled the deeds of every man, as He still does now."[17] John R. Clark Hall's translation is perhaps the most accurate, in that he maintains the division between "gumena gehwylcum" and their "dædum": "For men of all degrees God's judgment ruled their deeds, just as it still does now."[18]

---

[16] *Beowulf*, trans. Michael Alexander (Harmondsworth and New York: Penguin Books, 1973), 141.

[17] *Beowulf: A Dual-Language Edition*, trans. Howell D. Chickering, Jr. (Garden City: Anchor Books, 1977), 221. There is some poetic justification for taking "he" as referring to God, rather than His *dom*, if one seeks to maintain consistency with passage B.

[18] *Beowulf and the Finnesburg Fragment*, trans. John R. Clark Hall, new ed. rev. C. L. Wrenn (London: George Allen & Unwin Ltd., 1950), 163.

Klaeber recognized the problem in these lines and suggested (though without further explanation) that "dædum" be understood in an instrumental sense.[19] This reading would require a translation like "The judgment of God would rule all men by deeds (or, actively)," which is similar to the gloss provided by Hoops: "mit Taten walten über."[20] However, the distinction between God ruling "by deeds," as opposed to by will or intent, seems overly subtle within the theological purview of the *Beowulf*-poet, particularly in comparison to the other deistic *sententiae*, so I would adopt the other grammatically acceptable solution: "The judgment of God ruled (or, was wont to rule) deeds, [and] each of men, just as it still does now." Normal word order (even in poetry) precludes the modifying of "dædum" by "gehwylcum,"[21] so it seems best to consider the two words in apposition, with "gumena" qualifying "gehwylcum."[22]

Although passage C shares the same underlying structure as A and B—God ruled humanity, and still does—it differs from them in its heightened level of specificity. God is no longer the subject of the sentence, as the nominative position is occupied by God's *dom*, His judgment or authority. Similarly, the activity of this divine authority is not defined simply as "ruled" (*weold*), but as "was wont to control" (*wolde ... rædan*); the object of God's attention likewise undergoes a narrowing of focus, from "mankind" in general to "deeds" and "each of men" (*dædum ... gumena gehwylcum*). Thus, the poet seems to have begun with a simple, proverbial paradigm and embellished it (without changing the core meaning) by the addition of specifying details. Unfortunately for our purposes, these added details render impossible the collection of analogues, as passage C represents the "personalized" variant of a base *sententia*.

As would be expected from a sentence so tailored to a specific poetic use, C blends into its context more smoothly than our previous two examples. Beowulf has fallen in his battle with the dragon, and the cowardly retainers return from the sheltering trees to witness the touching scene of Wiglaf bathing the brow of his lifeless lord. The

---

[19] Klaeber, *Beowulf*, p. 221.

[20] Hoops, *Kommentar*, 299.

[21] See the chart showing the relative position of qualifiers in Bruce Mitchell, *Old English Syntax*, 2 vols. (Oxford: Clarendon Press, 1985), 1.68, ¶ 143.

[22] The somewhat unusual dative plural of *gehwylcum* may also be explained by its use in apposition to *dædum* and by the fact that *rædan* governs the dative case.

audience learns that despite his best intentions, Wiglaf could not alter the will of God with respect to Beowulf's demise; the thought is then expanded by our passage to include God's jurisdiction over all men. The appeal to divine authority increases the pathos of the scene by reinforcing the futility of Wiglaf's efforts at resuscitation. As in example B, the sentence is suggested by an immediately preceding reference to God, but in this case the proverb serves more of an explanatory than a concluding function: the reference to divine judgment (*dom*) over human deeds (*dædum*) explains the demise of the previously invincible hero, while at the same time providing a more generalized lesson for the audience. The sentence does mark a minor shift in discourse, as it falls between a descriptive passage and the introduction to Wiglaf's speech.

God works wonders

D. (lines 930b–31):

a mæg God wyrcan
wunder æfter wundre, wuldres Hyrde.

With this passage, we move from generalized declarations of divine omnipotence to descriptions of some specific activities of God. Passage D takes a recognizable proverbial form, as it is a self-contained, present-tense, declarative sentence stating an obvious truth. Furthermore, it is over-generalized for its context, as God's miraculous abilities *in toto* are not at issue at this point, but only His role in Grendel's demise.

The most pertinent proverbial parallel to this passage appears in Otloh, who appropriated for his collection the verse of Ps. 71.18: "Benedictus Dominus, Deus Israel, qui facit mirabilia solus"[23] [Blessed be the Lord, the God of Israel, who alone works wonders]. Otloh has not recast the verse as a proverb—it more closely resembles an invocation or benediction—but its inclusion in a self-styled collection of proverbs might indicate that the verse was perceived as appropriate material for a *sententia*. *Mirabilia* is only an approximate parallel to *wunder æfter wundre*, but the Latin and Old English sentences share the device of providing two epithets for God; passage D is the only deistic *sententia* of *Beowulf* to do so. The construction "wuldres X" as a divine epithet occurs three other times in the poem, but in all of the other cases, the place of "Hyrde" is held by "W(e)aldend" (lines 17, 183, and

---

[23] Otloh, *Lib. prov.*, ed. Korfmacher, no. 4 (p. 8).

1753). Although the replacement of *Waldend* in line 931 is necessitated to some extent by the meter (to avoid a superfluous alliterating element), the poet's choice of *Hyrde* may have been influenced by the *Deus Israel* of the biblical verse. Psalm 71 describes the blessings that the "son of the king" (i.e., Messiah) will provide for his people, so the epithet *Deus Israel* in this context evokes the function of God as protector or guardian, that is, as *Hyrde*. On the other hand, *Hyrde* may simply be the most appropriate term at this point in Hrothgar's speech, as he thanks the Lord for helping to destroy the scourge of the Danes.

Like Hrothgar, Augustine links the miraculous abilities of God with the activities of human agents; in his commentary on Ps. 71.18, the bishop writes: "Ipse *facit mirabilia solus*; quoniam quicumque faciunt, ipse in eis operatur, *qui facit mirabilia solus*"[24] [He alone works wonders, because whoever does them, He works in them, He who alone works wonders]. Augustine expands the idea in his explication of the similar verse of Ps. 76.14 ("tu es deus qui facis mirabilia solus" [you are the God who alone works wonders]):

> Fecit et Moyses, sed non solus; fecit et Elias, fecit et Elisaeus, fecerunt et apostoli; sed nullus eorum solus. Illi ut facerent, tu cum eis; tu quando fecisti, illi non tecum. Non enim tecum fuerunt cum fecisti, quando et ipsos tu fecisti.[25]

> [And Moses did (work wonders), but not alone; and Elias did, and Elisaeus did, and the apostles did; but none of them alone. In order that they might do them, you were with them; when you did them, they were not with you. For they were not with you when you did them, and when you created those very men.]

A consistent theme of Hrothgar's speech is his understanding that Beowulf was able to kill Grendel not on his own, but with the assistance of God. If passage D is, in fact, based on the expression of divine power found in Psalms 71 and 76, Augustine provides a precedent for interpretation of the verses along the same lines.

Sections of the liturgy incorporated the phrasing of Psalms 71 and 76 into a more extended invocation to God, thus exemplifying another way in which this particular expression of divine power could have

---

[24] Aurelius Augustinus, *Enarrationes in Psalmos*, ed. D. Eligius Dekkers, O.S.B., and Johannes Fraipont, CCSL 38, 39, 40 (Turnhout: Brepols, 1956), 39.985 [ps. 71, par. 20].

[25] *Enarr. in Psal.*, CCSL 39.1062 [ps. 76, par. 16].

become common currency. The relevant passages are those for "Missa in monasterio" and "Missa in domo" found in three Frankish recensions of the Gelasian Sacramentary; I quote here from the eighth-century *Liber sacramentorum Gellonensis*, but parallel passages appear in the sacramentaries from Angoulême and Autun:

> Omnipotens sempiterne deus, qui facis mirabilia magna solus, pretende super famulus tuus spiritum gratiae salutaris, et ut in ueritate tibi conplaceant, perpetuum aeis rorem tuae benedictionis infunde.[26]

> [Omnipotent, eternal God, who alone works great wonders, extend the spirit of saving grace over your servant, and as they truly please you, pour out the dew of your blessing over all the generations.]

Although Anglo-Saxon liturgical usage is notoriously difficult to establish, G. G. Willis has discerned Gelasian elements in the Lindisfarne Gospels, St. Cuthbert's Gospels, the Gospels of St. Burchard, in Bede, in the *Old English Martyrology*, and in St. Willibrord's Kalendar.[27] Willis concludes that both Old Gelasian and mixed types (Old and St.-Gall) of Gelasian sacramentaries were used in England during the eighth century.[28]

Leaving aside the Psalter, we find another biblical proverb which may have influenced *Beowulf* passage D; in contrast to the phraseological simplicity of the preceding example, this expression assumes two forms: "To God nothing is impossible" (based on Luke 1.37), and "All things are possible with God" (Matt. 19.26, Mark 10.27, Luke 18.27).[29]

---

[26] *Liber sacramentorum Gellonensis*, ed. A. Dumas, O.S.B., CCSL 159 (Turnhout: Brepols, 1981), "Orationes monasticae," rubrica 2587 (p. 403). For a similar passage "ad missa in domum," see CCSL 159.444 (rubrica 2826). For the other two recensions, see *Liber sacramentorum Augustodunensis*, ed. O. Heiming, O.S.B., CCSL 159B (Turnhout: Brepols, 1984), 195 (rubrica 1601) and 230 (rubrica 1852); and *Liber sacramentorum Engolismensis: Manuscrit B.N. Lat. 816, Le Sacramentaire Gélasien d'Angoulême*, ed. Patrick Saint-Roch, CCSL 159C (Turnhout: Brepols, 1987), 344 (rubrica 2204).

[27] G. G. Willis, *Further Essays in Early Roman Liturgy*, Alcuin Club Collections, no. 50 (London: S. P. C. K., 1968), 214–19.

[28] Willis, 230.

[29] The first form and the relevant biblical verses are cited in Whiting, *Proverbs ... before 1500*, G269; and *Deutsches Sprichwörter-Lexikon: Ein Hausschatz für das deutsche Volk*, ed. Karl Friedrich Wilhelm Wander, 5 vols. (Darmstadt: Wissenschaftliche Buchgesellschaft, 1964), 2.3.53 (hereafter *DS-L*).

The first form enjoyed some currency at least in late-medieval England, as Whiting cites examples from the Towneley *Prima Pastorum* and Coventry *Annunciation*.[30] The second variant was popular with Bede, who inserted the verse of Luke 18.37 in several places in his commentary on that gospel, in order to explain certain of Christ's miracles. For example, he anticipates disbelief of the raising of Jairus's daughter by asserting "Sed quae inpossibilia sunt apud homines possibilia sunt apud Deum"[31] [But those things which are impossible with men are possible with God], and later appends the same phrase (minus "sed") to the less remarkable story of Zacheus in the sycamore tree.[32]

This second variant is also found on the Continent, in a later and more substantially altered form, in the *Proverbia communia*:

> God es alle dings machtich
> Cuncta potest facere deus omnipotens scio vere[33]

> [God is powerful over all things; All-powerful God can
> do all things, I know truly].

Although this proverb is still more generalized than D—"alle dings / cuncta" versus "wunder æfter wundre"—its transformation from the biblical "apud Deum autem omnia possibilia sunt" (Matt. 19.26) [but with God all things are possible] may be considered a developmental analogue for the type of change undergone by the proverb as it appears in *Beowulf*. The syntax may be altered to some extent, and the vocabulary as well, but the sentence preserves its basic intent.

One final aspect of passage D calls for comment; that is its use of the adverb *a*. The word is not required by the meter (the line alliterates on "g" and 930b is metrically complete), nor does the expression of temporal continuity serve the same purpose as in our earlier examples (A-C), for the verb (*mæg*) is, this time, in the present tense. Thus, I would attribute the "always" of 930b to a tendency in the deistic passages of *Beowulf* to link the omnipotence of God with His eternal

---

[30] Bartlett Jere Whiting, *Proverbs in the Earlier English Drama, with Illustrations from Contemporary French Plays*, Harvard Studies in Comparative Literature 14 (Cambridge, Mass.: Harvard Univ. Press, 1938), 17 and 30.

[31] *In Lucae euangelium expositio*, bk. 3, chap. 8, in *Bedae Venerabilis Opera*, part 2.3: Opera exegetica, ed. D. Hurst, O.S.B., CCSL 120 (Turnhout: Brepols, 1960), 191.

[32] *In Lucae euangelium*, bk. 5, chap. 19, CCSL 120.333.

[33] *Prov. comm.*, ed. Jente, p. 70. The *Proverbia communia* is also cited by Wander, *DS-L* 2.3.53.

nature.[34] This tendency is not unique to the *Beowulf*-poet, as it is taken even further by the glossator of the Paris Psalter:

> Wese Israhela   *ece* drihten
> and hiora sylfra god   *symble* gebletsad,
> se þe wundor mycel   wyrceð ana;[35]

(emphasis mine)

[Blessed be always the eternal Lord of Israel, their own God, He who alone works great wonders].

The use in the Paris Psalter of "wundor" for *mirabilia* parallels that of passage D. It seems, then, that this *sententia* of *Beowulf* represents a variant of an originally biblical proverb (whether from the Psalms or the Gospels) that was particularly open to paraphrase and revision.

The place of passage D within its narrative context requires little explication. Hrothgar has just espied Grendel's severed arm hanging in Heorot, and he thanks the Lord for this welcome sight. Hrothgar explains his joy and gratitude by referring to his long suffering from the ravages of Grendel, and then intones our sentence, which reiterates his attribution of Grendel's downfall to divine power. God maintains a high profile in Hrothgar's speech, as we hear that Beowulf has done the deed "þurh Drihtnes miht" (line 940) [through the power of the Lord] and that the hero's mother may consider God good to her for providing such a son (lines 945–46). Hrothgar concludes his speech with the hope that God will reward Beowulf with blessings. Therefore, passage D forms part of a complex of references revealing how the influence of God is exerted through human agents, from the birth of the hero through his current success and future glory.

---

[34] The use of temporal adverbs in *Precepts* is discussed by Elaine Tuttle Hansen, *The Solomon Complex*, 54: "*A* and *simle* also appear in nonimperative utterances ..., where they seem to serve the same purposes as *oft* ... or *seldan* ..., specifying the characteristic or typical manner in which events or behavior are frequently or habitually observed to result from a given condition or situation, and once again constructing the predictability and stability of reality—for those human beings who are wise enough to perceive, and perpetuate, its order."

[35] *The Paris Psalter* 71.19 (ASPR 5.31). See also Alfred's formulation: "he [God] wæs a, and a byd, undeadlic and æce," in *King Alfred's Version of St. Augustine's 'Soliloquies'*, ed. Thomas A. Carnicelli (Cambridge, Mass.: Harvard Univ. Press, 1969), 82.

No plan (action) avails against the will of God

E. (lines 705b–7):

> þæt wæs yldum cuþ,
> þæt hie ne moste,   þa Metod nolde,
> se scynscaða   under sceadu bregdan.

F. (lines 967–68a):

> ic hine ne mihte,   þa Metod nolde,
> ganges getwæman.

For the most part, these two passages may be treated in conjunction, as they are not proverbs *per se*, but both derive from the same proverbial sentiment. Despite the fact that E is voiced by the narrator, and F by Beowulf, the parallels between the passages are striking: both employ a negative construction with respect to action by the subject ("ne moste … bregdan" and "ne mihte … getwæman"), and, of course, both utilize the half-line phrase "þa Metod nolde." The repetition of this latter phrase reveals the common sentential background of E and F, the idea that "(Someone) could not (do something) if God did not so desire," or more simply, that no human activity achieves its end without (or against) God. Although the subjects of these passages— Grendel and Beowulf—and their intended actions, may be assumed to find varying degrees of favor in God's eyes, the difference between them is ultimately insignificant, as in the proverbial corpus both benevolent and malicious actions are equally subject to the will of the divine. The sentential examples I have gathered also demonstrate the prevalence of negative syntactic or semantic constructions in developing this theme. That is, these mottoes and *sententiae* refer to failure if God does *not* approve or assist, rather than to success if He does.

An early medieval example of this proverbial sentiment is attributed to Charlemagne: "Contra Christum cuncta consilia cadunt"[36] [All plans fail against Christ]. The naming of Christ is unusual, but is explained in this case by the equally unusual complete alliteration of the motto (alliteration is a frequent device even of modern proverbs, but its use seems more frequent in the vernacular than in Latin). That

---

[36] Ludwig Herhold, *Lateinischer Wort- und Gedankenschatz* (Hannover: Verlag der Hahn'schen Buchhandlung, 1887), 49; Walther, no. 35725. Herhold provides no source for the attribution to Charlemagne.

the idea of reliance on divine favor continued (or reappeared) as the foundation of mottoes throughout the Middle Ages is exemplified by that of Dietrich von Erbach, archbishop-elect of Mainz in the second quarter of the fifteenth century: "Omnia cum Deo et nihil sine eo"[37] [All things with God and nothing without Him]. The concept of all things ("omnia") being possible with God's help was frequently employed in mottoes,[38] but Dietrich also included the inevitable corollary to it, that nothing is possible without God. Thus, his motto is more closely aligned to that of Charlemagne and to passages E and F. As mottoes were phrases invented or adopted essentially for public display, it is very possible that knowledge of them would circulate widely, and that in some cases the sentences would lose their original context and enter the proverbial repertoire of a region, whence they might even be re-adopted as new mottoes.

A more particularized branch in the development of this sentence declares specifically that human efforts fail without the express assistance of God. King Alfred articulated the idea twice in his translation of Augustine's *Soliloquies*:

> ... forðam man naþer ne ða god ne nane don ne mæge buton hys fultume.

> [Because a man cannot do good or anything at all without His help.]

> We witon þæt nan man mæg nawyht goodes wyrcan buton hym god myd wyrce.[39]

> [We know that no man can do any good at all unless God work with him.]

Alfred's sentences display the negative construction common to this sentential complex, along with the application to good and not-good activities that allows the same basic sentence to apply to both Beowulf and Grendel. In the twelfth-century *Pamphilus de amore*, we find expression of the sentiment that underlies Beowulf's declaration in F:

---

[37] Herhold, 183; Walther, no. 39226.a.2. See also Henri Tausin, *Dictionnaire des devises ecclésiastiques* (Paris: Lechevalier, 1907), no. 1391 (p. 138).

[38] See Herhold, 54 and 183.

[39] *King Alfred's Version of St. Augustine's 'Soliloquies'*, ed. Carnicelli, 68 and 69.

"Proficit absque deo nullus in orbe labor"[40] [No labor in the world succeeds without God]. The same idea is stated plainly in the Middle English *King Alisaunder* of *circa* 1300:

> Ac sooþ it is, cayser ne king
> Ne may ageins Goddes helpyng.[41]

A later Latin version of the proverb reads "Frustra conatur, cui non Deus auxiliatur"[42] [He whom God does not help labors in vain]. These wide-ranging examples should make clear that this sentential concept, although it seems never to have attained a standard expression, was current throughout the entire medieval period. These *sententiae* are equally applicable to passages E and F, although some (like Charlemagne's) seem more directed against the type of malevolent behavior intended by Grendel, while others (e.g., that from *Pamphilus*) are more easily applied to Beowulf's laudable efforts.

Still, the origin of this sentential thought remains obscure. Certain variants probably represent individual developments from separate sources, one of which may be a line from Ps. 126.1: "Nisi Dominus custodierit ciuitatem, in uanum uigilat qui custodit eam" [Unless the Lord protects the city, he who guards it watches in vain]. The psalmic verse describes a more detailed situation than the sentences I have cited above, but it is no less proverbial (at least potentially) in its form; that is, it describes no particular city, nor any individual watchman, in any specific time. However, we need not rely on our own judgments of proverbiality, as Otloh evidently considered the verse proverbial enough for his eleventh-century collection. Otloh's version of the *sententia* is noteworthy for displaying the sort of small alterations undergone by biblical proverbs: in place of the Vulgate "in vanum" he writes "frustra".[43]

More authoritative (and widely-read) ecclesiastical writers than Otloh were also struck by this biblical sentence, chief among them being Augustine, who used the line proverbially—that is, without identifying it as Scripture—in his letters,[44] in his tract on holy virgin-

---

[40] Cited from Jakob Werner, *Lateinische Sprichwörter und Sinnsprüche des Mittelalters aus Handschriften gesammelt* (Heidelberg: Carl Winter, 1912), 130.

[41] *King Alisaunder*, lines 1407–8, cited from Whiting, *Proverbs . . . before 1500*, G276.

[42] Walther, no. 10042.

[43] Otloh, *Lib. prov.*, ed. Korfmacher, no. 6 (p. 48).

[44] *S. Aureli Augustini Hipponiensis episcopi Epistulae*, ed. Al. Goldbacher, CSEL 57, part 4 (Vienna: Tempsky, 1911), epist. 186 (p. 49).

ity,[45] and in his sermons.[46] Fulgentius of Ruspe's letter "Ad Probam" typifies epistolary use of Ps. 126.1:

> Solus igitur Deus potest omnibus quibus uoluerit dare unde uera salus acquirit possit; et ideo solus potest in accipiente custodire quod dederit: Nisi enim Dominus custodierit ciuitatem, in uanum uigilant qui custodiunt eam.[47]

> [Therefore God alone is able to give, when He wishes, all those things through which true salvation may be acquired; and He alone can watch over what He has given: for unless the Lord protects the city, those who guard it watch in vain.]

Like Augustine and Otloh, Fulgentius declines to identify the source of the sentence, thus endowing it with a more proverbial than scriptural status. In the Anglo-Saxon period, Bede, too, found the verse noteworthy, as it is the only verse from Psalm 126 included in the "Collectio psalterii" attributed to him.[48]

The prospective relevance of this sentence to Beowulf's situation as defender of Heorot is self-evident. What is less clear is whether the *Beowulf*-poet knew and used (as a general sentiment) this biblical verse. The striking similarity between the psalm and the context of Beowulf's remark tempts one to reach a positive conclusion, and as we have seen (and will continue to see) with respect to the other deistic *sententiae* of *Beowulf*, these passages often resemble proverbs of biblical (and especially psalmic) origin. Thus I would suggest, although tentatively in the absence of further proof, that passage F may well represent the poet's reworking of Ps. 126.1, or of a sentence based on it.

One phrase requiring special attention is the "under sceadu bregdan" of E (707b). Hoops provides the gloss "in die Schatten hinunter schleudern ... dh. 'töten' " and cites Klaeber's suggestion of the influ-

---

[45] "De sancta uirginitate," in *Sancti Aureli Augustini De fide et symbolo* etc., ed. Iosephus Zycha, CSEL 41 (Vienna: Tempsky, 1900), chap. 40 (p. 285).

[46] *Sermones*, ed. J.-P. Migne, Patrologia Latina 38: sermon 105 ("De verbis Evangelii Lucae"), col. 622; sermon 297 ("In Natali apostolorum Petri et Pauli, III"), col. 1362.

[47] *Sancti Fulgentii episcopi Ruspensis Opera*, ed. J. Fraipont, CCSL 91 and 91A (Turnhout: Brepols, 1968), epist. 4, chap. 4 [CCSL 91.230]. See also his "De ueritate praedestinationis et gratiae," bk. 2, chap. 29 [CCSL 91A.509].

[48] "Collectio Psalterii Bedae," in *Bedae Venerabilis Opera*, part 4: Opera rhythmica, ed. J. Fraipont, CCSL 122 (Turnhout: Brepols, 1955), 468. Admittedly, the attribution of this work to Bede is not positive.

ence of the Latin idiom "ad umbras adigere."[49] In his edition, Klaeber
proposes that "The 'shades' might well be of classical origin" and refers
to *Aeneid* xi.831 and xii.952; he also offers similar phrases from the
Heliand and *Paradise Lost*.[50] Marie Hamilton prefers the Christian
interpretation of "under sceadu," and draws a parallel to *Guthlac*, lines
673–77:[51]

> Ne þurfun ge wenan,   wuldre biscyrede,
> þæt ge mec synfulle   mid searocræftum
> under scæd sconde   scufan motan,
> ne in bælblæsan   bregdon on hinder
> in helle hus.[52]

> [You sinful ones, deprived of glory, need not expect
> that you can shove me under the shadow of shame,
> using evil artifices, nor draw me down into the fire,
> into the house of hell.]

Hamilton draws attention to what she perceives as the two poems'
common usage of *under scæd/sceadu ... motan/moste ... bregdon/ bregdan*, but the similarities are looser than she implies, as "bregdon" of
Guthlac 676b is modified not by "under scæd" but by "on hinder in
helle hus," and the feminine noun "sconde" of 675a could as easily be
used genitively as adverbially. In that case, the line would be translated
as "may thrust (me) under the shadow of shame," a likely goal for
Guthlac's tempters, but not an analogue to the "under sceadu" of
Beowulf 707b.[53] Hamilton goes on to relate the phrase to the *in obscu-
rum* of the Offertory in the Daily Mass for the Dead, and to Gregory's
commentary on Job 40.22.[54] These analogues are cited by Hamilton in
order to establish the phrase in *Beowulf* as "a theological commonplace
on the Creator's protection of the just from the power of demons," but
as she notes, this protection did not prevent Grendel from devouring

---

[49] Hoops, *Kommentar*, 90.

[50] Klaeber, *Beowulf*, p. 154.

[51] Hamilton, 131.

[52] *Guthlac*, lines 673–77, in ASPR 3.68.

[53] Furthermore, the "ne" of *Guthlac* 676a may imply a difference between the
actions described in 675 and 676b–77a; if they were intended in simple variation, the
conjunction would be rendered otiose.

[54] Hamilton, 131–32.

Hondscio.[55] Thus, the use of this "theological commonplace" in *Beowulf* would imply that Hondscio was not among "the just." We may maintain the link to the liturgy while avoiding this problematic characterization of Hondscio if we consider that the terms *obscurus* and *umbra* are associated in the liturgy not with "the just" but with original sin.[56] Hondscio may or may not be the moral equivalent of Guthlac, but he certainly would be encumbered by this unfortunate result of the Fall. Whatever the origin of this phrase in *Beowulf*, we may be certain that it did not derive from the Latin proverbial tradition, as Hans Walther's collection provides no instances of *obscurus* as a metaphor for death, and only one of *umbra* being used in this way.[57] Perhaps we should be content with noting that *under sceadu* achieves great poetic success in *Beowulf*, as it evokes an image of Grendel's dark den at the same time as that of the metaphoric nether regions.

The scene in which Beowulf's companions fall asleep while waiting for Grendel to attack them has occasioned some consternation among critics of the poem,[58] but none have noted that the phrase "þa Metod nolde" provides useful clues to the moods both of the retainers and of the hero. If it was "known to men" ("yldum cuþ") that Grendel's depredations were dependent on the will of God, they might as well sleep, as any action on their part would be either superfluous in light of God's more effective protection, or futile in the absence of His assistance; as it is explained in the late-thirteenth-century *Jacob and Joseph*, "Þat oure Louerd wole habben ido mai no man binime."[59] Beowulf's wakefulness, however, is introduced with the contrastive conjunction *ac* (708a), suggesting that he intends to rely not only on divine providence but on his own martial skills as well. This "belt and suspenders" approach is not frowned upon by the poet, as the narrator himself later states that Grendel's killings were stopped by God *and* Beowulf's *mod* (1056–57). This interpretation need not negate the possible significance of analogues adduced by Panzer and Holthausen (see n. 58), but sug-

---

[55] Hamilton, 130–31.

[56] Albert Blaise, *Le vocabulaire Latin des principaux thèmes liturgiques*, rev. Antoine Dumas, O.S.B. (Turnhout: Brepols, 1966), 76 and 461 (*obscurus*), and 107, 170, and 369 (*umbra*).

[57] Walther, no. 19079: "Nullus homo lacrimis umquam revocatur ad umbris."

[58] See, for example, Hamilton, 130, and Klaeber, *Beowulf*, 154. Hoops (*Kommentar*, 90) cites Panzer's suggested Bear's-Son Tale analogues, along with Holthausen's parallel to the disciples of Christ in Gethsemane.

[59] *Jacob and Joseph*, line 62, cited from Whiting, *Proverbs ... before 1500*, G276.

gests that if the *Beowulf*-poet was including a traditional scene, he did so to the benefit of his hero's characterization. Beowulf himself comes to recognize the limits of his power as compared to that of God, when in F he explains to Hrothgar that he would have preferred to keep the mortally-wounded Grendel within Heorot, but was unsuccessful "þa Metod nolde." Thus passages E and F function similarly to D in describing the interaction of divine will and human agency in dealing with the crisis precipitated by Grendel, but E and F do so with particular reference to the hero's response to the enemy.

He whom God helps none can harm

G. (lines 2291–93a):

> Swa mæg unfæge   eaðe gedigan
> wean ond wræcsið,   se ðe Waldendes
> hyldo gehealdeþ.

With this passage we return to a sentence of truly proverbial form: note the unnamed "unfæge ... se ðe," the present tense of the verbs in both clauses, and the level of generalization above that of the surrounding text. Like the other deistic *sententiae* of *Beowulf*, this one has undergone a transformation as it was incorporated into the poem; in this case the alteration comes in the form of elaboration, as "unfæge" defines "se ðe," and "wean ond wræcsið" appears as a poetic formula for "danger" or "trouble." "Swa," of course, marks the sentence as a general explication of the preceding narrative.

The nearest parallel to this sentence, in time and substance, appears in the ninth-century *Heliand*, as a closing remark on Christ's raising of Lazarus:

> Sô mag hebenkuninges,
> thiu mikile maht godes   manno gehuilikes
> ferahe giformon   endi uuið fiundo nîð
> hêlag helpen,   sô huemu sô he is huldi fargibid.[60]

> [The great might of God, the king of heaven, can protect the life of every man, and against the enmity of enemies the holy one can help him to whom He grants His favor.]

---

[60] *Heliand*, fitt 49, lines 4114b–17, in *Heliand und Genesis*, ed. Otto Behaghel, 9th ed. rev. Burkhard Taeger (Tübingen: Max Niemeyer, 1984), 147.

Although the subject of the sentence has been reversed from the assisted man to the assisting God, these lines correspond remarkably well to
Beowulf passage G. Both *sententiae* begin with identical wording—"Swa
mæg/sô mag"—and introduce their final clauses with correlative constructions altered only to reflect their different subjects—"se þe/sô
huemu sô." In each instance it is His favor—"hyldo/huldi"—that God
chooses to grant. Significantly, the two *sententiae* perform the same
narrative function, that of closing an episode and extracting a moral
from it. The comparison of these lines from the *Heliand* to *Beowulf*
passage G suggests very strongly that both poets knew and used a
proverb or sentence along the lines of "He who receives God's favor is
safe from any injury." The parallel also clarifies some of the ways in
which poets altered existing *sententiae* to fit specific poetic environ-
ments: in this case, subject and object may be reversed, and the nature
of the averted injury may be redefined. While the *Beowulf*-poet's "wean
ond wræcsið" is relatively vague, the composer of the *Heliand* has
opted to direct a more pointed message to his audience by defining the
potential trouble as "the enmity of enemies" (*fiundo nîd*). The plurality
of "fiundo" successfully switches the focus of the sentence from Lazarus to the audience, as the only conceivable enemy in the biblical
episode is death, a singular entity, whereas a warrior-class audience
might be receptive to the idea that God's help could be forthcoming
and effective in struggles against more earthly foes.

Although the written record does not preserve other early-medieval,
vernacular examples of this *sententia*, some form (or various forms) of
the sentence had become very popular in England by around 1300.
Whiting cites three examples from that period, the first of which comes
from *Havelok the Dane*: "Ther God wile helpen, nouht ne dereth."[61]
The other examples derive from two versions of the *South English
Legendary*: the legend of Saint Brendan provides "Þing þat God wol
habbe ywest . ne ssel noþing sle,"[62] and that of Saint Eustace "For þat
þou (Lord) i-saued habbe wolt: no-þing ne schal fur-pere."[63] The form
of the sentence is remarkably similar in all three cases, as each begins
with a subordinate clause, uses some form of the verb "wille" in that

---

[61] *Havelok*, line 648, cited from Whiting, *Proverbs ... before 1500*, G276.

[62] *South English Legendary*, 1:195.438, cited from Whiting, *Proverbs ... before
1500*, G276.

[63] *South English Legendary* (Laud) 400.260, cited from Whiting, *Proverbs ...
before 1500*, G276.

clause, and concludes with a variant of "nothing (shall) harm." The possibility of direct literary borrowing is small, as the sentence appears in different sections of the *Legendary* collections, and no one, to my knowledge, has suggested a direct connection between *Havelok* and the *Legendary*. The possibility that these high-medieval examples reflect the continuation of an oral tradition reaching back as far as *Beowulf* and the *Heliand* is strengthened by the undefined nature of the potential harm, which I have suggested was the form known to the earlier poets.

Unfortunately, attempts to locate intermediate examples of the sentence meet with less success. It is not found elsewhere in the corpus of Old English literature, and Latin versions display greater variation than the Middle English analogues. For example, Otloh supplies a negative version of the idea: "Absque Deo nullus poterit consistere solvus (saluus)"[64] [Without God, none can remain safe]. Icelandic letters record the sentence only later, and in two vastly different forms. From the late-medieval period we find "Þann má ei kefja er guð vill hefja"[65] [No one may sink what God will raise], and from the early-modern, "Guds Vin skadar eingenn Skepna"[66] [No creature harms God's friend]. Still, it is clear that the basic idea of the sentence was widespread in proverbial form.

The plundering of the gold cup from the dragon's hoard is a narrative episode serving an essential function for the plot—it explains the angry awakening of the long-dormant *wyrm*—but it also exhibits some of the characteristics of a fable or exemplum. The thief is unidentified by name or social status: the terms used to describe him are "feasceaft" (2285a) [destitute] and "hæft hygegiomor" (2407a) [sad-minded captive], and we know only that he took the pilfered vessel to his similarly unnamed "hlaford" (2283a) [lord] as a conciliatory offering. The requested boon is granted, and passage G, appearing after the dragon has discovered its loss and the escape of the thief, provides a moral to this broadly-sketched episode: "So may an undoomed man easily survive woe and misery, he who holds the favor of the Lord." The undefined identities of the main actors in this episode characterize it as

---

[64] Otloh, *Lib. prov.*, no. 70 (p. 7); also cited by Walther, no. 189. Korfmacher suggests as Otloh's source John 15.5: "Sine me nihil potestis facere."

[65] From *Þáttr af Hemingi Áslákssyni*; cited in Bjarni Vilhjálmsson and Óskar Halldórsson, *Íslenzkir Málshættir* (Reykjavík: Almenna Bókafélagið, 1966), 122.

[66] *Gudmundi Olaui Thesaurus adagiorum linguae septentrionalis antiquae et modernae*, ed. Gottfrid Kallstenius, Skrifter utgivna av Vetenskaps-Societete i Lund 12 (Lund: C. W. K. Gleerup, 1930), no. 1319 (p. 67).

exemplary or vaguely fictional (even within the fictional framework of the poem as a whole), and like a fable, it is "told in the past tense ... and ... purport(s) to be a particular action or series of actions ... that took place once upon a time through the agency of particular characters."[67] A frequent structural feature of the fable is a proverbial moral at the conclusion, and as I have shown, the episode of the theft concludes with just such a proverbial sentence.

Of course, if this passage (2278-93b) is cast in fabular form, the question remains as to its intended lesson or thematic purpose. In light of Beowulf's less fortunate experience with the dragon, the poet may have intended the wretched thief as a contrast to (and thus an explanation of) the character and fate of the more powerful king of the Geats. The thief is "unfæge" [undoomed], as Beowulf clearly is not, and, according to the moral/*sententia*, he "gehealdeþ hyldo Waldendes," as Beowulf fears he does not.[68] As do passages E and F, passage G implies that victory or success is dependent upon the favor of God; Beowulf's demise can be attributed to the withholding, for whatever reason, of that favor.

What general conclusions may be drawn from this examination of deistic *sententiae* in *Beowulf*? First let us consider the functions of these passages within the narrative structure of the poem; most frequent is their use to explain or clarify an element of plot or characterization. Thus, passages A and D explain Beowulf's victory over the previously invincible Grendel as the result of divine providence, while the hero's failure to hold Grendel in Heorot is likewise attributed to the will of God (F). The death of the hero himself is rendered more significant by becoming part of the divine plan (C and G). The *sententiae* provide for a developed characterization of Beowulf by contrasting him with the retainers sleeping in Heorot (E) and the hoard-pilfering thief (G).

Furthermore, the deistic sentences may provide a sense of closure (A), or mark a transition either between two distinct narratives (B) or between two different forms of discourse (A and G). Finally, the sententious passages may summarize a series of actions (A) or simply set them in a global perspective.

---

[67] *Babrius and Phaedrus*, ed. and trans. Ben Edwin Perry, Loeb Classical Library, no. 436 (Cambridge, Mass.: Harvard Univ. Press, 1965), p. xx. I do not mean to imply that the episode *is* a fable, but rather, that it is treated as one in the construction of the narrative.

[68] "wende se wisa,   þæt he Wealdende
     ofer ealde riht   ecean Dryhtne
     bitre gebulge;"   (2329a–31a).

The thematic functions of the deistic *sententiae* are more difficult to describe. In general, the sentences propound the omnipotence of God in deciding human affairs, so they enjoin acquiescence by thief, retainer, and king alike. Of course, human uncertainty regarding what constitutes the will of God requires heroic efforts in any endeavor, efforts involving a trust both in God and in one's own skill. The sentences also create a link between the action of the poem and the world of the audience, as they stress the continuity of divine providence over the intervening generations.[69] Thus, the lessons exemplified by the poetic characters become immediately relevant to the later audience.

As I have demonstrated above, the deistic sentences of *Beowulf* exhibit frequent similarities of vocabulary, syntax, and semantics; these internal parallels indicate that the poet used a common verbal source or background in his construction of these phrases. I would offer that this background was constituted by a tradition of deistic proverbs in both Latin and the vernacular. Most of the analogues I have adduced are Latin, but that circumstance is accounted for both by the more widespread transmission and preservation of Latin texts and by the near hegemony of Latin as the language of Christian religious discourse. Such deistic proverbs were numerous and widely disseminated throughout the medieval period, and therefore would have been available to the *Beowulf*-poet for the composition of his poem.

Not surprisingly, the *Beowulf*ian sentences and their analogues hint strongly of a biblical, and especially psalmic, origin (see A, D, and F). However, the nature of this relationship is sometimes difficult to determine, as "In proverbs of Biblical origin we see all stages of the disintegration of a phrase: the Biblical quotation gradually becomes a vague, inaccurate reminiscence."[70] The vagueness of these "reminiscences" is well-illustrated by the *Beowulf* passages, while the differences between them and their analogues can be attributed in part to the particular fluidity of this type of proverb.

The actual use of the Bible as a source of proverbs should not come into question, as its verses would have been available not only through direct contact with the text itself (in worship and liturgy as well as in devotional reading), but also through preaching, ecclesiastical writ-

---

[69] On this point, see Leslie Harris, "The Vatic Mode in *Beowulf*," *Neophilologus* 74 (1990): 594–96.

[70] Archer Taylor, *The Proverb*, 54.

ings,[71] and school collections such as that compiled by Otloh. In fact, the use of psalms as the first texts for beginning readers was nearly ubiquitous in the west by the seventh or eighth century, with the result that, as Pierre Riché puts it, "Savoir lire c'est connaître son psautier."[72] This early training seemed to stay with medieval pupils, as citations from the psalter can be found in such diverse venues as bits of tile, the heads of royal diplomas, and the margins of manuscripts.[73] Not surprisingly, then, the Book of Psalms seems to have proved an especially fruitful source of deistic sentences, both because it enjoyed most frequent transmission and because its generalized mode of expression is particularly suited to proverbial extraction. While it may be impossible in individual cases to determine whether the composer of *Beowulf* drew on his own knowledge of the Bible or on other variants of biblical *sententiae*, it is clear that this proverbial tradition offered him a model for creating these phrases as they appear in the poem.

---

[71] Taylor, *The Proverb*, 58.

[72] Pierre Riché, *Éducation et culture dans l'Occident barbare, VIe–VIIIe siècles*, 3rd ed., Patristica Sorbonensia 4 (Paris: Editions du Seuil, 1962), 516; see also his "Le Livre Psautier, livre de lecture mérovingien," *Etudes mérovingiennes, Actes des Journées de Poitiers, 1952* (Paris, 1953): 253–56.

[73] Ibid.

3

Joy and Sorrow

One of the most frequently invoked proverbial contrasts, in the vernacular as well as the Latin corpus, is that between joy and sorrow. This dichotomy, so basic to the human condition, is likewise treated frequently in Old English (and other medieval) literature, and has its place in the thematic structure of *Beowulf*. The thematic use of joy and sorrow in *Beowulf* has been addressed by earlier scholars, who have explicated it in several ways. In the first instance, such scholars as Kemp Malone, Arthur Brodeur, and Herbert Wright have pointed out the alternation of joy and sorrow in the overall thematic structure of the poem.[1] That is, the first part of *Beowulf*, the narrative which portrays the cleansing of Heorot, is perceived as ultimately joyful, cheerful, and celebratory; however, this joy is fleeting. Brodeur writes that "In Part II, ... the unrelieved darkness of the theme contrasts bleakly with the recollected splendor and glory of Part I."[2] As a comprehensive view of the poem, especially with respect to the career of the hero, such an interpretation is valid and useful. Of course, it does not take into consideration the hints of disaster that pepper "Part I": for example, the Finnsburh episode, the warnings of Hrothgar's ser-

---

[1] Kemp Malone, "Beowulf," *English Studies* 29 (1948): 161–72, repr. in *An Anthology of Beowulf Criticism*, ed. Nicholson, 137–54; Arthur Gilchrist Brodeur, *The Art of Beowulf* (Berkeley: Univ. of California Press, 1959), esp. 82–87 and 116–29; Herbert G. Wright, "Good and Evil; Light and Darkness; Joy and Sorrow in *Beowulf*," *Review of English Studies* 8 (1957): 1–11, repr. in Nicholson, 257–67.

[2] Brodeur, 123.

mon, and Beowulf's misgivings about a continued peace between the Danes and Heathobards.

In a short article published in 1962, Jack Durant continues the thematic treatment of joy in *Beowulf*, but provides a somewhat different interpretation.[3] Durant categorizes the joys of the poem as social, diabolic, and spiritual, and concludes that while social joys—those based on "participation in the *comitatus*" and a sense of personal achievement—do decline at the end of the poem, they are replaced by the spiritual joy of the hero. This spiritual joy is, according to Durant, "perceived in terms of social joy"—that is, "comfort in the universal principles of brotherhood and service"—but is removed from the social into the universal realm by the imminence of Beowulf's death.[4]

In a more convincing argument, Theodore Andersson has analyzed the structure of *Beowulf* while concentrating on what he perceives as the "cultivation of mood and emotional resonance."[5] By dividing the entire poem into traditional episodes (e.g., battle scenes, hall scenes, consultations, flytings), Andersson has identified a wave pattern of alternating hope and despair, or in the terms of this study, of joy and sorrow. The wave pattern structures the entire poem, but still ends on an ebb tide: "the notion that life is unstable and is lent stability only by trust in the hereafter."[6] Andersson does not, however, examine the role of our proverbial or sentential passages in the development of this structure.

Casting his net somewhat wider, Joseph Harris has studied the elegiac aspects and passages of *Beowulf* in their literary-historical context. By proposing the existence of a West Germanic elegiac tradition, Harris has linked two passages of *Beowulf*—"The Lament of the Last Survivor" (lines 2231–70) and "The Old Man's Lament" (2444–62)—to a poetic form in which the speaker bemoans his or her current misery and contrasts it to an earlier, happier time.[7]

---

[3] Jack Durant, "The Function of Joy in *Beowulf*," *Tennessee Studies in Literature* 7 (1962): 61–69.

[4] Durant, 63 and 68. It should be noted that Durant perceives spiritual joy in *Beowulf* as entirely secular in nature. For another optimistic view of the poem, see Bruce Mitchell, " 'Until the Dragon Comes . . .': Some Thoughts on *Beowulf*," in *On Old English: Selected Papers* (Oxford: Basil Blackwell, 1988), 3–15 (repr. from *Neophilologus* 47 [1963]: 126–38); see also Mitchell's 1987 postscript in the same volume, esp. 42–43, 53–54.

[5] Theodore M. Andersson, "Tradition and Design in *Beowulf*," in *Old English Literature in Context: Ten Essays*, ed. John D. Niles (Cambridge: D. S. Brewer; Totowa, N.J.: Rowman and Littlefield, 1980), 94.

[6] Andersson, 105.

[7] Joseph Harris, "Elegy in Old English and Old Norse: A Problem in Literary

Thus, most approaches to the themes of joy and sorrow in *Beowulf*, whether thematic, structural, or literary-historical, stress a progression from earlier joy to later sorrow. Andersson devotes the most attention to the continued interplay between joy and sorrow in the poem, but even he interprets the joyful passages primarily as foils for the inevitable onset of disaster. The identification of this progression is comforting to modern readers in that we expect Old English heroic poetry to be ultimately pessimistic in its outlook, and we may be pleased to point out the Christian theme of *sic transit gloria mundi*. However, a look at the three passages in *Beowulf* where joy and sorrow are treated together reveals a more complex set of possibilities:

> H. Hwæt, me þæs on eþle   edwenden cwom,
> gyrn æfter gomene   (1774–75a)
>
> [Listen, a reversal came to me in my native land, grief after joy]
>
> I. hwæþer him Alwalda   æfre wille
> æfter weaspelle   wyrpe gefremman   (1314–15)
>
> [Whether the Almighty will ever wish to bring about a change for him after the time of sorrow]
>
> J.   Fela sceal gebidan
> leofes ond laðes   se þe longe her
> on ðyssum windagum   worolde bruceð   (1060b–62)
>
> [He who here enjoys the world for a long time in these days of strife must experience many pleasant and hateful things].

We are told by the poet that sorrow does indeed follow joy, but we also learn that better times may follow sorrowful ones, and finally, that good times and bad may be consecutive or even concurrent. These multiple possibilities may seem mutually contradictory in the context of a single poem, but such apparent contradiction is not at all surprising in the corpus of proverbial analogues (or, for that matter, in the life experience of the average person). For that reason, I will examine these passages in relation

---

History," in *The Vikings*, ed. R. T. Farrell (London: Phillimore & Co., Ltd., 1982), 157–64; *idem*, "Hadubrand's Lament: On the Origin and Age of Elegy in Germanic," in *Heldensage und Heldendichtung im Germanischen*, ed. Heinrich Beck (Berlin and New York: Walter de Gruyter, 1988), 81–114, esp. 97–101, 105.

to those analogues, even though only passage J itself takes a proverbial form. The ideas expressed in these passages and their analogues are simple, commonplace, even banal, but their individual phrasings may be examined and compared in an attempt to determine whether the poet drew his expressions from any specific proverbial tradition.

Sorrow after joy

H. (lines 1774–75a):

> Hwæt, me þæs on eþle   edwenden cwom,
> gyrn æfter gomene.

These lines, spoken by Hrothgar as he describes his troubles to Beowulf, constitute too particularized and personalized an expression to be considered proverbial. Hrothgar relates a change in his situation, and goes on to qualify that change (attributed to Grendel) as one of "sorrow after joy." However, the brevity of the reference to "gyrn æfter gomene" leads one to suspect that the poet is relying on a proverbial contrast easily recognized by his audience.

One early, and subsequently widespread, instance of the proverbial contrast of joy and sorrow is Prov. 14.13: "Risus dolore miscetur, et extrema gaudii occupat luctus" [Laughter will be mixed with sorrow, and tears occupy the end of joy]. The verse begins with the statement that joy and sorrow are mingled together, but it goes on to stress the progression from joy to sorrow, rather than the reverse. Although Otloh and Defensor included the entire verse in their collections,[8] Latin and vernacular proverbial usage tends to favor the second, more pessimistic, half. For example, Bede created a new sentence of his own on the pattern of Prov. 14.13 and including some of its wording: "Stultus est igitur qui gaudet in scelere, sapientis autem est et eius qui uiri nomine dignus sit praeuidere *quia risus dolore miscebitur et gaudia peccandi poena sequetur ultionis*"[9] [Therefore he is foolish who rejoices

---

[8] Otloh, *Lib. prov.*, ed. Korfmacher, no. 9 (p. 72); and Defensor, *Liber scintillarum*, ed. D. Henricus M. Rochais, O.S.B., in *Defensoris Liber Scintillarum, Desiderii Cadurcensis Epistulae, Epistulae Austrasicae aliaeque*, CCSL 117 (Turnhout: Brepols, 1957), 55.8 (p. 179). The entire verse also appears, attributed to Solomon, in the *Florilegium Frisingense*, in *Florilegia*, ed. Albert Lehner, CCSL 108D (Turnhout: Brepols, 1987), no. 363 (p. 31).

[9] Bede, "In Proverbia," in *Bedae Venerabilis Opera*, part 2.2B: Opera exegetica, ed. D. Hurst, O.S.B., and J. E. Hudson, CCSL 119B (Turnhout: Brepols, 1983), 21–163; here (bk. 2, chap. 10, p. 68) Bede is explicating Prov. 10.23.

in sin, because it is for the wise and for him who is worthy to be called
a man to foresee that laughter will be mixed with sorrow and the joy
of sinning results in an avenging punishment (emphasis mine)]. Bede's
"quia" introducing "risus dolore miscebitur" as a piece of accepted
wisdom, which indeed it is, lends authority and logic to his subsequent
statement that joy (in sinning) is followed by the pain of retribution.
He has used the biblical proverb as a model for constructing his own,
more specific, didactic expression. The tenth-century bishop Rather of
Verona found Prov. 14.13 a useful prooftext for his assertion that
sadness is "utilior" than joy:

> Ipso, inquit, nostro Deus gaudet lamento; unde dicitur: Ante rui-
> nam exaltatum cor; et illud quod tametsi de futura perditione
> maxime, tamen et de presenti potest intellegi euentuum uarietate:
> Risus dolore miscebitur, et extrema gaudii luctus occupat.[10]

> [He says, "God rejoices in our sorrow," whence it is said: the
> heart exulted before a fall; and although that concerns the great-
> est ruin in the future, nevertheless it also can be understood in
> regard to the variety of events in the present: Laughter will be
> mixed with sorrow, and tears fill the extremes of joy.]

As one would expect, Rather goes on to counsel moderation in both
joy and sorrow.

The movement from "joy and sorrow are mixed" to "sorrow
replaces joy" was also exploited in a poem by Alcuin:

> Tristia se laetis inmiscent tempora nostris:
> Utque vices faciunt noxque diesque suas,
> Gaudia iam veniunt, veniunt et tristia statim,
> Non est qui fuerat, transiet omnis homo.[11]

> [Sad times mingle with our happy ones: and as night
> and day fulfill their functions in alternation, now come
> joys, and at once come sorrows. He who had been is
> no longer; everyone will pass away.]

The last line presents the replacement of joy by sorrow as related to the
Christian elegiac theme of the transitoriness of the world.

---

[10] *Ratherii Veronensis Praeloquiorum libri VI*, ed. Petrus L. D. Reid, CCCM 46A
(Turnhout: Brepols, 1984), bk. 6, chap. 18 (p. 185).

[11] Alcuin, *Carmina*, in MGH *Poetae latini aevi carolini*, ed. Ernest Dümmler
(Berlin: Weidmannos, 1881), Carmen 48, lines 27–30 (pp. 1:260–61).

Sententiae based on Prov. 14.13 seem not to have enjoyed continuous vernacular transmission, but rather, appear to represent repeated adaptation from the biblical Latin form. Chaucer used the proverb in three different versions, none of them differing greatly from the biblical verse in their translation. In *Troilus and Criseyde*, Chaucer puts the proverb, characteristically, in the mouth of Pandarus: "The ende of blisse, ay sorwe it occupyeth."[12] The Man of Law expands on the proverb in his usual sententious fashion, but still retains a close translation of the biblical source:

> O sodeyn wo! that ever art successour
> To worldly blisse, spreynd with bitternesse;
> Th' ende of the joye of our worldly labour;
> Wo occupyeth the fyn of our gladnesse.[13]

Chaucer's third use of the proverb is similarly expanded, but omits the Latinate verb "occupyeth":

> But sodeynly hym fil a sorweful cas,
> For evere the latter ende of joye is wo.
> God woot that worldly joye is soone ago.[14]

In this last case, the proverb appears in the *Nun's Priest's Tale* just before the fox makes himself known to Chauntecleer; thus, it is used in similar fashion to what we have already seen (chapter 2) in *Beowulf*, that is, to introduce or anticipate some dramatic episode of the narrative.

Other Middle English versions of the sentence based on Prov. 14.13 exhibit greater variation in their wording. Whiting cites a variant from an Oxford manuscript of around 1350, wherein the movement from joy to sorrow is duplicated in parallel phrases: "The ende of lagthre is woth, and the ende of bliz is sorege."[15] Gower notes the customary nature of the contrast, and imbues it with a touch of metaphor:

---

[12] Chaucer, *Troilus*, 4.836; cited in Walter W. Skeat, *Early English Proverbs: Chiefly of the Thirteenth and Fourteenth Centuries* (Oxford: Clarendon Press, 1910), no. 193, and Whiting, *Proverbs ... before 1500*, E80.

[13] Chaucer, *Man of Law's Tale*, B.421–24; cited in Skeat, no. 193, and Whiting, *Proverbs ... before 1500*, J61.

[14] Chaucer, *Nun's Priest's Tale*, B.4394–96; cited in Skeat, no. 193, and Whiting, *Proverbs ... before 1500*, E80.

[15] Magdalen Oxford MS 27; cited by Whiting, *Proverbs ... before 1500*, E80.

It hath ben sen and felt fulofte,
The harde time after the softe.[16]

As this multiplication of examples shows, vernacular sentences originating from Prov. 14.13 were in frequent use in England by the fourteenth century; for that reason, we may assume that the verse circulated as a proverb somewhat earlier there, and that proverbs in general did, in fact, pass over from biblical Latin to vernacular English use.

Another likely biblical source for complaints lamenting the onset of sorrow is the book of Job. Hans Walther suggests Job 30.31 as the source of a sentence found in a fifteenth-century Munich manuscript: "Gaudium meum versum est in luctum"[17] [My joy has been turned into weeping], and cites as an earlier analogue the first lines of a poem by Walter of Châtillon:

Versa est in luctum
cythara Waltheri.[18]

[Walter's lute has been turned to weeping.]

A much earlier reflex of the biblical phrasing appears in Jerome's commentary on Isa. 23.1–3, as he addresses those people who desire the wealth of the world more than the lasting good of heaven; these should weep, knowing that worldly affairs are doomed to perish, "et contemplationem gaudii atque laetitiae in luctum lacrimasque uertendam"[19] [And the contemplation of joy and gladness must be changed to sorrow and tears]. Jerome has expanded the phrase considerably, but the defining elements of "gaudium," "luctus," and "verto" are still evident. The "versa est in luctum" formula does not seem to have produced many cognate *sententiae*, but it does provide an analogue to the reversal of fortunes evoked by Hrothgar's "edwenden cwom."

---

[16] Gower, *Confessio amantis*, 2.252.979–80; cited by Whiting, *Proverbs ... before 1500*, T302.

[17] Walther, no. 2777.

[18] *Moralisch-satirisch Gedichte Walters von Châtillon aus deutschen, englischen, französischen und italienischen Handschriften*, ed. Karl Strecker (Heidelberg: Carl Winter, 1929), Poem 17, st. 1, lines 1–2 (p. 148); Walther, no. 2777. Walter's use of this verse again illustrates the transitional function of such *sententiae*: the line closes Job 30, but opens Walter's poem.

[19] *Commentarii in Isaiam*, in *S. Hieronymi presbyteri Opera*, part 1: Opera exegetica, ed. M. Adriaen, CCSL 73 and 73A (Turnhout: Brepols, 1963), bk. 7, chap. 23 [CCSL 73.308].

The element of change, albeit a more voluntary alteration of mood, is also expressed in James 4.9. Bede quoted this verse in several of his commentaries,[20] but a more interesting use is in his "Homilia in Theophania seu Epiphania Domini," where he reshapes and alludes to various lines of Scripture, rather than quoting them directly:

> Miseri simus et lugeamus et ploremus coram domino qui fecit nos. Risus noster in luctum conuertatur et gaudium in maerorem. Beati enim lugentes quoniam ipsi consolabuntur.[21]

> [Let us be wretched and cry out in our hearts to the Lord who has created us. Let our laughter be converted to tears and our joy into lamentation. For blessed are those who mourn, because they will be consoled.]

Although Bede alters the syntax of James 4.9, he maintains the spirit of the verse. Caesarius of Arles had also alluded to the verse in one of his sermons, but used it as a thinly veiled threat against those who might tend to neglect their pursuit of virtue:

> Ergo nec ille desperet qui malus est, quia cito potest resurgere; nec ille qui bonus est, aut neglegens remaneat, aut aliquid de sua virtute praesumat, ne gaudium suum convertatur ad luctum.[22]

> [Therefore he who is evil should not despair, because he can soon rise again; nor should he who is good remain unwatchful or presume anything about his virtue, lest his joy be converted to sorrow.]

The proverbial expression is provided with a more imaginative and dramatic setting by Eusebius 'Gallicanus', in a homily on the Resurrection; the demonic denizens of Hell see Christ approaching for the Harrowing, and are understandably perturbed:

> O princeps noster: illas tuas diuitias, quas primo acquisieras per paradisi amissionem, nunc perdedisti per crucem. Perit omnis laetitia tua: in luctum conuersa sunt gaudia tua. Dum tu Chris-

---

[20] *In primam partem Samuhelis*, bk. 2, chap. 15; *In cantica canticorum*, bk. 1, chap. 2.

[21] "Homeliarum euangelii libri ii," in *Bedae Opera*, part 3: Opera homiletica, ed. D. Hurst, O.S.B., CCSL 122 (Turnhout: Brepols, 1955), bk. 1, hom. 12 (p. 86).

[22] "Sermo de templo vel consecratione altaris," in *Sancti Caesarii Arelatensis Sermones*, ed. D. Germanus Morin, O.S.B., CCSL 103 and 104 (Turnhout: Brepols, 1953), sermon 228, chap. 4 (p. 903).

tum suspendis in ligno, ignoras quanta damna sustineas in infer-
no.[23]

[O prince of ours, these your riches, which you first acquired
through the loss of paradise, now you have lost through the
cross. All your joy perishes: your joys have been converted to
tears. While you hang Christ on the cross, you disregard how
many damned you maintain in hell.]

In this case, the phrase serves primarily to invoke a reversal of fortune,
rather than to express any absolute state of happiness or misery, as the
"gaudia" of the Prince of Hell are difficult to imagine and must be
relatively small. These three homiletic variants illustrate one way in
which biblical sayings were disseminated, in rhetorical contexts similar
to or farther removed from their original setting. Although the entire
verse of James 4.9 was available not only in the Bible, but also in such
collectanea as that of Defensor,[24] the most common Latin version of
the phrase in question emerges as somewhat of a blending of James 4.9
with Job 30.31, maintaining the verb of the former, but stripping the
substantive elements down to the "gaudium" and "luctus" of the latter.
We may see the result of this process in Augustine's "Epistola ad
virgines": "non apud uos uerbis sed apud deum lacrimis agerem, ne
conuertat in luctum gaudium meum"[25] [I must serve God among you
not with words but with tears, lest my joy be converted to sorrow].

Returning to vernacular poetry, we find two Middle High German
expressions of the succession of sorrow after joy. The earlier dates from
the 1190's, in Hartmann von Aue's Der arme Heinrich: "Nu sehent wie
unser lachen mit weinen erlischet"[26] [Now behold how our laughter
is drowned in tears]. The theme of Hartmann's poetic image was repeated in more literal, and more dire, terms by Thomasin von Zerclaere: "An swiu grôze vreude lît, dâ lît grôz leit zallen zît"[27] [Wher-

---

[23] "Homilia Eusebii De resurrectione Domini," in Sermones extravagantes, ed.
Fr. Glorie, CCSL 101B (Turnhout: Brepols, 1971), sermon 8 (p. 884).

[24] Lib. scin., 55.4 (CCSL 117.179).

[25] Epistulae, CSEL 57, epist. 211 (p. 357).

[26] Hartmann von Aue, Der arme Heinrich, line 106; cited by Carl Schulze, Die
biblischen Sprichwörter der deutschen Sprache (Göttingen, 1860); repr. ed. Wolfgang
Mieder (Bern and New York: P. Lang, 1987), no. 65.

[27] Thomasin von Zerclaere, Welscher Gast, line 3989; cited by Ignaz v. Zingerle,
Die Deutschen Sprichwörter im Mittelalter (Vienna: Wilhelm Braumüller, 1864), 38;
Wander, DS-L, Freude 84.

ever great joy lies, there always lies great sorrow]. Neither of these sentences seems definitely based on a biblical verse, and only that of Thomasin assumes proverbial form; both, however, evoke the proverbial progression of sorrow following joy.

Having established that the theme of sorrow following joy was widespread in proverbial form, in both Latin and vernacular manifestations,[28] we may return to Hrothgar's speech to consider what use the *Beowulf*-poet has made of this contrast. The phrase "gyrn æfter gomene" occurs near the end of Hrothgar's sermon, as he describes how his long military success was interrupted. Hrothgar refers to his reversal of fortune with the essentially neutral term "edwenden," then succinctly defines this reversal as the accession of grief after joy. As he then goes on to recall the ravages of Grendel, Hrothgar's qualification of the reversal is hardly necessary; as a proverbial reference, however, the brief phrase "gyrn æfter gomene" would recall a familiar pattern to the minds of the audience. Thus the phrase performs the proverbial function of summarizing a narrative, and creates a relation between Hrothgar's experience and that of the reader or listener.

Joy after sorrow

I. (lines 1314–15):

> hwæþer him Alwalda   æfre wille
> æfter weaspelle   wyrpe gefremman.

This passage bears a closer similarity to proverbial form than did the last: the omission of the first two words of line 1314 would leave a perfectly regular proverb or sentence, in part because of the present tense of the verb.[29] Although the contrast of joy and sorrow is implied, rather than stated outright in this passage, the combination of

---

[28] Of course, the theme is closely enough related to common experience that it may be practically universal, but we are concerned here with its *proverbial* manifestations.

[29] Klaeber's note on these lines refers one to his statement that in *Beowulf* "Lack of concord as shown in the ... violation, or free handling, of the *consecutio temporum* should cause no surprise or suspicion" (*Beowulf*, p. xciii). However, Hoops (*Kommentar*, 160) lists only six other places in the poem where the tense shifts from preterite to present within a narrative segment: lines 381, 1923, 1928, 2486, 2495, and 2719. If, as I suspect, the change of tense in line 1314b is related to the proverbial background of the lines, some other explanation must account for the shift in its remaining occurrences.

wyrpe, which almost always connotes a change for the better,[30] with *weaspelle*, makes the sense unmistakable. As in the deistic *sententiae* of *Beowulf*, the activity of God in this case depends upon His will; thus, sentential analogues to this passage take two forms: either "joy follows sorrow" or "joy is granted by God."

As proverbs declaring that joy follows sorrow are not based on a specific biblical verse (or on any other single identifiable model), their wording displays greater variation than in my previous examples; however, their syntax, tense, and generality mark them as clearly proverbial or sentential. We may examine these analogues in roughly chronological order.

The eighth-century *Florilegium Frisingense* offers three sentences promising that sorrow will be followed by joy; two of these are drawn from Isidore of Seville's *Synonyma*, and the third from the Bible:

Tribulatio huius temporis finem habet   (*Syn.* 1.25)

[The tribulation of this time has an end]

Quanto in praesenti adfligimur, tanto in futuro gaudebimus
                                                              (*Syn.* 1.28)

[As much as we are distressed in the present, that much will we rejoice in the future]

Mundus gaudebit, et uos tristis eritis, sed tristitia uestra
uertetur in gaudium   (John 16.20)

[The world will rejoice, and you will be sorrowful, but your sorrow will be changed into joy].[31]

Although the sentences here cited from the *Florilegium* are provided with source designations in the manuscript ("Esidorus," "In Evangelio") and cannot, therefore, be considered proverbial, this collection is remarkable for reversing the usual monastic proportions of optimistic to pessimistic *sententiae*. That is, this *florilegium* presents sorrow turning to joy more often than the reverse. From our point of view, the *Florilegium Frisingense* is also notable for its compiler, an Anglo-Saxon or Irish scribe named Peregrinus, who copied out his selections

---

[30] Compare *Guthlac*, lines 47, 509, and 636, and other analogues, below.
[31] *Flor. Fris.*, nos. 238 (CCSL 108D.22), 239 (ibid.), and 250 (CCSL 108D.23).

in an Anglo-Saxon minuscule script.[32] For this eighth-century insular monk, sentences describing the alternation of joy and sorrow represented excerptible, potentially useful sayings. From around the same time, or perhaps somewhat earlier, the Irish *Audacht Morainn* contains a list of negative things yielding to the positive; included in this early *speculum principum* is the simple sentence "To-léci brón do fáilti" ("Sorrow yields to joy").[33]

In the late twelfth century, the proverb appears in a lyric by Hartmann von Aue, who characteristically embellishes it with a metaphorical image: "Nach ungewitter lichte tage, freude und heil nâch grôzer klage"[34] [After storms, bright days; joy and happiness after great sorrow]. The parallelism and elision of the verb combine to give proverbial form to Hartmann's expression.

Heinrich von dem Türlin offers the earliest German vernacular example of a sentence eschewing metaphor, but stating simply that "Joy often follows sorrow": "Einem leide volget dicke liep."[35] Heinrich was succeeded by Hugo von Trimberg—"Nach grôzem trûren kumt oft heil"[36] [Happiness often comes after great sorrow]—and by the Latin sentence in a fourteenth-century Kremsmünster manuscript, "Eveniunt homini post luctus gaudia sepe"[37] [Joys often come to a man after sorrows]. These *sententiae* exhibit significant variation in their diction, but all express the idea of joy *after* sorrow (*volget*, *nach*, *post*) and employ some form of an adverb meaning "often" (*dicke*, *oft*, *sepe*). Thus, these Middle High German and Latin analogues must represent variants of a common *sententia* lacking a fixed form.

Two fourteenth-century expressions of joy following sorrow employ parallel phrasing along with metaphorical elaboration. A Basel manuscript of the *Vocabular* of Jacobus Argentinensis offers a sentence similar to that of *Beowulf*, in that it expresses a sense of hope or expectation in connection with the proverbial reversal of fortune: "Gaudium post luctum spero, post germina fructum"[38] [I hope for joy after

---

[32] *Florilegia*, ed. Lehner, CCSL 108D.xiii–xiv.

[33] *Audacht Morainn*, ed. and trans. Fergus Kelly (Dublin: Institute for Advanced Studies, 1976), §54b (pp. 14, 15).

[34] Hartmann von Aue, *Klage* 2.444; cited by Schulze, no. 65.

[35] Heinrich von dem Türlin, *Diu Krône*, line 7304; cited by Zingerle, 88.

[36] Hugo von Trimberg, *Der Renner*, line 11111; cited by Zingerle, 149.

[37] Walther, no. 8222.

[38] Walther, no. 10227.

sorrow, fruit after the seed]. Like Hartmann, Chaucer compares sorrow and joy to darkness and light:

> And next the derke night the glade morwe;
> And also joye is next the fyn of sorwe.[39]

In this case, Chaucer seems to have reversed the meaning of the biblical proverb described earlier by maintaining the basic form and vocabulary—compare "the fyn of sorwe" to "the fyn of our gladnesse"—but inverting the places of the relevant emotions. His treatment of the sentence exemplifies the flexibility associated with this proverbial contrast.

The role of God in dispensing human happiness or misery may be stated explicitly (as in passage I) or implicitly. As an example of the latter we may consider Matt. 5.5 as it was excerpted by the accomplished Carolingian scholar Sedulius Scottus for his *Collectaneum Miscellaneum*: "Beati qui lugent nunc, quoniam et ipsi c(onsolabuntur)"[40] [Blessed are those who weep now, because they will be consoled]. Although the Beatitudes were a well-known part of the Gospels, or perhaps *because* they were, varied *sententiae* seem not to have developed from this verse. Sedulius, however, considered the theme as appropriate for inclusion under the chapter-heading "De lacrimis et lvcris," which also included Basil's pronouncement that "Presens luctus leticiam generat sempiternam"[41] [Present sorrow engenders eternal joy]. The implication that God rewards earthly sorrow with heavenly joy did not subsequently develop into a proverb, although the idea was widespread and may provide part of the foundation for *sententiae* linking happiness to God. Sedulius's interest in collecting sentences linking joy and sorrow in various ways parallels that of Defensor, whose chapter "De risu et fletu" contains twenty-two items, and together they may reflect an eighth- to ninth-century intellectual trend.

Any Latin proverbs that I have found ascribing to the will of God the onset of joy or sorrow on earth alone have been attested only in late-medieval or early-modern texts, and resemble the form recorded by

---

[39] Chaucer, *Troilus*, 1.951–52; cited by Skeat, no. 154.

[40] From Sedulius Scottus, *Collectaneum Miscellaneum* 13.21.1, ed. Dean Simpson, CCCM 67 (Turnhout: Brepols, 1988), 91. The verse also appears in Defensor's *Lib. scin.*, 55.1 (CCSL 117.179); for another biblical verse (John 16.20) expressing joy after sorrow, see *Lib. scin.*, 52.1 (p. 175).

[41] Basil, *Admonitio ad Filium Spiritualem* 17, in Sedulius, *Coll. Misc.* 13.21.14 (CCSL 67.92).

Jan Gruter: "A Deo omnis prospera, omnis res acerba a Deo est"[42] [Everything blissful and everything grievous is from God]. However, a line from *Maxims I* illustrates the currency of this theme in an Old English sentential context. Describing the plight of a blind man, the poet declares that "Waldend him þæt wite teode, se him mæg wyrpe syllan"[43] [The Lord gave him that punishment, He may give him a reversal]. The sentiment is exactly parallel to passage I from *Beowulf*, and the form and diction are also very similar. *Wyrpe* is used in both passages to connote a positive change, and in both, God's potential assistance is qualified: "God can (*mæg*) grant relief," and "God may desire (*wille*) to grant relief." The similarities between these passages outweigh the differences, particularly if one considers the fluidity of this sentence as I have already demonstrated. Thus, the progression of joy after sorrow had acquired proverbial status by the Anglo-Saxon period, and continued to be expressed through the high and late Middle Ages.

As I mentioned briefly in connection with Chaucer's *Nun's Priest's Tale* (and in chapter 2, above), proverbs are often inserted in a narrative in order to mark a change in the action. In the case of passage I, Hrothgar has suffered a great loss in the death of Æschere, but the proverbially-based passage anticipates Beowulf's upcoming victory by reminding the audience of God's proven ability to turn suffering into joy. Hrothgar is portrayed as expecting just such a divinely-initiated reversal, as he waited ("bad") to see "hwæþer him Alwalda æfre wille...." Similarly, familiarity with the usual sentential treatment of this theme, along with the help of God already expressed in relation to Beowulf's earlier victory, would incline a reader or listener to assume that if God's providence is being invoked, then it is likely to be forthcoming.[44]

---

[42] Walther, no. 34292.f; see also nos. 34293.g and h, and 39222.d, all collected by Walther from Jan Gruter's compilations. But see also *Deor*, lines 31–34 (ASPR 3.179), where we learn that God distributes blessings to some people and woes to others.

[43] *Maxims I*, line 43 (ASPR 3.158). The blindness referred to may be physical or spiritual; in either case its cure represents a divinely effected change for the better. For the argument in favor of spiritual blindness, see Frederick M. Biggs and Sandra McEntire, "Spiritual Blindness in the Old English *Maxims I*, Part I," *N&Q* 35 (Mar. 1988): 11.

[44] Nowhere in the Latin or vernacular proverbial corpus, to my knowledge, does God inflict suffering on humanity without compensatory joy; He may balance joys with woes, but He never plunges people into misery and leaves them there.

Joy and sorrow linked

J. (lines 1060b–62):

> Fela sceal gebidan
> leofes ond laðes,   se þe longe her
> on ðyssum windagum   worolde bruceð!

Unlike passages H and I, these lines are truly proverbial in form: they employ the indefinite subject *se þe*, along with a modal verb in the present tense and an overall sense of generalization. The diction of passage J also seems largely traditional, as "leofes ond laðes" has the air of a proverbial formula,[45] and the initial phrase—"Fela sceal gebidan"—is paralleled in *Maxims II*: "se þe ær feala gebideð"[46] [He who has endured much]. The sense of the passage is clear: "He who long enjoys the world in these days of strife must experience many pleasant and painful things," or in a proverbial short-form, "Life brings both joy and sorrow."

Analogues to passage J again take two forms,[47] the first of which states simply that joy and sorrow are mingled together, and dates back at least to Ovid: "Miscentur tristia letis"[48] [Let sorrow be mingled with joys]. In a more complex formulation, the poetical wisdom dialogue *Solomon and Saturn II* personifies the emotions, represented by their respective physical manifestations, as "companions":

> Saturnus cwæð:
> Ac forhwan beoð ða gesiðas   somod ætgædere,
> wop and hleahtor?   Full oft hie weorðgeornra
> sælða toslitað.   Hu gesæleð ðæt?

---

[45] I have counted twelve instances where *leof* and *lað* appear in the same line of Old English poetry; however, these phrases are quite varied, and the two words rarely occur in the same half-line. Thus, I would characterize the contrast as proverbial rather than formulaic. See Jess B. Bessinger, *A Concordance to the Anglo-Saxon Poetic Records*, programmed by Philip H. Smith (Ithaca: Cornell Univ. Press, 1978).

[46] *Maxims II*, line 12b, ASPR 6.56; the parallel is pointed out in Klaeber, *Beowulf*, 170, note to lines 1060–62.

[47] Actually, there exists a third form, less closely related to the *Beowulf* passage, which declares that neither joy nor sorrow is a permanent state. An early appearance of this form is in Sedulius, *Coll. Misc.* 80.17.2 (p. 336): "Nemo perpetuo felix. Omnium rerum uicissitudo est. Nemo perpetuo miser … Nec tristia, nec leticia perpetua est." According to Simpson, Sedulius garnered these sentences from the *Glossae Consentaneae*, an "otherwise unknown collection of synonymous phrases" (p. xx).

[48] Ovid *Ars* 3.580; cited by Walther, no. 14913.

Salomon cuæð:
Unlæde bið and ormod   se ðe a wile
geomrian on gihðe: se bið Gode fracoðast.[49]

[Saturn said: But why are those companions always together, weeping and laughter? Very often they destroy the
felicity of those who are eager for honor. How does that
happen?
Solomon said: Wretched and despairing is he who always
wishes to complain in grief: he is most hateful to God.]

The basis of Saturn's question is the proverbial concept that "sadness
accompanies joy," and he goes on to explore the negative connotations
of the connection by pointing out that these companions often "destroy the happiness of those eager for honor." Robert Menner, the
editor of the poem, considered Saturn's question "unanswerable," and
perceived Solomon's rejoinder as a condemnation of "improper *tristitia*."[50] However, recourse to the proverbial tradition I have outlined
helps to explain the aptness of Solomon's response. The famous sage
does condemn excessive mourning, but his reference is probably to the
sin of despair, that sin which is, as an aspect of pride, "most hateful to
God." For Solomon, then, joy accompanies sorrow in order that
unrelieved misery should not lead a person to despair. He evokes the
positive connotations of the *sententia*, countering Saturn's pagan and
hence pessimistic point of view, and implies that the potential accession
of joy after sorrow may be attributed to the will of God. Thus, this
brief exchange explores the same range of possible movements and
causes that we have seen expressed elsewhere in the proverbial corpus.

Finally, we might note a late-medieval variant of this proverb, cited
by Hans Walther from the *Proverbia communia* and a sixteenth-century
Wolfenbüttel manuscript: "Hoc est consuetum: comitantur tristia
letum"[51] [This is usual: sadness accompanies joy]. Here, the juxtaposition of joy and sorrow is explicitly marked as customary.

The second proverbial form in which joy and sorrow are linked
together describes them explicitly as alternating in a somewhat circular

---

[49] *Sol. and Sat. II*, lines 339–44, in *The Poetical Dialogues of Solomon and Saturn*, ed.
Robert J. Menner (New York: Modern Language Association of America; London:
Oxford University Press, 1941; repr. New York: Kraus, 1973), 97 [macrons omitted].

[50] *Solomon and Saturn*, ed. Menner, p. 135.

[51] *Proverbia communia*, 126; Walther, no. 10994.

fashion; this version finds its clearest vernacular expression in the *Canterbury Tales*: "Joye after wo, and wo after gladnesse."[52] However, an earlier and intriguing variant is found in the Latin of the *Carmina burana*, in the third stanza of the poem beginning "O Antioche":

'Post tristitiam fient gaudia,
post gaudium erit tristitia':
   sunt vera proverbia,
   que fatentur talia.
     dicta veritatis,
     dicta claritatis
     amantur.[53]

['Joys will occur after sorrow, sorrow will appear after joy': these are true proverbs which acknowledge such things. Sayings of truth, sayings of clarity, are loved.]

This stanza clearly implies that the alternation of joy and sorrow was expressed proverbially at least by the second quarter of the thirteenth century, the date of the *Codex Buranus*. Still, the Latin poet's reference to the proverbs is tantalizing in the plurality of "proverbia" and "dicta"; do the plural nouns refer to the *sententiae* of the first two lines as separate entities, or do they merely imply the existence of variant expressions of a single base *sententia* encompassing the bilateral movement of joy and sorrow? Either interpretation is possible, especially in light of the analogues I have already adduced.

The situation of this stanza within "O Antioche" is also relevant to the use of proverbs in *Beowulf*. The Latin poem begins as a planctus, and then switches to narrative discourse. Bernt notes the change as occurring at stanza 6,[54] as this is where the first-person plaint of Apollonius gives way to third-person narration, but it could be argued that stanza 3 also marks a change in the poetic mode of expression. In stanzas 1 and 2, Apollonius's planctus is typically allusive and exclamatory, whereas in stanzas 4 and 5 he begins to tell the story of his

---

[52] Chaucer, *Knight's Tale* A.2841; cited by Skeat, no. 225, and Whiting, *Proverbs ... before 1500*, J61.

[53] "O Antioche," *Carmina burana*, no. 97, st. 3, in *Carmina Burana: die Gedichte des Codex Buranus lateinisch und deutsch*, ed. and trans. Carl Fischer, Hugo Kuhn, and Günter Bernt (Zurich and Munich: Artemis Verlag, 1974), 336. Cited by Schulze, no. 65 (who refers to the old numbering of the poem—148); see also Wander, *DS-L*, Freude 1165.6.

[54] Fischer, Kuhn, and Bernt, 921.

troubles. Thus, stanza 3 with its proverbial reference provides a transition between lyric and narrative in the context of Apollonius's speech. Furthermore, the relation of the proverb(s) to the narrative resembles that which we have already seen in connection with *Beowulf* (lines 2291–93a), in that Bernt notes that the Apollonius legend is recounted "(w)ie als Exempel zu dem Sprichwort."[55]

Like stanza 3 of "O Antioche," our *Beowulf* passage J also occurs in a non-narrative setting introducing the beginning of a narrative passage. The poet describes Hrothgar's distribution of treasure at the feast (1050–55a), makes a brief reference to the roles of God and Beowulf in eliminating Grendel (1055b–57a), and then indulges in a series of proverbial statements, of which our passage is the last (1057b–62).[56] Immediately after this series, the poet returns to the feast and the scop's song about the fight at Finnsburh. As the last sentence of the sentential series, passage J serves a transitional function not only between two narrative episodes (the feast and the fight), but also between a non-narrative and a narrative segment. The analogy with "O Antioche" shows that this proverbial function is not unique to *Beowulf*.

Finally, this third *Beowulf* passage provides a sense of anticipation not unlike what we have seen in passage I, but somewhat more complex in nature. As the feast in Heorot is a happy occasion, the introduction of sorrow or unpleasantness seems somewhat out of place, and recalls Krikmann's description of textual incongruity as a proverb marker. In this case, the hint of misfortune is taken up and developed in the Finnsburh episode, which itself foreshadows the future tribulations, both imminent and ultimate, of the Danes.

This desire to link narrative strands through a sententious statement may explain the form of passage J, which seems created out of two proverbial complexes. The greater part of the *sententia* (minus "leofes ond laðes") is paralleled by the lines from *Maxims II* mentioned at the beginning of this discussion:

> ... and gomol [bið] snoterost,
> fyrngearum frod,   se þe ær feala gebideð.[57]

> [And an old man is wisest, experienced in former years,
> he who has endured much.]

---

[55] Ibid. Note that Bernt seems to interpret 3.1–2 as a single proverb.

[56] See my discussion of this passage in chap. 2, above.

[57] *Maxims II*, lines 11b–12b (ASPR 6.56).

Passage J echoes "feala gebideð" with its "fela ... gebidan," and reflects
the temporal element of "gomol" with "longe ... worolde bruceð."
Thus, the two passages may represent separate developments of a base
sententia along the lines of "He who lives long experiences many
things." The full sense of the sentence from *Maxims II*—that age and
experience bring wisdom—would apply well to Hrothgar, but the
Beowulf-poet has chosen to replace the element of wisdom with a brief
description of the types of experiences the long-lived must encounter:
leofes ond laðes. If, as I suspect, the *Maxims II* version reflects a more
common proverbial sentiment regarding the collocation of age and
experience, that meaning would present itself to the minds of the
audience, allowing them to apply the sentence to Hrothgar, but the
poet has extended its frame of reference by adducing the proverbial
complex of joy and sorrow.

I hope to have shown that a widespread proverbial tradition juxta-
posing joy and sorrow existed at least from the early Middle Ages and
continues through to the modern period. Unfortunately, the origins of
this tradition are not entirely discernible. Certain proverbs and sentences treating joy and sorrow are clearly based on a biblical verse (I refer
to the influence of Prov. 14.13 on examples from groups H and J), but
others seem, in their variation, more remote from a single source (e.g.,
group I). In some vernacular cases—Gower, Hartmann, Thomasin—it
remains impossible to tell whether a proverb represents the vernacular
variant of an originally biblical sentence, or whether it reflects a parallel
tradition. The same is sometimes true of Latin proverbs, even those
clearly marked as such: the description of joy and sorrow in "O Antioche" could be an expansion of the biblical "Risus dolore miscetur,"
but it could just as easily derive from Ovid's "Miscentur tristia letis" or
some other, as yet unidentified source. Still, there should remain no
question that proverbs treating the relations of joy and sorrow (in all of
their possible arrangements) were available to the *Beowulf*-poet.

This being said, we may return to the poem to see what use the poet
has made of these proverbs *qua* proverbs; I will begin with passage J, as
it is the first to appear in *Beowulf* and the most clearly sentential of the
lot. One useful concept for the interpretation of passage J is what Betty
Cox calls gnomic "extension," that is, "generalizations which have
been classified specifically and demonstrated by a particular model."[58]
According to Cox, these extensions "absorb a particularity from the

---

[58] Betty S. Cox, *Cruces of Beowulf* (The Hague: Mouton, 1971), 120.

narrative" and show "how a particular person or a particular situation relates to a wider or different group of situations or people."[59] Something to this effect had already been described by Arthur Brodeur, whose perceptive commentary deserves to be quoted at length:

> Twice, in his account of the feast in Heorot, the poet stresses the theme of human suffering directly, and emphasizes man's ignorance of the decrees of Fate (lines 1057-62; 1233 ff.)—with the intimation that woe must follow joy, and that God is man's only refuge. The immediate application is general, to the necessary dependence of man upon God in an uncertain world; the secondary application is to the imminent death of Æschere. But for Danes and Geats alike there is a deeper meaning, in those successive passages which report Hygelac's death and Wealtheow's appeal to Beowulf.[60]

Brodeur succinctly points out three levels of application or relation, but his overall interpretation of the elegiac movement of the poem leads him to stress only the progression from joy to sorrow in this passage. As we have seen, the proverbial analogues to lines 1060-62 allow for movement in both directions, and a second look at the relation of the *sententia* to the Finn episode and feasting scene will show that the poet made full use of this bilateral expression.

As I described earlier, passage J effects a transition between a sentential series and the resumption of narrative. In serving that function, the lines introduce both the theme of the Finnsburh episode and its relation to the framing story; the sentence is part of what Stanley Greenfield calls the "authenticating voice," which "validates the way or ways in which it understands and wishes its audience to understand [reported events]."[61] Perceived in that light, the sentential passage, with its equilateral balance of joy and sorrow, should point us to a similar balance in the narrative that "models" it. Thus, the *sententia* pronouncing the alternation of joy and sorrow in life is immediately followed by a description of joy:

> Þær wæs sang ond sweg   samod ætgædere
> fore Healfdenes   hildewisan   (1063-64)

---

[59] Cox, 120-21.

[60] Brodeur, 121.

[61] Stanley B. Greenfield, "The Authenticating Voice in *Beowulf*," in *Hero and Exile*, ed. George H. Brown, 45.

[There was song and music together before the battle
leader of the Danes].

In the midst of this merriment, Hrothgar's scop takes up his *gomen-
wudu* and begins to relate the Finnsburh episode, a narrative of unrelieved sorrow. The tale ends with the doubly-bereaved Hildeburh being
transported home by the Danes, and is closed by the remark "Leoð
wæs asungen, gleomannes gyd" (1159b–60a) [The song was sung, the
singer's story]. If this heroic but tragic lay had any dampening effect on
the high spirits of the revelers, we are not told so, for the noisy celebra-
tion of the feast resumes immediately after the closure of the episode:

> Gamen eft astah,
> beorhtode bencsweg,   byrelas sealdon
> win of wunderfatum   (1160b–62a)

[Joyous clamor rose up again, the noise resounded from
the benches, the cupbearers provided wine from won-
derful vessels].

The Finn episode may, as Brodeur explains, foreshadow in Hildeburh
the losses later sustained by Wealhtheow,[62] but he interprets at a
further remove from the *sententia* in question, which seems best to
apply to the alternation of joy and sorrow inherent in the Finnsburh
episode and its immediate context, and perhaps, more generally, to the
contrast between the joyous evening and the sorrowful morn.[63] Cox's
theory of extension prescribes interpretation of a gnomic sentence in
connection with a "particular model"—in this case, the story of Finn,
Hengest, and Hildeburh—and it would seem overly ambitious to apply
our short three-line passage to the movement of the poem as a whole.
However, a wider use of the concept of extension, and one hinted at by
Cox, might help to establish a functional distinction between *sententiae*
(or gnomes) and proverbs. In gnomic poetry, or in any deliberately
compiled collection of sentences, *sententiae* usually lack a narrative or
situational context that would provide a specific meaning; inserted into
narrative or conversation, proverbs accrue meaning (different in each
case) through their contexts. In other words, a decontextualized sentence asserts universal and perhaps descriptive authority, but only in

---

[62] Brodeur, 119.

[63] For another discussion of the relationship between this *sententia* and the Finn
episode, see Karkov and Farrell, "The Gnomic Passages of *Beowulf*," 30–31.

application does a proverb acquire an interpretative, prescriptive, or proscriptive focus. Standing alone, "Life brings both joy and sorrow" can carry a positive, negative, or simply admonitory connotation; only when it is applied to a specific case is the intended meaning clear.[64]

The immediate context of passage I also points out the vacillation between joy and sorrow in the plot of *Beowulf*. Hrothgar, having discovered the death of Æschere, sits "on hreon mode" (line 1307b) [with a sad spirit] and summons Beowulf to his chamber; meanwhile, he ponders whether the Lord will effect an improvement in his sad situation. The hero arrives, and having politely asked Hrothgar if he has spent a pleasant night, receives the vehement reply:

> Ne frin þu æfter sælum!   Sorh is geniwod
> Denigea leodum.   (1322–23a)

> [Do not ask about joys! Sorrow is renewed for the Danish people.]

Thus, Beowulf's innocent expectation of continued joy is countered by the old king's explanation of renewed sorrow. What role, though, does our proverbial reference play in this scene? As I explained in my initial treatment of this passage, the invocation of divine providence, along with familiarity with the proverbial tradition of joy following sorrow, would lead the audience to expect that Hrothgar's hoped-for *wyrpe* will eventually occur; hence the sentence may be perceived as foreshadowing or predicting the next movement of the storyline. Indeed, Beowulf's cheerful and promising appearance is the first sign of an optimistic turn, and he does, in due course, avenge Æschere's death and complete the cleansing of Heorot. Like passage J, the sentential reference of passage I garners meaning from its immediate context, and from an episode at one remove from it.

In passage H, we have our only proverbial expression of unalloyed grief after pleasure—"gyrn æfter gomene." However, the phrase occurs in Hrothgar's brief summary of his career, and immediately after describing the misery he endured at the claws of the Grendel-kin, the Danish king thanks God for sending Beowulf and victory. Once again we see, not a unidirectional movement, but an alternation between joy and sorrow, with the joy again being provided by the Lord. This seems

---

[64] For a provocative discussion of the relationship of the proverbial refrain to the narrative references of *Deor*, see Harris, " 'Deor' and its Refrain," 37–44.

to be the total meaning of all three proverbial passages as they are extended by their contexts: that joy and sorrow alternate in anyone's life (and secondarily, that joy in life is the gift of God). As all three *sententiae* appear in what is considered Part One of *Beowulf*, this alternation need not affect the perception of the overall thematic movement of the poem as leading from victory to downfall, or from joy to sorrow. However, it would be well to exert caution in describing that movement as "elegiac," as the earlier part of the poem, as I have shown, does not simply set up a happy edifice to be knocked down and reminisced about later, but explores the inevitable, and proverbial, variation of joy and sorrow in human existence.

Therefore, these sentential passages support Andersson's perception of a wave-like structure in *Beowulf*, but we might, as a final point, consider how the proverbs relate to the narrative episodes. There are two possibilities: either the proverbial references were included by the poet to strengthen and focus the alternating mood pattern of the narrative, or they are antecedent to and inspire that pattern. I have already explored the first option, but the second also deserves consideration. Although the narrative episodes and elegiac passages of *Beowulf* are traditional in nature, I hope to have shown that the proverbial references are no less so. One could argue that a proverbial tradition carries even greater weight than a heroic or poetic one, in which case the alternation of joy and sorrow in *Beowulf* may be predicated on the proverbial treatments of that theme, and the narrative episodes serve not merely, but primarily, to illustrate the truth of these expressions of accepted wisdom.

4

Fate and Death

In the preceding chapter, joy and sorrow were treated together, because the two consistently appear in a complementary relationship. Fate and death are likewise linked together, not because their relationship is complementary, but because the connection between them is consistent, and in a sense inevitable. As explained in *Beowulf* and in the proverbial tradition surrounding the poem, all human beings are subject to the power of fate, and the ultimate fate of each person is to die. As the operations of fate precede death in the unfolding (or closing) of an individual's life, we may also proceed in that order.

The nature of *wyrd* as a pagan or Christian phenomenon, like the nature of the divine in *Beowulf*, has occasioned much discussion. The most recent scholarship seems to tip the scales on the side of a Christian interpretation—*wyrd* as a sort of Providence—although the issue is by no means settled.[1] I will not attempt here a thorough study of the concept of *wyrd* in *Beowulf*; first, because the non-sentential appearances of *wyrd* in *Beowulf* are outside my purview, and second, because the aspects of fate in *Beowulf* which are paralleled by proverbial analogues would give only a partial view of *wyrd* itself in the poem.

---

[1] For a useful review of the scholarly literature on *wyrd* in OE, see Jerold C. Frakes, *The Fate of Fortune in the Early Middle Ages: The Boethian Tradition*, Studien und Texte zur Geistesgeschichte des Mittelalters 23 (Leiden: E. J. Brill, 1988), 83–100; as might be predicted from the subtitle of his book, Frakes himself favors Boethian or Christian interpretations of *wyrd*.

The fatalistic *sententiae* of *Beowulf* are as follows:

K.   Gæð a wyrd swa hio scel   (455b)

[Fate always happens as it must]

L.   ... ac unc furður sceal
weorðan æt wealle,   swa unc wyrd geteoð,
Metod manna gehwæs   (2525b–27a)

[but further, it must happen to us at the wall as fate,
(and) the Lord of every man assigns us]

M.   ... Wyrd oft nereð
    unfægne eorl,   þonne his ellen deah   (572b–73)

[Fate often saves the undoomed man, when his courage
avails].

The first of these statements is the most general pronouncement on
fate, whereas the second applies the concept to a more specific situation, as well as equating fate with God.[2] Both passages emphasize the
inexorability of fate. Passage M affords a more refined description of
the activities of fate, presenting a positive result, but attaching condi-
tions to it (the *eorl* must be *unfæge* and courageous).

K. (line 455b):

    Gæð a wyrd swa hio scel.

This half-line represents the most "perfect" proverb in all of *Beowulf*: along with its brevity, it employs a generalization of time (*a*) and
two verbs in the present tense, one of which (*scel*) carries an imperative
sense.

The inevitability of fate is stated plainly in Latin literature as early
as Manilius: "Certum est et ineuitabile fatum"[3] [Fate is certain and
inevitable]; the same sentence served much later as the somewhat unin-
spiring device of Albrecht, sixteenth-century Graf of Hohenlohe.[4] Wal-

---

[2] While "Metod manna gehwæs" may simply paraphrase "wyrd," the proverbial analogues discussed below support a correspondence of fate with God.

[3] M. Manilius, *Astronomicon*, ed. Franciscus Semi, Scriptorum Romanorum quae
extant omnia 224–25 (Pisa: Giardini, 1975), bk. 2, line 113.

[4] *Die Wahl- und Denksprüche, Feldgeschreie, Losungen, Schlacht- und Volksrufe
besonders des Mittelalters und der Neuzeit*, ed. J. Dielitz (Frankfurt: Wilhelm Rommel, 1884), 42; Wander, *DS-L*, Bescheren 4.

ter of Châtillon used the unwavering "ordo fatorum" to explain a turn
of plot:

> Sed quia fatorum stat ineuitabilis ordo
> Euentusque hominum series immobilis artat,
> Errauit temulenta manus, ferroque perire
> Non patitur Lachesis. ...[5]

> [But because the order of the fates stands inevitable and
> a stiff chain confines the fortunes of men, the unsteady
> hand has strayed and Lachesis does not suffer (Alexan-
> der) to perish by the sword.]

Walter's "quia" implies the authority of the sentence by introducing it as
a given; that is, as an unimpeachable fact that explains the ensuing event.

A similar formulation may be found in Lydgate's *Troy Book*, where
Fortune (instead of fate) appears steadfast in its operations:

> But Fortune wil have hir cours alwey,
> Whos purpos holt, who seyth ye or nay.[6]

Lydgate has added to the simple statement of fate/fortune's inexorability the comment that this power is not subject to the desires of mere
humans. The proverbial expression of the helplessness of humanity
before fate was not original with Lydgate, as it appears in the pseudo-
Ovidian *Consolatio ad Liviam*—"non ullis vincere fata datur"[7] [no one
is granted to conquer fate]—and, more importantly, in Aldhelm's fire
riddle. One suspects that Aldhelm was familiar with a "vincere posse"
version of the sentence, as he includes the phrase twice in two lines,
referring to fortune and fate respectively:

> Me pater et mater gelido genuere rigore,
> Fomitibus siccis dum mox rudimenta uigebant;
> Quorum ui propria fortunam uincere possum,
> Cum nil ni latices mea possint uincere fata.[8]

---

[5] *Galteri de Castellione Alexandreis*, ed. Marvin L. Colker, Thesaurus Mundi:
Bibliotheca scriptorum latinorum mediæ et recentioris ætatis 17 (Padova: Antenore,
1978), 3.352–55 (p. 81); Walther, no. 8892.a.

[6] Lydgate, *Troy Book* 1.239.3307–8; cited from Whiting, *Proverbs ... before 1500*,
F537.

[7] Ovid, *Consolatio ad Liviam* 234, in *The Art of Love and Other Poems*, ed. J. H.
Mozley, Loeb Classical Library (Cambridge, Mass.: Harvard Univ. Press, 1947), 340;
Walther, no. 39008.c.1.

[8] Aldhelm, *Aenigmata*, in *Tatvini Opera omnia; Variae collectiones Aenigmatum*

[My father and mother begot me of cold and hardness,
but I quickly grew strong upon dry tinder, by the
strength of which I can conquer my own fortune;
nothing but water can extinguish my destiny.]

Aldhelm first stresses the inexorable power of fire by inverting the
expected meaning of the "vincere posse" phrase, claiming that fire can
conquer even fortune. That the destiny ("mea fata") of fire can be overcome only by water both presents an essential clue to the riddle's solution and frames it in the terms of an elemental struggle. The riddle
acquires added meaning from the (probable) proverbial phrase: because
under normal circumstances no one can conquer fate, we are led to understand that the riddle does not describe a normal human condition.[9]

The power of fate or fatality is sometimes expressed as a law: in the
Metamorphoses, Ovid's Apollo laments that "fatali lege tenemur"[10] [we
are held by the fatal law], and Manilius provides yet another *sententia*
in his *Astronomicon*: "Fata regunt orbem, certa stant omnia lege"[11]
[The fates rule the world, all stands fixed by their laws]. Like the
Beowulf passage, all of these *sententiae* stress the immutability and
inevitability of fate.

The primary function of passage K is, as for other sentential passages
we have seen, to provide closure to Beowulf's address to Hrothgar. The
proverb adds to the characterization of the hero as one capable of fore-
sight—he has provided for the disposal of his person and property in
the event of defeat—a dimension of fearlessness in the face of imminent
danger. Beowulf's catalogue of past victories (lines 419–24) implies his
self-confidence, but the greater part of his speech delineates the horrible
treatment he and his men may expect if he fails in his self-appointed
role as cleanser of Heorot. The speech is designed, not to predict victory, but to add to the suspense carrying through to Grendel's ultimate
defeat. In this context, the proverb bears the extended connotation of

---

merovingicae aetatis; Anonymus De dubiis nominibus, ed. Maria De Marco et al.,
CCSL 133 (Turnhout: Brepols, 1968), aenigma 44, lines 1–4 (p. 429).

[9] A different verbal tradition is represented in Nigel Wireker's *Speculum
stultorum*:

Contra naturam vel sortem querere quicquam,
Nemo potest illud reddere vel facere.

See *The Anglo-Latin Satirical Poets and Epigrammatists of the Twelfth Century*, ed.
Thomas Wright, 2 vols. (London, 1872), 1.145; Walther, no. 3337.

[10] Ovid, *Metamorphoses* 10.203; Walther, no. 8888.

[11] *Astronomicon*, ed. Semi, 4.14.

"I know that I may die in this endeavor, but I am not afraid to proceed." As in passage L (see discussion below), the proverb implies that the outcome of the battle depends on forces external to the actual combatants.

Finally, the evocation of fate in passage K gives added life to the brief mentions of Hreðel and Weland that immediately precede it. The legendary histories of both of these characters involve changes of fortune that can perhaps best be explained by the machinations of fate (i.e., the accidental death of Hreðel's son and the revenge ultimately achieved by Weland). The proverb thus recalls their stories to the audience, and links Beowulf to these heroic figures.

L. (lines 2525b–27a):

> Ac unc furður sceal
> weorðan æt wealle,   swa unc wyrd geteoð,
> Metod manna gehwæs.

These lines, part of Beowulf's announcement of his intention to fight the dragon, constitute too specific a statement to be considered truly proverbial: note, for example, the use of the dual pronoun *unc* rather than the plural *us*, and the localizing phrase "æt wealle." However, the lines are influenced by proverbial expression in several structural and thematic ways; that they partake of traditional heroic language is beyond question, as evidenced by the correspondence of *Beowulf* 2525 with *Maldon*, line 247. The use of *sceal* is, of course, common in proverbial expression, and the poet generalizes the operation of fate from its influence over the two combatants to the power of God over every man, "manna gehwæs." Proverbial analogues illustrate several of the themes of this passage: that fate rules over men, that a man must acquiesce to his fate, and that fate and God often work in conjunction.

Juvenal provides one concise sentence on the power of fate over men—"Fata regunt homines"[12] [The fates rule men]—that was later cited by John of Salisbury.[13] In the *Captivi* of Plautus, Tyndarus illustrates a proverb on fate with the example of his own career:

---

[12] Juvenal, *The Satires: A Text with Brief Critical Notes*, ed. E. Courtney (Rome: Edizioni dell' Ateneo, 1984), 9.32 (p. 88); Walther, no. 8882.

[13] *Polycraticus* 5.4.

Fortuna humana fingit artatque ut lubet:
me, qui liber fueram servom fecit, e summo infimum.[14]

[The fortune of men shapes and constricts as it pleases:
it turned me from a free man into a slave, from the
highest to the lowest.]

As one might expect, Latin tragedy also makes use of *sententiae* on fate,
particularly on the necessity of resignation to it; one such warning is
found in Seneca's *Oedipus*:

Fatis agimur: cedite fatis!
non sollicitae possunt curae
mutare rati stamina fusi.[15]

[We are driven by the fates: submit to the fates! No
anxious cares can change the threads of that determined
spindle.]

Although any direct contact between the *Beowulf*-poet and the works
of Juvenal, Seneca, or especially Plautus is, at the very least, extremely
dubious, these examples may serve as representative of the use of such
proverbs in classical Latin literature.

    One classical text that has been suggested as a possible influence on
Beowulf is the *Aeneid*. Although scholars have presented perceived similarities on the levels of scene, motif, vocabulary, syntax, and even polit-
ical background,[16] the problem of Virgilian influence still resembles
that of Christian influence on *Beowulf*; that is, the nagging question

---

[14] *Captivi* 2.2.53 (lines 304–5), in *Plautus in Five Volumes*, ed. and trans. Paul
Nixon, Loeb Classical Library (Cambridge, Mass.: Harvard Univ. Press, 1966),
1:490; see Walther, no. 9848.a, and Wander, *DS-L*, Glück 204.

[15] Seneca, *Oedipus* 980–82, in *L. Annaei Senecae Tragoediae*, ed. Otto Zwierlein,
Scriptorvm Classicorvm Bibliotheca Oxoniensis (Oxford: Clarendon Press, 1986),
249.

[16] See Georg Zappert, *Virgils Fortleben im Mittelalter* (Vienna, 1851); Fr. Klaeber,
"Aeneis und Beowulf," *Archiv* 126 (1911): 40–48, 339–59; Tom Burns Haber, *A
Comparative Study of the "Beowulf" and the "Aeneid"* (Princeton: Princeton Univ.
Press, 1931); Alois Brandl, "Beowulf-Epos und Aeneis in systematischer Verglei-
chung," *Archiv für das Studium der neueren Sprachen und Literaturen* 171 (1937):
161–73; Rudolf Sühnel, "Vergil in England," in *Festschrift für Walter Hübner*, ed.
Dieter Riesner and Helmut Gneuss (Berlin: Erich Schmidt, 1964), 129; Richard J.
Schrader, "Beowulf's Obsequies and the Roman Epic," *Comparative Literature* 24
(1972): 237–59; and Theodore A. Andersson, *Early Epic Scenery: Homer, Virgil, and
the Medieval Legacy* (Ithaca: Cornell Univ. Press, 1976).

remains as to why, if the *Beowulf*-poet made extensive use of the *Aeneid* in his own composition, he has included no reference to it, or even an unambiguously Virgilian allusion. There can be no question that the works of Virgil were well known in the early Middle Ages, and in Anglo-Saxon England specifically, as citations are frequent in Donatus and Priscian, the two most popular Latin grammars,[17] and allusions to and discussions of Virgil are common in the writings of Augustine and Alcuin.[18] He was known by Bede,[19] and praised by Alfred the Great.[20] In fact, Rudolf Sühnel's assessment of Virgil's status in rhetorical and metrical handbooks could almost be extended to the whole of early-medieval Latin literature: "auf ein Ovid-Zitat und zwei Horaz-Zitate kamen zwanzig Vergil-Zitate."[21] If the *Beowulf*-poet benefited from any Latin learning at all, he is almost certain to have encountered the *Aeneid*—or parts of it—in some form.[22]

Invocations of Fortune or the Fates appear even more frequently in the *Aeneid* than in *Beowulf*; several of these pronouncements bear not only a semantic similarity to our *Beowulf* passages, but also a proverbial, or at least loosely formulaic, aspect that can best be ascertained by examining them *en masse*:

1) Fata viam invenient   (III.395 and X.113)

[The fates find a way]

2) Vixi, et, quem dederat cursum fortuna, peregi (IV.653)

[I have lived and followed the course shown by fortune]

3) Superat quoniam Fortuna, sequamur,
   Quoque vocat, vertamus iter   (V.22–23)

---

[17] See Domenico Comparetti, *Vergil in the Middle Ages*, trans. E. F. M. Benecke (London: Swan Sonnenschein & Co., 1895), 70.

[18] See Comparetti, 90–91, and Haber, 13–16.

[19] Haber, 12–13.

[20] Comparetti, 131.

[21] Sühnel, 127.

[22] For the transmission of *sententiae*, excerpts from an author would serve just as well as, if not better than, complete texts. Thus, Peter Hunter Blair's argument that even Bede would have derived most of his Virgil from grammars, florilegia, and other secondary sources need not affect our present discussion; see "From Bede to Alcuin," in *Famulus Christi: Essays in Commemoration of the Thirteenth Centenary of the Birth of the Venerable Bede*, ed. Gerald Bonner (London: SPCK, 1976), 239–60.

[Because Fortune rules, let us follow, and turn down the road she offers]

4) Nate dea, quo fata trahunt retrahuntque, sequamur;
   Quidquid erit, superando omnis fortuna ferendo est
                                                (V.709–10)

[Goddess-born, where the fates push and pull let us follow; whatever will be, all fortune is to be won by endurance]

5) Et, quaecumque viam dederit Fortuna, sequatur (X.49)

[And whatever way Fortune will give, he will follow]

6) Et te, si qua viam dederit fortuna, Latino
   Iungemus regi   (XI.128–29)

[And if fortune gives a way, we will ally you with king Latinus]

7) Quo deus et quo dura vocat Fortuna, sequamur
                                                (XII.677)

[Let us follow where god and stern Fortune command].[23]

These passages display a remarkable number of parallels of diction and phraseology: *viam* (passages 1, 5, 6), forms of *dedo* (2, 5, 6), of *supero* (3, 4), of *sequor* (3, 4, 5, 7), and in the case of (5) and (6), an entire phrase—*qua(ecumque) viam dederit fortuna*. Although these parallels may simply reflect Virgil's tendency to refashion his own phrases, they may also hint at a proverbial background to these lines—something like "One must follow the way given by fate/fortune"—which seems very similar to the sentiment and expression of our *Beowulf* passage L (*Aeneid* passage [1] perhaps more closely resembles *Beowulf* passage K).[24] Like pas-

---

[23] All citations of the *Aeneid* are from *The Works of Virgil*, ed. John Conington, rev. Henry Nettleship, 3 vols. (Hildesheim and New York: Georg Olms, 1979), vols. 2 and 3.

[24] For the purposes of this study, it is not important whether such a proverb existed *before* Virgil's time, but only *after*. Four of the passages are cited elsewhere as medieval proverbs: 1) Walther, no. 8887; 4) Eduardus Margalits, *Florilegium proverbiorum universae latinitatis* (Budapest: Ludovicus Kókai, 1895), 209; 5) Walther, no. 8154; 7) Walther, nos. 25624, 25624.a, 25624.b.

sage L, the lines from the *Aeneid* seem to apply beyond the specific narrative situation; John Conington notes of (4) that "[t]he sentiment is general, not ... confined to the special occasion of the burning of the ships. '*Every* contingency ... is to be surmounted not by resistance but by submission.' "[25] This same submission to fate is expressed sententially at the close of *Resignation B*—"Giet biþ þæt selast, þonne mon him sylf ne mæg / wyrd onwendan, þæt he þonne wel þolige"[26] [Yet it is best for a man to suffer his fate well, when he cannot himself change it]—and seems to inform our *Beowulf* passage.

Perhaps the most intriguing correspondence between L and the *Aeneid* appears with respect to *Aeneid* (7). Here, as in L, fortune works in cooperation with God. Tom Haber has described the similar functioning of God and fate in *Beowulf* and the *Aeneid*: "the success and defeat of the characters of both epics seem to depend upon a three-fold set of factors: God or Jupiter, Fata or Wyrd, and individual courage."[27] Haber also correctly identifies *Aeneid* (7) as the line quoted by Aldhelm in his riddle on fate:[28]

> Facundum constat quondam cecinisse poetam:
> "Quo Deus et quo dura vocat Fortuna; sequamur!"
> Me veteres falso dominam vocitare solebant,
> Sceptra regens mundi dum Christi gratia regnet.[29]

> [It is true that the eloquent poet once sang: "Let us
> follow where god and stern Fortune command!" The
> ancients were wont wrongly to call me lord, when the
> grace of Christ rules the scepters of the world.]

Aldhelm declares explicitly that the Christian God supersedes, and is thus more powerful than fate, a hierarchy that obtains also in Alfred's translation of Boethius,[30] and in *Beowulf* lines 1057–58 and 2291–93, though not necessarily in our current passage L, where God and fate

---

[25] Conington/Nettleship, 2:403–4.

[26] *Resignation*, lines 217–18 (ASPR 3.218).

[27] Haber, 57. The other sentential passages of *Beowulf* where God, fate, and courage are linked are lines 930–31 and 2291–93 (see chap. 2, above).

[28] Haber, 11–12.

[29] *The Riddles of Aldhelm: Text and Verse Translation with Notes*, ed. and trans. James Hall Pitman, Yale Studies in English 67 (New Haven: Yale Univ. Press, 1925), 6.

[30] See Frakes, note 1 above.

seem coequal. Aldhelm's position against undue belief in the power of
fate parallels that of Augustine, who twice expresses disapproval of
what he perceives as a common, but erroneous, equation of God with
fate or fortune. In his *Enarrationes in Psalmos*, Augustine scornfully
presents the types of deterministic excuses offered by sinners: "O si
Deus hoc nollet, non facerem! Hoc uoluit Deus, fortuna hoc uoluit,
hoc uoluit fatum"[31] [O, if God had not willed this, I would not have
done it! God willed it, fortune willed it, fate willed it]. In his Retrac-
tions, Augustine is more explicit in his condemnation of the error:
"cum uideam homines habere in pessima consuetudine, ubi dici debet:
hoc deus uoluit, dicere: hoc uoluit fortuna"[32] [as I see men hold to the
worst custom, when they ought to say "God willed this," to say
instead "Fortune willed this"]. Judging from our *Beowulf* passage,
Augustine and Aldhelm did not succeed in rooting out this well-entrenched and customary correspondence.

Another interesting sentential collocation of Christ and *wyrd* appears in *Maxims II*, set among a series of naturalistic superlatives:

> ... Wind byð on lyfte swiftust,
> þunar byð þragum hludast.   Þrymmas syndan Cristes
>   myccle,
> wyrd byð swiðost.   Winter byð cealdost,
> lencten hrimigost ...[33]

[Wind is the swiftest in the sky, thunder is sometimes
the loudest. The powers of Christ are great, fate is the
strongest. Winter is the coldest, springtime the frosti-
est].

By virtue of its parallelism with surrounding half-lines, "wyrd byð
swiðost" would seem to constitute the base *sententia* modified by
"þrymmas syndan Cristes myccle."[34] The juxtaposition of the positive
adjective *myccle* with the superlative *swiðost* could be perplexing (is
wyrd stronger than the powers of Christ?), unless one understands *wyrd*
as one among Christ's powers. Thus, the powers of Christ are great,

---

[31] *In Psalmos* 140.9 (CCSL 40.2032).
[32] *Sancti Aurelii Augustini Retractationum libri II*, ed. Almut Mutzenbecher,
CCSL 57 (Turnhout: Brepols, 1984), 7. Augustine's comment appears in his
correction to the definition of fortune he had offered in *De academicis* 1.1.1.
[33] *Maxims II*, lines 3b-6a (ASPR 6.55).
[34] It is treated as such by Whiting, *Proverbs ... before 1500*, W182.

wyrd is the strongest of these. Still, the proverb, if such it is, remains oddly placed in an ongoing description of meteorological and seasonal phenomena. Although *Maxims II* has never been praised as a showpiece of rhetorical or poetic finesse, it may be that the poet (or compiler, as he is sometimes called) deliberately placed the Christ/*wyrd* sentence here specifically because of its problematic nature. If "Wyrd byð swiðost" or some similar expression were a very ancient (perhaps pre-Christian) and well-entrenched proverb, the poet would have to take pains—as did Augustine and Aldhelm—to demonstrate to his audience the supremacy of the Christian God. No reader or listener is likely to dispute the fact that thunder is (sometimes) the loudest sound, winter the coldest season, summer the warmest, etc., so these patently true observations lend credibility and authority to a possibly more controversial statement embedded among them.[35]

Before returning to the question of Virgilian influence on *Beowulf*, I should point out two other Old English analogues for a connection of fate with God. The first, an admonition against the casting of lots and concomitant recommendation of acquiescence to the divine will, was very widespread in the Middle Ages, as it originates in the *Disticha Catonis*. The Old English version of the distich reads: "Ne sec ðu no þurh lietas hu þe gewurðan scyle, ac do swa ðu betst mæge; eaðe gerædeþ god his willan be ðe [and] þine ðearfe, þeah he hit þe ær ne secge" [Do not seek to discover through lots what will happen to you, but do the best you can; God easily designs His will for you and your needs, although He may not make it known to you beforehand] and the Latin,

> Quid deus intendat, noli perquirere sorte:
> quid statuat de te, sine te deliberat ille[36]

> [Do not seek what God intends by lot: what He ordains for you, He determines without you].

Although divination is not referred to in our *Beowulf* passage, the addition in the Old English *Disticha* of the phrase "do swa ðu betst mæge" as an alternative to attempts to circumvent what is fated implies

---

[35] I am indebted to Thomas D. Hill for suggesting the use of this device in *Maxims I* and *II*.

[36] R. S. Cox, ed., "The Old English Dicts of Cato," *Anglia* 90 (1972): no. 30 (p. 9); see also Walther, nos. 25003, 25130, 25773, 25775, and Sedulius Scottus, *Coll. Misc.*, 25.26.4 and 25.26.5.

the same attitude towards fate as that developed at greater length in the heroic poem. Finally, God's power over fate is revealed by the Deity Himself, when He informs Abraham (in *Genesis A*) of the impending birth of Isaac; God assures the patriarch that

> Þu sceal wintrum frod   on woruld bringan
> sarra sunu[,]   soð forð gan
> wyrd æfter þissum   wordgemearcum.[37]

> [You, advanced in age, shall bring a son into the world with Sarah, the true fate will proceed according to these predictions.]

Although *wyrd* in this passage has the sense of "future" or "event," it does refer to Abraham's fortune or lot in life, and is clearly an operation or result of the divine will.

By this excursus on the sentential linkage of fate and God, I hope to have shown that the connection between *Beowulf* and the *Aeneid*, while it remains a tantalizing possibility, does not appear necessary in this case. Although the influence of the *Aeneid* on early-medieval *Latin* composition is well-documented, the same cannot be said for its use by vernacular poets. Even if passage L were a reflex of *Aeneid* (7), the poet's source need not have been a full text of Virgil, but is just as likely to have appeared as an excerpt in a florilegium, grammar, or other school-text.[38] Indeed, the similarities of the Virgilian passages to each other, and their easy fit into the wider tradition of *sententiae* on fate, would seem to mark them as particularly apt for excerpting or repetition. It should also be noted that Germanic literature preserves equally relevant proverbs that are almost certainly free from Virgilian influence, such as the Old Norse "Verðr hverr eptir sínum forlögum at leita" [Each person must seek after his fate] and "scöpom viðr mangi" [no man can withstand fate].[39] It is safe to say that passage L of *Beo-*

---

[37] *Genesis A: A New Edition*, ed. A. N. Doane (Madison: Univ. of Wisconsin Press, 1978), lines 2355–57 (p. 193); Klaeber ("Aeneis und Beowulf," 350) suggests the parallel to *Beowulf* 455b.

[38] J. D. A. Ogilvy (*Books Known to the English, 597–1066*, Medieval Academy of America, publ. no. 76 [Cambridge, Mass.: Medieval Academy of America, 1967], 259) notes that "MSS of Virgil in English libraries are few, late, and of uncertain provenance. Probably Virgil, like other schoolbooks, was frequently worn out and replaced." Another possibility is that students learned their Virgil through excerpts in miscellanies.

[39] The first proverb is found in *Vatnsdæla saga*, chap. 5, and *Reykdæla saga*,

wulf reflects some tradition of proverbs on fate, a tradition that even early in the Middle Ages displayed a remarkable interplay (or at least correspondence) between Latin and vernacular expression.

Like passage K, passage L is spoken by Beowulf as he announces his intention to engage in battle against a formidable foe; hence the inclusion of a fatalistic proverb (passage K) and a subsequent allusion to it (L) link two conflicts which are separated by over fifty years and a long expanse of narrative. In both cases, the proverb removes from the hero some responsibility for the outcome of the battle, and the two fights provide exempla illustrating the different directions in which fate (and God) can operate. Common sense (and some recent criticism) would dictate that an aged Beowulf is less assured of success than the hero in his younger days, and furthermore, that a fire-breathing *wyrm* constitutes a more dangerous opponent than a humanoid wrestler, but no hint of these potentially significant factors is provided by the poet. In his speech, Beowulf himself equates the two fights (2918b–24a), adding only that this time he will require armor against the fire of the dragon. His heroic stance is the same before both battles, right down to the point of including the proverb on fate. That this stance is conventionally expressed becomes clear in comparison with Leofsunu's pledge in *Maldon* 247; the proverbial reference of *Beowulf* L augments the traditional nature of the scene.

M. (lines 572b–73):

> Wyrd oft nereð
> unfægne eorl,   þonne his ellen deah.

These lines stand out from the poem not only because of their sentential form, but also for their similarity to the modern proverb, "Fortune favors the brave."[40] The *Beowulf*ian version is somewhat complicated by the added condition that the *eorl* be *unfæge*, but I will address the proverbial connection of fate and death below, and concentrate here on the relationship between fate and courage.

---

chap. 6; cited here from *Íslenzkir Málshættir*, 92 (*Reykdæla saga* reads "fylgja" instead of "leita," but the meaning is the same in each case); the second proverb is cited from *Atlamál in grœnlenzco*, st. 48, in *Edda: Die Lieder des Codex Regius nebst verwandten Denkmälern*, ed. Gustav Neckel, 4th ed. rev. Hans Kuhn, Germanische Bibliothek (Heidelberg: Carl Winter, 1962), 1:254.

[40] For modern English examples, see Bartlett Jere Whiting, *Modern Proverbs and Proverbial Sayings* (Cambridge, Mass.: Harvard Univ. Press, 1989), F243.

One of the earliest and most influential uses of the proverb appears in the *Phormio* of Terence: "Fortes fortuna adiuvat" [Fortune helps the brave]; the sentence was subsequently cited by Cicero as a "vetum proverbium"[41] [old proverb]. The Latin proverb underwent many transformations (as will be seen below), but the alliterative phrasing employed by Terence seems to be the base from which variations were created. According to Heinrich Reichert, who tried to reconstruct the prehistory of Terence's sentence, this particular wording stood out from many others:

> Die Römer wußten um die geheimnisvolle Kraft des Geschickes. Die griechische Tyche, die Schickung, war ihnen ein geschichtlich und im Alltag erwiesener Begriff. Sie kannten die Bereitschaft des Glückes, die zu fördern und geheimnis voll zu lenken, die würdig sind und entschlossen zu wagen. Das Volk übersetzte diese Erfahrung in mannigfachen Wendungen in die Sprachen des Alltags. Im FORTES FORTUNA ADIUVAT ... fand es seine Prägung.[42]

This "Prägung" was still used as a device as late as the sixteenth century.[43]

However, the proverb underwent literary variation as early as the time of Virgil and Tibullus. In the *Aeneid*, Virgil altered "fortes" to "audentis,"[44] while Tibullus worked what one editor has called "an elegiac variation of the old alliterative proverb":[45] "Audendum est; fortes adiuvat ipse Deus"[46] [It is to be ventured; God himself helps the brave]. Tibullus's version exhibits the replacement of fate by God that is also typical of *Beowulf*ian *sententiae*. Ovid rang several changes on the proverb, typical among them being "Audentes deus ipse iuvat" [God himself helps the brave] and "Audentem Forsque Venusque iuvat"[47] [Both luck and love help the brave].

---

[41] *Phormio* 1.4.203; Walther, no. 9804.

[42] Heinrich G. Reichert, *Lateinische Sentenzen: Essays* (Wiesbaden: Dieterich, 1948), 80.

[43] Dielitz, 109.

[44] *Aeneid* X.284, ed. Conington/Nettleship, 3:263.

[45] *The Elegies of Albius Tibullus: The Corpus Tibullianum edited with introduction and notes on Books I, II, and IV, 2-14*, ed. Kirby Flower Smith (Darmstadt: Wissenschaftliche Buchgesellschaft, 1971), note to 1.2.16 (p. 210).

[46] Walther, no. 1699, and Margalits, 11.

[47] *Metamorphoses* 10.586 (cited from Walther, no. 1702), and *Ars Amatoria* 1.608 (from Smith, *The Elegies*, 210).

A somewhat different version of the proverb found expression in Ennius—"Fortibus est fortuna viris data" [Fortune has been given to brave men]—and was cited, along with Virgil, by Macrobius.[48] In the twelfth century, the object of Fortune's assistance was likewise altered by Otto of Freising: "Fortuna iuvante virtutem"[49] [With fortune assisting virtue]. Manuscripts from the thirteenth and fourteenth centuries provide versions of the sentence expanded almost to the point of explication, thus indicating that the proverb was still well established at that time:

> Audacem fortuna iuvat, nil grande cor audax
> Terret, nil animus, quidquid abhorret, habet.

> [Fortune helps the brave; the brave heart fears nothing greatly; courage has nothing whatever that it dreads.]

> Audaces fortuna iuvat non omnibus horis;
> Ergo boni solet esse comes discretio moris.[50]

> [Fortune does not help the brave at all times; therefore discretion is wont to accompany good conduct.]

The fourteenth century also witnessed what might be called a revival of this proverb in English narrative. Chaucer included it frequently: in the *Legend of Good Women*—"Hap helpeth hardy man alday"—in *Troilus and Criseyde*—"Fortune . . . helpeth hardy man to his enprise"—and in the *Reeve's Tale*—"'Unhardy is unseely,' thus men sayth."[51] Gower used the proverb in his *Confessio Amantis*—"Fortune unto the bolde Is favorable forto helpe"—as did Barbour in his *Bruce*:

> . . . it is all gret certante[,]
> That ure helpis ay hardy men.[52]

A vernacular example of perhaps greater relevance to *Beowulf* is that found in *Andreas*, lines 458–60. To assuage the fears of his sea-faring

---

[48] Walther, no. 9812.

[49] *Gesta Friderici* 2.35, in *Ottonis et Rahewini Gesta Friderici I. Imperatoris*, ed. G. Waitz, 2nd ed. (Hannover: Hahn, 1884), 115.

[50] Walther, nos. 1685 and 1687.

[51] *Legend of Good Women*, line 1773 (Whiting, *Proverbs . . . before 1500*, H96); *Troilus* 4.600–601 (Whiting, F519); and *Canterbury Tales* A.4210 (Whiting, U3).

[52] *Confessio Amantis* 3.4902–3, and *Bruce* 1.16–17; both cited from Whiting, *Proverbs . . . before 1500*, F519.

companions, the saint reminds them that God favors their works, and
recalls to them one past example of God's help, the stilling of the
waves by Christ. Andreas summarizes the moral of this inset narrative
with a version of our proverb:

> Forþan ic eow to soðe   secgan wille,
> þæt næfre forlæteð   lifgende god
> eorl on eorðan,   gif his ellen deah.[53]

> [Therefore I wish to tell you truly, that the living God
> never deserts a man in the world, if his courage is
> good.]

In its replacement of fortune by God, the variant from *Andreas* resembles those of Tibullus and Ovid, but the final half-line proves its relationship to *Beowulf* passage M. The two variants illustrate the ways in
which a proverb can be altered to fit thematic needs; the poet of
Andreas desires his hero to impart perfect faith in God, hence "God
never abandons a man of courage," whereas the *Beowulf*-poet puts the
proverb in the hero's mouth as an off-handed explanation for a deed
long past, "Fate *often* saves a brave and undoomed man." Unlike passages K and L, Beowulf's use of the proverb in this case does not serve
to remove personal responsibility for the outcome of a hazardous con-
flict. The hero recalls how the sun rose and the seas subsided (another
parallel to *Andreas*?), thus bringing his watery ordeal to an end. The
proverb would seem to attribute his success to fate, but Beowulf immediately follows it with a description of his own fortitude, beginning
"Hwæþere me gesælde" (574b) [But it befell me] and going on to elaborate on the extraordinary nature of his feat. The oppositional use of
hwæþere provides the full meaning of the proverb in this context; that
is, "Fate often helps a brave man, but I deserve full credit for this victory," or in Klaeber's paraphrase, "Fate does not render manly courage
unnecessary."[54]

The proverbial nature of passage M has been recognized for long
enough, and sufficiently documented, that some speculation as to its
source might be in order. The parallels between passage L and the
Aeneid make that possibility attractive in this case as well, but on the

---

[53] ASPR 2.15; the parallel is noted by Dobbie (ASPR 4, note to line 573b) and
Klaeber (*Beowulf*, note to lines 572f.).
[54] Klaeber, *Beowulf*, note to lines 572f.

other hand, the wide range of variants makes it less likely that passage M needs to be grounded in Virgil, or in any other classical author. Because the proverb was cited in so many different forms (e.g., fortuna/deus, fortes/audentes), and because its appearances usually lack an accompanying attribution, it is safe to suppose that "Fortune favors the brave" existed as a common and orally transmitted proverb from early on, and continued as such through the Anglo-Saxon period.

As I stated at the beginning of this chapter, it has not been my intention to define the concept of *wyrd* as it appears in *Beowulf*. However, the variety of analogues that I have introduced into the discussion does raise one issue: the relationship among *fatum, fortuna,* and *wyrd*. Up to this point, I have used the terms fate and fortune indiscriminately, as they tend to be used interchangeably in the *sententiae* (the only exception is "*Fortune* favors the brave," which maintains a fairly stable diction). In general, passages K, L, and M refer to *wyrd* as a power more akin to fortune than the fates; *wyrd* is the guiding force of what happens to one in life. One's life does, of course, include one's death, but that is not the only object of *wyrd*, which can help or hinder in any endeavor. In fact, the state of being *fæge* or *unfæge* seems to supersede the powers of *wyrd*, as in passage M, or even of God, as in lines 2291–93a, where God helps the *unfæge* man only. In the sentential passages of *Beowulf*, then, God and fate seem to be not only frequently linked or alternated, but ultimately parallel in their functions.[55]

*Beowulf*ian *sententiae* on death exhibit greater differences, but at the same time closer similarities, than any other group. This paradox can be explained by the division of form and theme in the sentences: most of them present the simple and incontrovertible truth that all men must die, but they make this statement in varied forms and styles. Different aspects of death are stressed in various passages, so it is with respect to these shades of emphasis that I have divided them.

All men must die

N. (lines 1386–87a):

> Ure æghwylc sceal   ende gebidan
> worolde lifes

---

[55] For a discussion of this correspondence (wherein fate is a function of the divine will) in the *Heliand*, see Albrecht Hagenlocher, *Schicksal im Heliand: Verwendung und Bedeutung der nominalen Bezeichnungen*, Niederdeutsche Studien 21 (Cologne: Böhlau Verlag, 1975), 96–103, 138–44, 162–69.

[Each of us must experience an end to life in the world]

O. (lines 2590b–91a):

> Swa sceal æghwylc mon
> alætan lændagas

[So must each man relinquish his transitory days]

P. (lines 1002b–8a):

> No þæt yðe byð
> to befleonne   —fremme se þe wille—,
> ac gesecan sceal   sawlberendra
> nyde genydde,   niþða bearna,
> grundbuendra   gearwe stowe,
> þær his lichoma   legerbedde fæst
> swefeþ æfter symle.

[That is not easy to flee from—whoever may try—but
he must be compelled by necessity to seek the place
that lies ready for soul-bearers, the sons of men, dwell-
ers in the world, where his body will sleep after the
feast, fast on the bed of death.]

These three sentences all make the simple point that death is the end
of every earthly life, and make that point sententially. All three impart
the necessity of death with the verb *sceal*, and express their subjects
with generalized terms: *æghwylc* in passages N and O, and a series of
general nouns in passage P. This last passage adds to the deadly imperative the nuance that no one can escape death by flight; but let us first
examine the proverbial basis for the more basic statement.

The *Sententiae* of Publilius Syrus, collected after his death in the first
century BC and then widely disseminated (although sometimes combined or confused with the pseudo-Senecan *De moribus*), enjoyed a
fruitful afterlife throughout the Middle Ages; manuscripts still extant
from as early as the ninth century attest to its use as a school text, with
Christianizing alterations as needed.[56] Publilius sets forth the basic
facts of life without sentiment or elaboration: "Lex universa est, que

---

[56] On manuscripts and textual history, see Publilius Syrus, *Sententiae*, ed. R. A.
H. Bickford-Smith (London: C. J. Clay & Sons, 1895), pp. xx–xxi; and M. D.
Reeve, "Publilius," in *Texts and Transmission: A Survey of the Latin Classics*, ed. L.
D. Reynolds (Oxford: Clarendon Press, 1983), 327–29.

iubet nasci et mori"[57] [It is a universal law that orders to be born and to die]. Lucan also entered the curricular canon at an early date,[58] and his lines on death—

> Libera Fortunae mors est; capit omnia tellus
> quae genuit; caelo tegitur qui non habet urnam[59]

> [Death is free of Fortune; the earth takes in all to whom it gives birth; who has no urn is covered by the sky]

—were repeated in the *Moralium dogma* of William of Conches, and in a fourteenth-century Leiden collection of Lucanian proverbs.[60] The Bible provides a sentence on the generality and finality of death— "Omnes morimur, et quasi aquae dilabimur in terram, quae non revertuntur" (2 Kings 14.14) [We all die, and fall into the earth like waters that do not return]—that may have formed the basis for Augustine's "Ista vita morientium est: hinc transimus, sed interest, quo" (*In Psalmos* 145.7) [This life is of the dying: we pass away from here, but we do not know where] and Egbert of Liège's "Sic an sic, fratres, nos hinc transibimus omnes"[61] [One way or another, brothers, we will all pass away from here]. Egbert seems to have been especially fond of such dismal reminders, as he included two others:

> Tendit ad occasum, quicquid precessit ad ortum.

> [Whatever proceeds from an origin moves towards an end.]

> Sorte licet dubia, cunctus tamen ortus obibit.[62]

---

[57] Publilius Syrus, ed. Bickford-Smith, L5 (p. 20); Walther, no. 13716, and Wander, *DS-L*, Geboren 26.

[58] Ernst Robert Curtius, *European Literature and the Latin Middle Ages*, trans. Willard R. Trask, Bollingen Series 36 (Princeton: Princeton Univ. Press, 1973), 49. See also Günter Glauche, *Schullektüre im Mittelalter: Entstehung und Wandlungen des Lektürekanons bis 1200 nach den Quellen dargestellt*, Münchener Beiträge zur Mediävistik und Renaissance-Forschung 5 (Munich: Arbeo-Gesellschaft, 1970); Glauche points out that Lucan was among the curricular authors listed by Jerome (p. 4) and Alcuin (p. 10).

[59] *De bello civili*, ed. D. R. Shackleton Bailey, Bibliotheca scriptorum Graecorum et Romanorum Teubneriana (Stuttgart: B. Teubner, 1988), 7.818–19 (p. 192).

[60] Walther, no. 13728.a.

[61] All three are cited by Ernst Voigt, *Egberts von Lüttich Fecunda ratis* (Halle: Max Niemeyer, 1889), 115.

[62] Voigt, 137 and 192.

[Although fortune may be unknown, nevertheless all
that has been born will die.]

Egbert, like Publilius, treats birth and death together, but this sub-class
of *sententiae* does not find expression in *Beowulf*, and need not be pursued further here.[63]

The absolute certainty of death was expressed proverbially in classical Latin writings, as witnessed by Plautus—"non moriri certius" [cer-
tain as death]—and Seneca—"nihil cuiquam nisi mors certum est"[64]
[nothing is certain for anyone but death]. At some point, this useful
idea entered Christian Latin parlance, perhaps through the medium of
the question-and-answer dialogue. The *Altercatio Hadriani Augusti et
Epicteti Philosophi*, an early series of brief questions and even briefer
answers, includes the set "H. Quid est certissimum? E. Mors"[65] [What
is most certain? Death]. The *Hadrian et Epictetus* was known to
Alcuin,[66] and served as a source for the Old English *Prose Solomon
and Saturn* dialogue. In that text, Saturn asks the question and Solomon
replies:

Saga me hwæt ys cuðost mannon on eorðan to witanne.

Ic þe secge, þæt nys nænygum men nanwyht swa cuð swa
he sceal deað þrowian.[67]

[Tell me what is the most certain knowledge for men on
earth.

I say to you that there is nothing so certain to a man as that
he must suffer death.]

Outside the realm of catechistic literature, Augustine contrasts the
uncertainties of earthly life to the certainty of death; he stresses the dis-

---

[63] Voigt, 137, gives further examples of this type; see also *Jezebel: A Norman
Latin Poem of the Early Eleventh Century*, ed. Jan M. Ziolkowski, Humana Civilitas
10 (New York: Peter Lang, 1989), p. 160.

[64] Plautus, *Captivi* 732; Seneca, Epis. 99.9; both cited from Morris C. Sutphen,
"A Further Collection of Latin Proverbs," *American Journal of Philology* 22 (1901):
241–60.

[65] *Altercatio Hadriani Augusti et Epicteti Philosophi*, ed. Lloyd William Daly and
Walther Suchier, Illinois Studies in Language and Literature 24.1–2 (Urbana: Univ.
of Illinois Press, 1939), no. 22 (p. 104).

[66] Daly and Suchier, pp. 75–76.

[67] *The 'Prose Solomon and Saturn' and 'Adrian and Ritheus'*, ed. James E. Cross
and Thomas D. Hill, McMaster Old English Studies and Texts 1 (Toronto: Univ.
of Toronto Press, 1982), no. 38 (p. 31).

tinction with repetitive wording that seems to reflect a proverbial background:

> Quid enim in hac terra certum est, nisi mors? Considerate omnia omnino uel bona uel mala uitae huius, uel in ipsa iustitia, uel in ipsa iniquitate; quid hic certum est, nisi mors?[68]

> [For what on this earth is certain except death? Consider all in all, both the good and the evil of this life, both the justice and injustice; what is certain here except death?]

And a few lines later, "Quocumque te uerteris, incerta omnia: sola mors certa"[69] [Wherever you turn, all things are uncertain: death alone is certain]. While Augustine's "Nothing is as certain as death" is not exactly the same as the *Beowulf*-poet's "Every man must die," it illustrates the tendency to express this rather ordinary idea in pithy, forceful wording. The same tendency can be seen in Defensor's abbreviated citation of Ecclus. 8.8: "Noli de mortuo gaudere, sciens quoniam omnes morimur"[70] [Do not rejoice over a death, knowing that all die].

Even the simplest of *sententiae* are open to revision and paraphrase, as the following example should make clear. Writing in the mid-twelfth century, Vitalis of Blois incorporated two such sentences into a short passage of his *Geta*:

> *Omnia mors tollit*; doctum cecidisse Platonem
> Atque ipsum Socratem occubuisse ferunt.
> Fama mei uiuet, sed et hec quoque morte peribit.
> *Omnia mors delet, omnia morte cadunt.*[71]

> [Death carries off all; learned Plato has lain sightless and Socrates himself has lain dead. My fame may live, but this too will perish in death. Death removes all, all fall in death (emphasis mine).]

---

[68] *Enarrationes in Psalmos*, CCSL 38.419–20 [ps. 38, par. 19].

[69] *Enarrationes in Psalmos*, 420.

[70] *Lib. scin.* 66.8 (CCSL 117.205). A similar sentiment appears in the OE *Disticha Catonis*: "Ne hopa ðu to oþres monnes deaðe: uncuð hwa lengest libbe" (Cox, "The Old English Dicts of Cato," no. 12 [p. 7]).

[71] Vitalis of Blois, *Geta*, ed. Ferruccio Bertini, in *Commedie Latine del XII e XIII secolo*, 5 vols. (Genoa: Istituto di Filologia Classica e Medievale, 1976–86), lines 179–82 (3.204).

The last line quoted here also appears by itself in a thirteenth-century Berlin manuscript and in the Pyramus-poem of Dietrich,[72] but a four-teenth-century Basel manuscript combines the lines to read "Omnia mors tollit, omnia morte cadunt"[73] [Death carries off all, all fall in death]. Vitalis's version of the sentence may have been misremembered by the later scribe, or perhaps he merely reproduced a version more familiar to him from elsewhere. In any case, this example of sentential transformation, though much later than *Beowulf*, illustrates a long-standing acceptance of sentential variation, even on such a basic subject as the death of every person.

A few more examples will complete this survey of seemingly self-evident *sententiae* in Latin letters. A thirteenth-century Paris manu-script yields "Nulla potest forti virtus resistere morti"[74] [No power can resist strong death], and two London manuscripts of the thir-teenth/fourteenth century point out that the law of death knows no divisions of class or sex:

> O mors, quam dura, quam tristia sunt tua iura!
> Parcere maiori tu nescis sive minori.

> [O death, how harsh, how sad are your laws! You do
> not know how to spare the greater or the lesser.]

> Mors cunctis dura, cunctos trahit in sua iura:
> Regem, reginam mors cogit inire ruinam.[75]

> [Death is harsh to all, it draws all under its laws: death
> forces both king and queen to be ruined.]

All of the examples I have cited combine to impress one with the fact that simple (or, as in *Beowulf* passage P, slightly elaborated) sentential expressions of the universal necessity of death were widespread, and hence readily available, in medieval Latin writings.

However, vernacular literature also preserves the remains of morbid proverbs. *Örvar-Odds saga* includes the same proverb twice, as first Hjálmarr and then Oddr laconically states that "Deyja skal hverr um

---

[72] Bertini, 3.205, cites Dietrich's poem, for which see Paul Lehmann, *Pseudo-antike Literatur des Mittelalters*, Studien der Bibliothek Warburg 13 (Leipzig: B. G. Teubner, 1927), line 284 (p. 45); Walther, no. 20005.

[73] Walther, no. 20010.

[74] Walther, no. 18938.c.

[75] Walther, nos. 19509 and 15124.

sinn"[76] [Every person must die sometime]. Use of the proverb characterizes a heroic attitude, but does not necessarily predict an imminent
demise, as Hjálmarr does succumb after his pronouncement, but Oddr
does not. A similar proverb, or another variant of the same one, is
spoken by Völsungr in response to a warning by Signý: "eitt sinn skall
hverr deyja, en engi má undan komaz at deyja um sinn"[77] [every person must die one time, and no one can escape dying once]. Likewise,
Sigurðr responds to Fáfnir's revelation of the curse on his treasure with
apparent unconcern, "þvíat eino sinni scal alda hverr / fara til heliar
heðan"[78] [because every man must leave the world once]. The only
verse included in Gisls þáttr Illugasonar uses a short version of the proverb—"hverr deyr seggr eitt sinn"[79] [every man dies one time]—as part
of a more complex heroic stance. The Middle High German Eraclius provides what one suspects is another example of an extended proverb:

> Den tôt enmag erwenden nieht,
> deheines mannes wîstuom,
> sîn gewalt noch sîn rîchtuom,
> bürge noch veste.[80]

> [No man's wisdom can avert death, nor can his
> strength, his wealth, castles or fortress.]

Finally, Chaucer includes in the Canterbury Tales two proverbs as
straightforward in their expression as those of Beowulf N and O: "Al
this thyng moot deye" and "Alle shul we deye."[81] There can remain
no doubt that "Each person must die" was a common proverb, in
Latin and the vernacular, in religious and secular use, throughout the
whole of the Middle Ages. It is no surprise, then, to find it in Beowulf,
even more than once.

One other set of proverbs may have influenced Beowulf passage P;

---

[76] Örvar-Odds saga, chap. 14 and 16; from Íslenzkir Málshættir, 54.

[77] Die Völsungasaga, ed. Wilhelm Ranisch (Berlin: Mayer & Müller, 1891), chap.
5, p. 6; Íslenzkir Málshættir, 54.

[78] Fáfnismál, st. 10, in Edda, ed. Neckel/Kuhn, 182.

[79] Gisls þáttr Illugasonar, chap. 4, in Íslendinga þættir, ed. Guðni Jónsson
(Reykjavík: Sigurðar Kristjánssonar, 1945), 44.

[80] Eraclius: deutsches und französisches Gedicht des zwölften Jahrhunderts, ed. H. F.
Massmann, Bibliothek der gesammten deutschen National-Literatur 6 (Quedlinburg:
Gottfr. Basse, 1842), lines 368–71 (p. 12); Zingerle, 148.

[81] Knight's Tale, A.3034, and Clerk's Prologue, E.38; both cited from Whiting,
Proverbs . . . before 1500, D243.

these sentences state explicitly that no one can flee (successfully) from
death. A famous example derives from Horace, "Mors et fugacem persequitur virum"[82] [Death also pursues the fleeing man], while Mat-
thew of Vendôme links the idea of flight with that of the immutable
natural law we have already seen: "Mors properat, fuga nulla potest
mortale tributum solvere: nature lege tenetur homo"[83] [Death hastens,
no flight can escape the mortal tribute: man is held by the law of
nature]. Another, somewhat less illustrious writer of the twelfth century, Henry of Settimello (or Henricus Pauper), reformulated the proverb
in elegiac terms:

> Quo fugiam vel quid faciam? Mors undique claudit,
> Ne fugiam, cunctas imperiosa vias[84]

> [Where will I flee and what will I do? Death, imperi-
> ous, shuts off all routes everywhere, lest I flee].

Finally, an eleventh- to twelfth-century manuscript of the *Disputatio
Adriani Augusti et Epicteti Philosophi*, which borrows from the *Hadrian
et Epictetus* cited above, records the question-and-answer set: "A. Quid
est mors? E. Quod omnes fugiunt et nemo evadere valet"[85] [What is
death? What everyone flees and no one manages to escape].

Klaeber notes that the proverb is "well known in ON. literature,"
and cites Saxo Grammaticus—"fatis arduum obstare"[86] [it is difficult
to resist the fates]. The Old Norse examples are worth examining, not
only because they help to establish the distribution of the proverb, but
also because they illustrate how death and fate can be proverbially
linked.

In some cases, the proverb refers specifically to death; two such uses
can be found in *Harðar saga*—"Eigi má feigum forða"[87] [One cannot

---

[82] *Carmina* 3.2.14; Walther, no. 15145. Compare Augustine's twice-repeated
"nos non persequitur nisi mors," *Enarrationes in Psalmos*, CCSL 39.623 (ps. 51, par.
1).

[83] *Tobias*, chap. 4; Walther, no. 15194.

[84] *Elegia de diversitate fortunae et philosophiae consolatione*, bk. 1, lines 87–88;
Walther, no. 25631.

[85] *Disputatio*, no. 14, in *Altercatio Hadriani et Epicteti*, ed. Daly and Suchier,
113. Daly suggests (p. 81) that the answer in the *Disputatio* is taken from *Altercatio*
27 ("Quid est vispillo? Quem multi devitant et nemo effugit," p. 105), but the two
sentences are not especially similar in their wording.

[86] Klaeber, *Beowulf*, note to lines 1002b–3a; Saxo, *Historia Danorum*, 8.295.

[87] *Harðar saga Grímkelssonar*, chap. 35; from *Íslenzkir Málshættir*, 81.

save the doomed]—and *Sverris saga*—"Ecki kemr vfeigum i hel ok ecki ma feigum forda"[88] [No undoomed person is sent to death and one cannot save the doomed]. However, another variant of the proverb states that it is difficult to flee from what is fated, which may refer only to the events of one's life. For example, in *Vatnsdæla saga* Grímr and Ingimundr are told by a seeress that they both will settle in Iceland. Grímr does move there, but Ingimundr initially refuses to follow suit. Despite Ingimund's resistance, Grímr expresses his expectation of seeing Ingimundr in Iceland at some point, because "Óhægt mun forlögin að flýja"[89] [It will be difficult to escape fate]. Grímr had already expressed his acquiescence to fate in a slightly different proverbial form just before this: "eigi mundi tjóa at brjótask við forlögunum"[90] [it does not help to struggle against fate]. When Ingimundr does, of course, finally land at Borgarfjörd, Grímr rides down to meet his ship, and notes, in explicitly proverbial terms, the fulfillment of the prophecy: "ok kemr hér nú at því, sem mælt er, at torsótt er at forðask forlögin"[91] [and now it happens according to the saying, that it is difficult to escape fate]. Grím's proverbs display, by their use of *óhægt* and *torsótt*, the understatement also notable in *Beowulf* passage P ("no þæt yðe byð"), which makes one suspect that they exist as variants within the same proverbial complex. The alternation of fate and death in the Old Norse proverbs also helps to explicate the way in which *wyrd* in *Beowulf* may or may not refer to a death, even when essentially the same *sententia* is used, as in passages K and L.

Proverbs and *sententiae* warning that fate and death are inescapable abound in early Irish literature; in one case the expression is as concise and generalized as the Old Norse examples: "Ní fhétar dul seoch an cindeamhain" [There is no escaping Fate].[92] However, more detailed versions, expanded into triads, specify that either the time or the place

---

[88] *Sverris saga Sigurðarsonar*, chap. 42, in *Flateyjarbók: En samling af Norske Konge-Sagaer*, ed. Guðbrandur Vigfússon and C. R. Unger, 3 vols. (Oslo: P. T. Malling, 1860-68), 2:575; cf. Guðmundur Olafsson's *Thesaurus Adagiorum*, ed. Kallstenius, no. 624 (p. 38).

[89] *Vatnsdæla saga*, ed. Einar Ól. Sveinsson, Íslenzk Fornrit 8 (Reykjavík, 1939), chap. 10, p. 31; *Íslenzkir Málshættir*, 92.

[90] *Vatnsdæla saga*, chap. 10, p. 30.

[91] *Vatnsdæla saga*, chap. 14, p. 38; *Íslenzkir Málshættir*, 91.

[92] From the "Voyage of Bran"; proverbial text and translation from *A Miscellany of Irish Proverbs*, ed. Thomas F. O'Rahilly (Dublin: Talbot Press, 1922), no. 282 (p. 86).

of one's death cannot be avoided. Two variants of the first type appear
in the "Battle of Magh Rath":

> Nī thesairg trú teiched, nī tarba éc d' ingabāil, uair trī huaire
> nach imgaibther .i. uair éca, uair gene, uair choimperta.

> [Flight saves not a man who is doomed to have his life cut short,
> it is profitless to shun death, for there are three times that cannot
> be avoided, the time of death, the time of birth, the time of con-
> ception.]

> > Trí uara ná tairiset
> > fri tráig ocus fri tuile,—
> > uair gene, uair choimperta
> > uair scartha anma duīne.

> > [Three times that stay not for ebbtide or for flood,—the
> > time of birth, the time of conception, the time when
> > the soul departs.][93]

Variants specifying the place of death also appear in the "Battle of
Magh Rath" and in the *Táin Bó Cualnge*:

> > Trí fótáin nach sechainter,
> > cia toiscet na habrochtair,—
> > fót in gene, fót in báis,
> > ocus fót ind adnacuil.

> > [Three places that cannot be avoided ... the place of
> > birth, the place of death, and the place of burial.]

> > Is ēicen do neoch a thecht
> > cosin fót forsa mbí a thiglecht.

> > [Everyone must go to the place where his final bed is
> > (destined to be).][94]

This last variant substitutes the idea of compulsion for that of unavoid-
ability, but provides a proverbial parallel to the inescapable "legerbedd"
of passage M.

Two final vernacular examples will round out the discussion of this

---

[93] Text and translation from O'Rahilly, pp. 86–87.
[94] Ibid.

proverbial variant. In Germany, the sentence appears in Freidank's *Bescheidenheit*,

> Wirn mugen mit keinen sinnen
> dem tôde niht entrinnen[95]

[We cannot escape death through any clever strategy]

and in fourteenth-century England, in the *Otuel and Roland*:

> By the Ensampyl, who mowe se
> That no man schall hys deth fle
> For none skynnes nede.[96]

Considering the entire corpus of proverbial analogues to *Beowulf* passage P, we may add to Klaeber's note that the referent of *þæt* in line 1002b is clarified by context, the observation that a medieval audience should immediately have recognized the lines as a reworking of the common proverb "One cannot flee from death."

Although passages N, O, and P all state essentially the same truism, that everyone must die, they are used by the *Beowulf*-poet to slightly different effects. Klaeber's punctuation obscures the fact that passage N is the second in a string of three *sententiae* mouthed by Beowulf in response to Hrothgar's speech lamenting the death of Æschere and describing Grendel's mere. Hrothgar closes his speech with an offer of yet more treasure if Beowulf will track down Æschere's murderer, and it is this offer to which the hero responds. His first proverbial statement—"It is better to avenge one's friend than to mourn him"—effectively conveys his intention to act as that avenger; the third *sententia* of the series—"He who is able should do glorious deeds before he dies"—provides a further rationale for his willingness to assist Hrothgar. Our passage N is strategically placed to mesh with both of these sentences, as it could be perceived as an addendum to the first or as a preface to the third. In either case, it allows all three *sententiae* to refer simultaneously to Beowulf and to Æschere. Passage N could have a consolatory function (i.e., don't mourn too much for Æschere, because we all die sometime), and at the same time reinforce Beowulf's heroic characterization as a warrior entering battle fearless of death (i.e., I recognize this

---

[95] Freidank, *Bescheidenheit* 175.22, ed. and trans. Wolfgang Spiewok (Leipzig: Philipp Reclam, 1985), 218.

[96] *Otuel and Roland*, lines 1916–18; cited from Whiting, *Proverbs . . . before 1500*, D97.

task as dangerous, but I am bound to die sometime). The first sentence of the series obviously refers to Beowulf and Æschere (as avenger and "avengee"), but the third sentence could do so as well, if Beowulf is not only announcing his own intention, but also tactfully praising Æschere as a doer of deeds before his death, in response and deference to Hrothgar's praise of his old companion. By their very generality, proverbs and *sententiae* are especially well-suited to such multiple interpretations.

Passages O and P are less complicated in their contextual placement. Passage O essentially completes the metaphor predicting Beowulf's death after the breaking of his sword; it explains the image of the hero having to leave the field and dwell elsewhere as the passage from life to death. However, it also provides a breather, so to speak, for the audience as they follow the progress of the battle, a short respite that the formula "Næs ða long to ðon" (2591b) [It was not long until] implies is taking place in the fight itself.

Passage P performs the transitional function that we have already seen with respect to several other *Beowulf*ian *sententiae*. In this case, the elaborated proverb concludes a description of Grendel's severed arm and of the interior of Heorot, in preparation for a resumed description of the pleasures of the victory feast. The unusual length of the sentential passage is explained by the poet's successful attempt to link it to what comes both before and after. The poet describes the destruction wreaked in Heorot by Grendel's attempt at flight from Beowulf, and follows immediately with the generalization that death is not easy to flee (*fleam/befleonne*). On the other end, the passage concludes with an image of the feast of life (*symle*), and then the feast in Heorot is resumed.[97]

The doomed must fall

Q. (lines 1753–55a):

> Hit on endestæf   eft gelimpeð,
> þæt se lichoma   læne gedreoseð,
> fæge gefealleð.

> [In the end it finally happens that the perishable body declines, the doomed one falls.]

---

[97] The extension of the sentence also results from the introduction of variation, essentially the poeticizing of a *sententia*.

This passage obtains its proverbial aspect from the present tense of its verbs (although the exemplum of which it forms a part is also related in the present tense), and, more subtly, from the nominal phrase "se lichoma." The latter implies a level of generalization higher than that surrounding the passage, in that Hrothgar's exemplum describes a particular (albeit fictitious) individual, so "his lichoma" would be the expected, non-sentential wording.

In my discussion of passage P, I gave examples of Old Norse proverbs stating that the doomed man cannot flee from death. To these examples can be added variants relating simply that the doomed person must die; such variants can be found in *Reykdæla saga*—"Þá mun hver deyja, er feigur er"[98] [Then must each die who is doomed]—in *Þiðreks saga af Bern*—"Þeir verða að falla er feigir eru"[99] [They who are doomed must fall]—and in *Grettis saga*—"Verður hver þá að fara, er hann er feigur"[100] [Each must die when he is doomed]. The poet of *Hamðismál* expanded the proverb and gave it a mythological cast: "qveld lifir maðr ecci eptir qvið norna"[101] [no man lives through the evening after the word of the norns]. Old Norse proverbs also treat the reverse situation, that of the undoomed man, as both *Íslendinga saga* and *Fóstbrœðra saga* include variants of "Hverjum bergur nokkuð, er eigi er feigur"[102] [He who is not doomed will escape somehow]. We have seen a similar formulation in *Beowulf* passage M, as "Fate often helps the undoomed man."

The Old Norse analogues by themselves would not suffice to establish the proverbial background to passage Q, of which the state of being doomed is not necessarily the main ingredient, but they are matched by an Old English sentence found in *Maxims I*: "Fus sceal feran, fæge sweltan"[103] [The eager one must go, the doomed one die]. A passage from *Guthlac A* lacks explicit mention of imminent doom but is nevertheless similar to *Beowulf* passage Q in its collocation of *lichoma*, *læne*, *sceal*, and *gedreosan*:

---

[98] *Reykdæla saga*, chap. 6; cited from *Íslenzkir Málshættir*, 54.
[99] *Þiðreks saga af Bern*, chap. 338; cited from *Íslenzkir Málshættir*, 81.
[100] *Grettis saga*, chap. 62; cited from *Íslenzkir Málshættir*, 80.
[101] *Hamðismál*, st. 30, in *Edda*, ed. Neckel/Kuhn, 274.
[102] *Íslenzkir Málshættir*, 81.
[103] *Maxims I*, line 27 (ASPR 3.157).

Ne mæg min lichoma   wið þas lænan gesceaft
deað gedælan,   ac he gedreosan sceal,
swa þeos eorðe eall   þe ic her on stonde.[104]

[My body cannot part from this perishable condition,
from death, but it must fall just like all this earth on
which I here stand.]

Thus, it seems that the *Beowulf*-poet has replaced the modal verb cus-
tomarily employed in variants of this sentence with a simple present or
consuetudinal, in order to fit it more easily into the context of the
exemplum. The sentence also introduces the idea that he who is strong
now will be dead later, a lesson that is continued by passage R.

Strong now, dead later, or, A thousand ways to die

R. (lines 1761b–68):

                    Nu is þines mægnes blæd
ane hwile;   eft sona bið,
þæt þec adl oððe ecg   eafoðes getwæfeð,
oððe fyres feng,   oððe flodes wylm,
oððe gripe meces,   oððe gares fliht,
oððe atol yldo;   oððe eagena bearhtm
forsiteð ond forsworceð;   semninga bið,
þæt ðec, dryhtguma,   deað oferswyðeð.

[Now the glory of your might exists for awhile; but it
will soon happen that sickness or a sword will deprive
you of strength, or the grasp of fire, or the welling of
the flood, or the bite of a sword, or the flight of a
spear, or terrible old age; or the brightness of your eyes
will diminish and dim; it will happen before long,
warrior, that death will overpower you.]

This passage appears to extend beyond the length of the average *sententia*, but the anomaly can be explained by its incorporation of two
separate sentential complexes. One of these, stating that present
strength is followed by future death, informs the beginning and end of
the passage, while the middle portion is related to *sententiae* warning

---

[104] *Guthlac*, lines 371–73 (ASPR 3.60).

that there are many ways to die. Both sets of *sententiae* are found most frequently in Latin versions.

A fourteenth-century Basel manuscript provides the most detailed variant of the sentence—

> Sis iuvenis fortis, dives, sapiens, veneratus!
> Cum mors ipsa venit, his omnibus es spoliatus[105]

> [You may be strong in youth, rich, wise, honored!
> When death comes, you are despoiled of all these things]

—but a contemporary variant from England neatly summarizes the lesson of Hrothgar's speech: "Esto memor mortis, cum tu sis corpore fortis!"[106] [Be mindful of death while you are strong in body!]. As Hans Walther notes, such sentences may derive from Ecclus. 14.12, "Memor esto, quoniam mors non tardat"[107] [Be mindful that death does not tarry]. In vernacular German, the proverbial "heute ... morgen ..." formula was used to express the same theme, in "Wer heut lebt, der stirbet morn"[108] [Who lives today, dies tomorrow]. A similar temporal opposition is produced in passage R by the poet's placement of *nu*, *eft sona*, and *semninga*.

Sententiae warning that death comes in a thousand (or many) ways, and often enumerating several of those ways, are even more common in Latin literature. As Hans Walther records, the sentence "Ubique mors est; mille ad hanc aditus patent" [Death is everywhere; a thousand ways lie open to it] became proverbial,[109] although the full Senecan passage reads:

> ubique mors est. optume hoc cauit deus:
> eripere uitam nemo non homini potest,
> at nemo mortem; mille ad hanc aditus patent.[110]

> [Death is everywhere. God has provided for this most graciously: one can take away a man's life, but not his death; a thousand ways lie open to it.]

---

[105] Walther, no. 29739.
[106] Walther, no. 8035.
[107] Walther, no. 5881.
[108] Zingerle, 196; see also Wander, *DS-L*, Heute 90.
[109] Walther, no. 32076.
[110] *Phoenissae* 151–53, in *Tragoediae*, ed. Zwierlein, 104.

A version of the sentence found its way into the pseudo-Senecan *Liber de moribus*, where it was read by Sedulius Scottus and included (twice) in his own *Collectaneum*:

> Multos defferentes uitam mors incerta preuenit.
> Itaque omnis dies uelud ultimus iudicandus est.[111]

> [Death, unpredictable, forestalls many who postpone life.
> Therefore, pass every day as if it were thought your last.]

Vincent of Beauvais cites Statius—"Mille modis leti miseros mors una fatigat" [One death plagues the wretches in a thousand ways]—and Prosper:

> Ferro, peste, fame, vinclis, ardore, calore,
> mille modis miseros mors rapit una homines.[112]

> [By the sword, pestilence, famine, fetters, heat, or cold,
> one death seizes wretched men in a thousand ways.]

Like Prosper, Albert von Stade included in his *Troilus* a variant of the sentence comprising both the "thousand ways" and the list of dangers:

> Mille modis mortis miseros mors una trucidat,
> Una morte mori sit quasi turpe sibi.
> Per gladios, per balistas, per tela, per enses
> Invitant mortem, dat quoque clava necem.[113]

> [One death slaughters wretches with a thousand ways
> to death, as if it were shameful for them to die through
> one death. Through swords, through crossbows,
> through spears, through foils they invite death, and the
> cudgel too brings about a violent demise.]

The same combination is found, more concisely, in a Basel manuscript:

---

[111] Sedulius Scottus, *Coll. Misc.*, 4.91 and 16.7 (CCCM 67.18, 132).

[112] Vincent of Beauvais, *De eruditione filiorum nobilium*, ed. Arpad Steiner, The Medieval Academy of America, publ. no. 32 (Cambridge, Mass.: Medieval Academy of America, 1938), chap. 41, p. 169; Statius *Thebaidos* 9.280; Prosper *Poema coniugis* 25–26; see Walther, nos. 9356 and 14865, and Margalits, 332.

[113] *Troilus Alberti Stadensis*, ed. Th. Merzdorf, Bibliotheca Scriptorum Medii Aevi Teubneriana (Leipzig: B. G. Teubner, 1875), lines 63–66 (p. 72); Walther, no. 14865.

Unda, peste, fame, gladiis, algore, calore,
Ac laqueis mille mors genus omne rapit[114]

[By water, pestilence, famine, swords, cold, heat, and a
thousand nooses, death captures all that is born].

In describing the victories of Baldwin in Jerusalem, William of Tyre
expands the list of dangers into realistic description, but still concludes
with the tell-tale tag:

ita ut nec qui de navibus exierant ad mare redire presumerent et
qui ad montes se contulerant, dum incaute fugiunt periculosa
incurrentes precipicia, inprovise mortis mille vias invenirent.[115]

[... in such a way that those who had gone out from the ships
would not presume to go back to the sea, and those who had
betaken themselves to the mountain would (as they flee heedless-
ly, rushing at perilous precipices) come upon a thousand ways of
unforeseen death.]

Although I have found no vernacular version of the list of dangers
(outside *Beowulf*), the concept appears in expanded form in the description of dismal prospects that makes up the bulk of the poem, *The
Fortunes of Men*. The topos of the thousand or many modes of death
does seem to have crossed over from Latin usage at some point. The
expression appears in Freidank,

Der mensche ist sô broede,
wol tûsent slahte toede,
die sint dem menschen beschert,
swaz er tuot od swar er vert[116]

[Man is so fragile, death comes to him in a thousand
ways, whatever he does or wherever he goes]

and in Gower, "Althogh ther be diverse weie To deth, yit is ther bot
on ende."[117]

---

[114] Walther, no. 32145.

[115] *Willelmi Tyrensis archiepiscopi Chronicon*, ed. R. B. C. Huygens, with H. E.
Mayer and G. Rösch, CCCM 63 and 63A (Turnhout: Brepols, 1986), bk. 10, chap.
6 (CCCM 63.460).

[116] *Bescheidenheit*, 177.9 (Spiewok, 222).

[117] *Confessio Amantis*, 4.2256; cited from *The Oxford Dictionary of English
Proverbs*, 3rd ed. rev. F. P. Wilson (Oxford: Clarendon Press, 1970), 225.

Thus, the *sententia* forming the core of *Beowulf* passage R can appear in any of three versions: it may warn of the thousand ways to die, it may list some of those ways, or it may combine both themes. Klaeber has noted that "the polysyndetic series [of this passage] suggests the rhetoric of a preacher,"[118] and indeed it does, but we have seen analogous *sententiae* appear in philosophical, dramatic, pedagogical, and narrative works as well. The homiletic tone of Hrothgar's speech may bear some of the responsibility for the length of passage R, but eight lines are none too many within which to fuse two different *sententiae*, one of which often assumes an extended form itself.

Hrothgar's sermon is, as befits the character's age, rank, and wisdom, highly sentential. The speech alternates exempla and *sententiae* or proverbial references, using the latter sometimes to expand the relevance of the former (as with passage Q), or, in the case of passage R, employing a sentence to introduce an exemplum. Passage R is composed in such a way as to apply directly to Beowulf (*þines, þec*), but it is followed and proven by a description of Hrothgar's own career. The specific references to hero and king disguise somewhat the exemplum/*sententia* relation, but the correspondence between general expression and specific example obtains nonetheless, as elsewhere in the poem.

Gain glory before death

S. (lines 1387b–89):

> Wyrce se þe mote
> domes ær deaþe;   þæt bið drihtguman
> unlifgendum   æfter selest.

> [Let he who can earn fame before death; that is afterwards best for the dead warrior.]

T. (lines 1534b–36):

> Swa sceal man don,
> þonne he æt guðe   gegan þenceð
> longsumne lof;   na ymb his lif cearað.

> [So should a man do, when he intends to gain lasting praise in a battle: care not about his life.]

---

[118] Klaeber, *Beowulf*, note to lines 1763ff.

The sentential form of passage S is clearly marked by the generality of "se þe" and "drihtguman," and augmented by the use of "selest." In fact, the entire second half of the passage, beginning with "þæt bið," serves mainly to point out the sentential and didactic nature of what precedes it. Passage T also includes such a marker, the formula "swa sceal man don." However, T expresses too specific a situation to be considered proverbial in a strict sense, as no analogues address the special case of earning praise through fearless combat. Both passages, and their analogues, express the opposition of fame to death, and the theme of contempt for life.

That passage S represents the variant of a proverbial expression current in the Anglo-Saxon period is proven by the existence of at least two Old English analogues; the first of these is found in *Maxims I*:

Deop deada wæg   dyrne bið lengest;
holen sceal inæled,   yrfe gedæled
deades monnes.   Dom biþ selast.[119]

[The deep way of death is secret for the longest; holly
must be burned, the dead man's inheritance shared out.
Fame is the best.]

These lines form a cohesive unit, being preceded by a description of the seasons and followed by a section delineating the proper behavior of a married, royal couple; thus, "dom biþ selast" must be interpreted with respect to the sentence that precedes it. In general terms, *dom* is "best" for a dead man, and more specifically, *dom* may be understood as the best *yrfe* of the dead man; *yrfe* represents the same idea as the "æfter" of passage S. Both *Maxims I* and our *Beowulf* passage reflect a proverb stating that "Glory is the best thing for a dead man to leave behind." A briefer version of the sentence appears in *Maxims II*, as "Til sceal on eðle / domes wyrcean"[120] [A good man should earn fame in his homeland].

A second Old English analogue to passage S appears in the *Seafarer*, as the lesson drawn from the fact that every man must eventually meet his end one way or another:

Forþon þæt bið eorla gehwam   æftercweþendra
lof lifgendra   lastworda betst,
þæt he gewyrce,   ær he on weg scyle,

---

[119] *Maxims I*, lines 78–80 (ASPR 3.159).
[120] *Maxims II*, lines 20b–21a (ASPR 6.56).

fremum on foldan   wið feonda niþ,
deorum dædum   deofle togeanes,
þæt hine ælda bearn   æfter hergen,
ond his lof siþþan   lifge mid englum
awa to ealdre,   ecan lifes blæd,
dream mid dugeþum.[121]

[Because the praise of those living and speaking afterwards is the best of last words for every man, he should
perform, before he must depart, good feats on the earth
against the enmity of enemies, brave deeds against the
devil, so that the sons of men will commend him afterwards and his praise may live forever among the angels,
his reward of eternal life, joy among the hosts.]

The first ("biþ") and fourth ("fremum") lines of this passage have
undergone emendation, and not all commentators or editors agree on
its grammatical niceties, but the burden of the passage is clearly that "A
man should perform praiseworthy deeds while alive, in order to achieve
good fame after his death." While the sentential form of this passage,
and its description of good fame as the best thing for a man to leave
behind him, clinch its relationship to the analogues from *Beowulf* and
Maxims I, the poet of the *Seafarer* has expanded the *sententia* by providing a description of the sort of praiseworthy deeds that a man should
perform. As is typical in the *Seafarer*, the poet has begun with a secular
ideal—that of achieving fame through brave feats—and manipulated the
image to give it a Christian significance. In this case, the poet has
appropriated not only a secular, heroic image, but what appears to be
a secular, heroic proverb.

Still, it is not enough to identify our proverb without considering
whence it might have arisen and how widespread it might have been.
Latin *sententiae* extolling fame after death are, as one might expect,
essentially restricted to secular works and manuscript collections of
miscellaneous sentences. The frequent connection of these sentences
with various heroic figures explains their wide distribution in spite of
an apparent lack of ecclesiastical sanction. Klaeber points out a possible
heroic analogue to passage S—*Aeneid* X.467ff.[122]—but I have found no
evidence that the Virgilian lines ever attained proverbial or sentential

---

[121] *Seafarer*, lines 72–80a (ASPR 3.145).
[122] Klaeber, *Beowulf*, note to lines 1386ff.

status. A different sentential variant appears in Ausonius: "Vita perit, meriti gloria non moritur"[123] [Life perishes, the glory of merit does not die]; close variants of this sentence are found in several later medieval manuscripts, replacing "meriti" with "mortis."[124]

One function of heroic narrative is, of course, to spread the fame of the warriors it describes; thus, when a narrator or character asserts that "fame never dies," the sentence is not only included as part of, but also proven by, the existence of the narrative. When Walter of Châtillon writes in his *Alexandreis*,

> Viuere per famam dabitur post fata sepultis.
> Sola mori nescit eclypsis nescia uirtus
>
> [To live on through their fame will be given after the
> fate of the grave. Valor alone knows no death nor
> eclipse],

or,

> Hoc solum releuamen inest, quod gloria mortem
> Nescit et occasum non sentit fama superstes[125]
>
> [This alone offers relief, that glory knows no death, and
> that fame survives and suffers no end],

the placement of such sentences in the mouths of characters affirms the purpose of the work as a whole. The same can be said of Albert's *Troilus*, where we read that "Post mortem sola fama superstes erit"[126] [Only fame will remain after death]. Poetic retellers of heroic legends help to disseminate the ethos embodied by their characters, and also participate in that ethos as the justification for their own works. This is not to say that *sententiae* reminding one of *post mortem* reputation can exist only in conjunction with heroic figures, as many manuscript collections contain such sentences as

---

[123] *Septem sapientum sententiae septenis versibus explicatae*, "Anacharis Scytha," line 2, in *D. Magni Ausonii Opuscula*, ed. Carolus Schenkl, MGH Auctores 5.2 (Berlin: Weidmannos, 1883), 249.

[124] Walther, no. 33860.

[125] *Alexandreis* 6.335–36 (Colker, 161), and 7.356–57 (188); Walther, nos. 33991 and 10324; cf. Singer, 1.15. Vernacular translations of the *Alexandreis* often maintain the sentential form of such passages; see Ulrich von Eschenbach, *Alexander*, lines 5004–5010, and *Alexanders saga* (ed. C. R. Unger), pp. 97 and 116.

[126] *Troilus*, 5.342 (p. 143); Walther, no. 22024.a.

> Mors hominem, requies animam, cisterna cadaver
> Suscipit, et nobis nil nisi fama manet
>
> [Death receives the man, rest the soul, a cistern the
> corpse, and nothing remains for us but fame],

and "Fac bene, dum vivis, post mortem vivere si vis"[127] [Do well, while you live, if you wish to live on after death].

Scandinavian literature is replete with proverbs and sentences extolling the achievement of fame lasting after death; Saxo provides one example in his translation of the old *Bjárkamál*:

> Gloria defunctos sequitur, putrique favillæ
> fama superstes erit, nec in ullum decidet ævum,
> quod perfecta suo patravit tempore virtus[128]
>
> [Glory follows the dead, and fame will outlast moulder-
> ing ashes, nor will ever perish what perfect valor ac-
> complished in his day].

Perhaps the most famous analogue appears in *Hávamál*:

> Deyr fé,   deyia froendr,
> deyr siálfr it sama;
> enn orðztírr   deyr aldregi,
> hveim er sér gódan getr.
>
> Deyr fé,   deyia froendr,
> deyr siálfr it sama;
> ec veit einn,   at aldri deyr:
> dómr um dauðan hvern.[129]
>
> [Cattle die, kinsmen die, one also dies oneself; but the
> good fame never dies for him who obtains it.
> Cattle die, kinsmen die, one also dies oneself; I know
> one thing that never dies: the judgment about every
> dead man.]

Like the *Beowulf* passages, the first stanza from *Hávamál* impresses its

---

[127] Walther, nos. 15157 and 8635.

[128] *Saxonis Gesta Danorum*, ed. J. Olrik and H. Ræder, 3 vols. (Hauniae, 1931), lines 37–39 (1:57); Singer (1.15) describes this and the other Old Norse analogues.

[129] *Hávamál*, st. 76–77, in *Edda*, ed. Neckel/Kuhn, 29; cf. *Gudmundi Olaui Thesaurus Adagiorum*, no. 2210 (p. 106).

audience with the importance of *earning* fame. A third native Norse example is used, like *Beowulf* T, to urge men to battle. King Sverrir confers with his followers at one point about whether they should engage in battle with the forces of King Magnús, and is told by a *karl* that "lifa orð lengst eptir hvern"[130] [Praise words live longest after each person].

Middle High German sentences opposing fame to death include one in Ulrich von Eschenbach's translation of Walter's *Alexandreis*,[131] but also two variants suggesting a proverbial formula of "lip/lebet/lop." The earlier of these appears in Hartmann's description of Arthur's enduring popularity:

> Er hat den lop erworben,
> ist im der lîp erstorben,
> sô lebt doch iemer sî name[132]

> [He has attained such fame that although his body has died, his name lives on forever].

A similar phrasing can be found in the poetry of Rûmelant:

> Tôt ist sîn lîp, noch lebet sîn lop,
> sîn name gestirbet nimer[133]

> [Dead is his body, but his fame lives on; his name will never die].

Although these passages refer too specifically to a single character to be considered sentential, the consistent alliteration and thematic similarity to *sententiae* we have seen suggest an underlying proverbial background.

The primary injunction of passage T is to set aside concern for the safety of one's life. Although a great deal of sentential, didactic, and poetic literature enjoins the reader or listener to take better heed of what happens after death than before, the topos most consistently used is that of *contemptus mundi*, a religious concept not perceptibly relevant to the passage at hand. Passage T does not teach contempt for all the matter of earthly existence, but only for the *lif* of the individual war-

---

[130] *Saga Sverris konungs*, chap. 47, Fornmanna sögur 8 (Copenhagen, 1834), 116. Compare Cúchulainn's "Is buaine bladh ná saoghal," "Fame endures longer than life," cited from O'Rahilly, *Miscellany of Irish Proverbs*, no. 134 (p. 38).

[131] See note 125, above.

[132] *Iwein*, ed. G. F. Benecke and K. Lachmann, 6th ed. (Berlin: Walter de Gruyter & Co., 1959), lines 15–17 (p. 1).

[133] Cited from Zingerle, 149.

rior. The closest sentential analogue to this aspect of T appears in the *Disticha Catonis*:

> Multum venturi ne cures tempora fati:
> non metuit mortem, qui scit contemnere vitam[134]

> [Do not give much care to the times of future fate: he who knows how to despise life does not fear death].

In this case, the *Beowulf* passage more closely resembles the Latin than the Old English version of the distich, as the latter shows the influence of the *contemptus mundi* topos, having translated "vitam" as "ðas world": "Ne rec ðu to swiðe hu sio wyrd wandrige; se ðe fullice ðas world forsihð, ne ondræt he him noht swiðe deað"[135] [Do not worry too much about how fate may proceed; he who fully despises this world does not much fear death]. In the absence of further analogues, it seems that passage T is, indeed, a specific application of the "Gain lasting fame" sentence illustrated by passage S (lines 1387b-89).

I have already discussed the context of passage S in conjunction with passage N (lines 1386–87a), above. Passage T occurs in a less formal and potentially sentential setting—the battle with Grendel's mother. The most interesting question with respect to T is why, given that the lines are not proverbial, and that they appear in the middle of a very active battle scene, the poet chose to endow them with sentential weight by his use of the phrase "swa sceal man don." The answer has to do with one purpose of *Beowulf* as a whole, and with the function of the monstrous battles within the poem. Passage T expresses approval of Beowulf's disposal of his failed sword, and his reliance (at least temporarily) on his own strength; the implied alternative would be for the hero to save his life by fleeing the scene of battle. The sentential form given to this brief comment on Beowulf's behavior both suggests that the hero is responding to a life-threatening situation in a culturally approved manner, and recommends such a response to the members of the audience. The sentential diction helps to characterize the hero as one worthy of emulation, and to point out the general lesson to listeners, many of whom will never engage in subaqueous combat with an enraged *merewif*.

---

[134] *Disticha Catonis*, ed. Marcus Boas (Amsterdam: North-Holland Publ. Co., 1952), 4.22 (p. 218); Walther, nos. 15594 and 18027.
[135] Cox, "The Old English Dicts of Cato," no. 73 (p. 14).

Death before dishonor

U. (lines 2891b–92):

Deað bið sella
eorla gehwylcum   þonne edwitlif.

[Death is better for every man than a shameful life.]

These lines are clearly and unmistakably proverbial: they employ
the consuetudinal "bið," the comparative syntactical structure "sella
... þonne," and a generalized reference to "eorla gehwylcum"; they are
concise in their expression, and correspond to many analogues. The
only significant difference between this passage and its analogues is that
the latter contrast an *honorable* death to a shamed life, whereas the
*Beowulf*ian lines omit the initial modifier.

Unlike the parallels to passages S and T, analogues to passage U
appear in both secular and ecclesiastical settings. Describing the death
of the Athenian general Chabrias, Cornelius Nepos explains his fatal
courage: "At ille præstare honestam mortem existimans turpi vitæ,
cominus pugnans telis hostium interfectus est"[136] [And preferring an
honorable death to dishonorable life, he was killed in close combat by
the weapons of the enemy]. Almost two centuries later, Tacitus put a
variant of the same proverb in the mouth of Agricola: "Proinde et
honesta mors turpi vita potior, et incolumitas ac decus eodem loco sita
sunt"[137] [Not only is an honorable death better than dishonorable
life, but in our case security and honor are present in the same place].
The biblical analogue, which was excerpted by Defensor and Sedulius
Scottus, is rather less warlike: "Melior est mors quam uita amara, et
requies aeterna quam languor perseuerans"[138] [Death is better than a
bitter life, and eternal rest better than persistent sickness].

Vernacular variants of the proverb, unlike *Beowulf* and the Latin
examples, tend to replace the nouns "death" and "life" with verbal
phrases. *Flóamanna saga* provides "Betra er að deyja virðulega en lifa
skammsamlega" [It is better to die honorably than to live shamefully],

---

[136] *Cornellii Nepotis Vitæ excellentium imperatorum*, ed. J. Fr. Fischer (London:
A. J. Valpy, 1822), chap. 4, p. 190; Margalits, 332.

[137] *Agricola*, ed. and trans. Maurice Hutton, Loeb Classical Library (Cambridge,
Mass.: Harvard Univ. Press, 1946), chap. 33, pp. 88–89; Margalits, 331.

[138] Ecclus. 30.17, cited from Sedulius, *Coll. Misc.*, 66.51 (CCCM 67.268); see also
Defensor, *Lib. scin.*, 47.9 (CCSL 117.164).

and *Flóvents saga*, "Betra er að deyja dýrlega en lefa við skömm"[139] [It is better to die gloriously than to live with shame]. Middle English examples are too numerous to require discussion, and need only be listed:

> For leovere us is here
> Mid manscipe to fallen,
> Thanne we heonne i-sunde farren,
> Ure frenden to scare [shonde]
>   (Lagamon's *Brut*, lines 5832–35)

> And levere al some is
> Vor to deye myd honour than libbe in ssame ywys
>   (Robert of Gloucester, lines 3417–18)

> For he hadde lover dye in fight,
> Than schond tholi and unright
>   (*Arthour and Merlin*, lines 2359–60)

> Bettir is, to sterve worthschipliche,
> Than long to liven schandfullice
>   (ibid., 9197–98)

> More honoure is faire to sterve
> Than in servage vilely serve
>   (*Alisaunder*, lines 3065–66)

> Better manly to be slayn,
> Than long to live in sorwe and pain
>   (*Horn Childe*, lines 166–67).[140]

The prevalence of verbal phrases in vernacular variants of this proverb does not necessarily indicate a Latin source for *Beowulf* passage U. Like the other writers quoted here, the composer of *Beowulf* altered the proverb to fit his precise poetic need, and it is common enough that oral transmission must have been extensive from an early date.

The array of literary uses for such a proverbial contrast as death

---

[139] *Flóamanna saga*, chap. 15; *Flóvents saga*, chap. 25; both cited from *Íslenzkir Málshættir*, 54.

[140] All cited from Whiting, *Proverbs ... before 1500*, D239; for Shakespearean examples, see Charles G. Smith, *Shakespeare's Proverb Lore: His Use of the* Sententiae *of Leonard Culman and Publilius Syrus* (Cambridge, Mass.: Harvard Univ. Press, 1963), no. 55; for modern English examples, see Whiting, *Modern Proverbs*, D99.

versus dishonor is consciously exploited by Chaucer, who presses the phrase and concept into the service of both rhetoric and characterization in the *Franklin's Tale*. Dorigen begins her long complaint by enumerating her traditionally-defined options and expressing her traditionally-conditioned decision:

> "Allas," quod she, "on thee, Fortune, I pleyne,
> That unwar wrapped hast me in thy cheyne,
> Fro which t'escape woot I no socour,
> Save oonly deeth or elles dishonour;
> Oon of thise two bihoveth me to chese.
> But nathelees, yet have I levere to lese
> My lif than of my body to have a shame...."[141]

The contrast provides both introduction and structure for the ensuing series of exempla, the bulk of which illustrate the principle embodied in the proverb underlying, but not expressly stated in, Dorigen's complaint. The proverb "Death is better than dishonor" explicitly provides Chaucer with the diction of Dorigen's complaint, but only implicitly— that is, as subtext—with the conclusion that Dorigen must inevitably draw. Dorigen's emotional distress is brought home by her representation of the proverbial contrast as a choice, rather than a mandate, a rhetorical strategy reflecting her indecision and hesitancy and concretized in her failure to take action for "a day or tweye" (5.1457).

The immediate context may also be invoked to explain the omission of a qualifier with *deað* in *Beowulf* passage U. The sentence closes Wiglaf's chastising speech to Beowulf's cowardly retainers, following just after his prediction of a foreign invasion as the consequence of their inglorious behavior. Thus, the immediate referent to *edwitlif* is the projected existence in exile for the warriors, rather than merely their loss of reputation; the latter is, however, a given fact in Wiglaf's speech, which places honorable or manly death outside the realm of possibility. Reputation once lost cannot be regained.

The sentential themes with which I have dealt in this chapter—the inevitability of fate and death, the desire for lasting fame, the upholding of honor—are not specific to any one cultural or religious tradition. Because they address broad and universal aspects of human existence, it would be difficult to demonstrate specific sources for any of these

---

[141] *Franklin's Tale*, 5.1355–61, in *The Riverside Chaucer*, ed. Larry D. Benson, 3rd ed. (Boston: Houghton Mifflin Co., 1987), 186.

*Beowulf*ian *sententiae*. The preceding survey of other, possibly relevant, proverbial treatments of these matters can make no claim to completeness, but should serve to indicate the rich proverbial tradition available on any of the topics treated in these passages of *Beowulf*. As for any characterization of the passages themselves, or of the culture they reflect, one must again take refuge in the multivalence of the tradition from which they stem. Such simple assertions as "Everyone must die" or "God and fate determine events" are equally valid in classical, Christian, or medieval heroic contexts, and it is primarily in their proverbial or sentential forms that they move from one to the other. *Beowulf* benefited from this cultural exchange.

5

Warnings and Advice

Proverbs and *sententiae* may adopt many strategies, even within a single work such as *Beowulf*. They may comment on supernatural phenomena (Metod eallum weold gumena cynnes; Gæð a wyrd swa hio sceal), they may describe universal aspects of human existence (Ure æghwylc sceal ende gebidan worolde lifes; Fela sceal gebidan leofes ond laðes se þe longe ... worolde bruceð), or they may provide directives for individual behavior (Wyrce se þe mote domes ær deaþe). It is this last category of proverbs and *sententiae*, those providing specific advice and warnings, that remain to be treated here.[1] I will begin by examining those passages for which relevant analogues provide a proverbial background, then consider a few passages of *Beowulf* which assume the form of sentential advice but appear to reflect authorial invention.

V. (lines 20–25):

> Swa sceal geong guma   gode gewyrcean,
> fromum feohgiftum   on fæder bearme,
> þæt hine on ylde   eft gewunigen
> wilgesiþas,   þonne wig cume,
> leode gelæsten;   lofdædum sceal
> in mægþa gehwære   man geþeon.
>
> [So should a young man bring about good with splen-
> did gift-giving in his father's house, so that when he is

---

[1] Two such passages have been discussed as S and T in chap. 4, above.

older his dear companions will in turn remain with
him when war comes, his people may serve him; a man
must prosper anywhere with praiseworthy deeds.]

The dual use of *sceal* in this passage might justify its treatment as
two distinct *sententiae*, but the sentiment of the last sentence is too
tautological to stand alone, and the *lofdædum* seem clearly to refer to
the *fromum feohgiftum* described earlier in the passage. Such is the
interpretation assumed by Chickering, who translates the last sentence
as "By such generosity any man prospers."[2] The basic connotation of
the passage seems to be that loyal friends are acquired through gift-
giving, but the complexities introduced by such qualifiers as the youth
of the person addressed and the predicted *wig* suggest connections with
other proverbial complexes.

The relationship between friendship and gift-giving is well established in three stanzas of *Hávamál*:

> Vápnom oc váðom   scolo vinir gleðiaz,
>   þat er á siálfum sýnst;
> viðrgefendr oc endrgefendr   erost lengst vinir,
>   ef þat bíðr at verða vel.
>
> Vin sínom   scal maðr vinr vera,
>   oc gialda giöf við giöf;
> ....
>
> Veiztu, ef þú vin átt,   þann er þú vel trúir,
>   oc vill þú af hánom gott geta:
> geði scaltu við þann blanda   oc giöfum scipta,
>   fara at finna opt.[3]

[Friends should gladden each other with weapons and
clothing, that is most visible on a man; those who give
repeatedly and in return are friends for longest, if that
endures to turn out well.

A man should be a friend to his friend, and repay gift
with gift.

Know, that if you have a friend whom you trust well,

---

[2] Chickering, *Beowulf*, line 25 (p. 49).
[3] *Hávamál*, st. 41, 42.1-2, 44, in *Edda*, ed. Neckel/Kuhn, 23-24. For typo-
graphical reasons, I have transliterated 'ǫ' as 'ö' here and elsewhere.

and you wish him to do well by you, you should open
your mind to him and exchange gifts, go often to meet
him.]

Middle English proverbs reflect the same idea, as the *Ancrene Riwle*
states that "Muchel yeove ofdraheth luve," and Gower suggests that
"With yifte a man mai frendes make."[4] One Latin sentence of this
type—"Audimus dici: donando simus amici"[5] [We hear it said: through
giving we may be friends]—appears in several thirteenth- to fifteenth-
century manuscripts, but in general, Latin proverbs are more cynical
regarding the connection of wealth to popularity, beginning with the
biblical Book of Proverbs: "Amici divitum multi" [The rich man has
many friends] and "Divitiae addunt amicos plurimos"[6] [Riches bring
many friends]. Although both verses also provide an explicit contrast to
the friendless state of the poor man, they were most often cited in these
truncated forms, as in Jerome's *In Osee* and Defensor's *Liber scintillarum.*[7] Apparently the mere connection of the ideas of friendship and
wealth sufficed to evoke the negative connotation of purchased, and
hence unstable, loyalty.

The social complications of gift-giving and -receiving are recognized
also in vernacular proverbs, in late-Middle English variants such as
"Bunden is that giftes takitz" and "Bountith askis rewarde,"[8] and even
in *Hávamál*:

> Betra er óbeðit,   enn sé ofblótið,
>   ey sér til gildis giöf[9]

---

[4] *Ancrene Riwle* 197.27–28 (cited from Whiting, *Proverbs ... before 1500*, G92),
and Gower, *Confessio Amantis* III 163.7726 (Whiting, G87).

[5] Walther, no. 1726; cf. no. 1731.

[6] Prov. 14.20 and 19.4; cf. Whiting, *Proverbs ... before 1500*, M637 and R108.

[7] Jerome, *In Osee*, in *S. Hieronymi presbyteri Opera*, part 1: Opera exegetica; no.
6: Commentarii in prophetas minores, CCSL 76 and 76A, ed. M. Adriaen (Turnhout: Brepols, 1969–70), bk. 3, chap. 12 (CCSL 76.135). Defensor, *Lib. scin.*, 64.6
(CCSL 117.198).

[8] Whiting, *Proverbs ... before 1500*, G74 and B474.

[9] *Hávamál*, st. 145, in *Edda*, ed. Neckel/Kuhn, 41. The similar attitudes here of
Hávamál and the Latin sentential corpus raise the possibility of foreign influence on
the Old Norse poem. For studies of this topic, see Rolf Pipping, "Hávamál 21 och
ett par ställen hos Seneca," *Acta Philologica Scandinavica* 20 (1949): 371–75; Elias
Wessén, "Ordspråk och lärodikt: Några stilformer i Hávamál," in *Septentrionalia et
Orientalia: Studia Bernardo Karlgren ... dedicata*, Kungl. Vitterhets Historie och
Antikvitets Akademiens handlingar 91 (Stockholm, 1959), 455–73; *idem, Hávamál:
Några stilfråger*, Filologiskt arkiv 8 (Stockholm: Almqvist & Wiksell, 1959); and

[Better unasked than too much offered, a gift asks repayment].

Of course, a return on one's investment is not always forthcoming, so one should discriminate among potential donees; as the eleventh-century Durham Proverbs note, "Leana forleosaþ se þe lyþran deð"[10] [He loses gifts who makes them to the wicked]. Our *Beowulf* passage, however, expresses no such misgivings about the efficacy of gifts in securing loyalty, and therefore seems most closely related to the proverbial complex advising the establishment of friendship through gifts.

The optimism of passage V extends to a prediction of assistance from the young man's *wilgesiþas* in the event of war; the contrast between the benevolent situation of *on fæder bearme* and the more threatening *þonne wig cume* suggests a parallel to the still current proverb, "A friend in need is a friend indeed."[11] Even in the early Middle Ages, the "family" of variants of this sentence was quite large, with different branches stressing different aspects of the basic idea, but the variant most closely related to *Beowulf* passage V can be found both in Sedulius Scottus's *Collectaneum* and in Publilius Syrus's *Sententiae*: "Habet in aduersis auxilia qui in secundis commodat"[12] [He who accommodates in times of safety has aid in times of adversity]. The exactness of the quotation indicates that Sedulius probably copied the sentence from Publilius, though he does not acknowledge his source; still, it is helpful to know, in view of the complex manuscript history of Publilius's *Sententiae*, that this particular proverb was known in the time of Sedulius—and of *Beowulf*. The similarity to passage V is striking, as both *sententiae* link the hope of assistance in trouble to a history of bestowal under more favorable circumstances; the syntactic reversal of these elements in the Old English version results from the more

---

Klaus von See, "Disticha Catonis und Hávamál," *Beiträge zur Geschichte der deutschen Sprache und Literatur* (Tübingen), 94 Sonderheft (*Festschrift für Hans Eggers*, ed. Herbert Backes), (1972), 1–18. For arguments against some suggested borrowings and influences, see Joseph Harris, "Eddic Poetry," in *Old Norse-Icelandic Literature: A Critical Guide*, ed. Carol J. Clover and John Lindow, Islandica 45 (Ithaca: Cornell Univ. Press, 1985), 68–156 (esp. pp. 106–11); and Carolyne Larrington, "*Hávamál* and Sources outside Scandinavia," *Saga-Book of the Viking Society* 23 (1992): 141–57.

[10] Durham Proverbs, 14.25 (Whiting, *Proverbs . . . before 1500*, G75).

[11] See Whiting, *Modern Proverbs*, F265 and F266.

[12] Sedulius Scottus, *Coll. Misc.*, 80.12.40 (CCCM 67.332), and Publilius Syrus, *Sent.*, H6 (Bickford-Smith, p. 15); Walther, no. 10532.

extended, almost linear narrative of that passage, as well as reflecting normal Old English syntax.

Another early variant of this proverbial sentiment addresses not the man in the position of the first Beowulf, but one like a *wilgesið*: Alcuin admonishes, "Rebus in adversis numquam dimittis amicum"[13] [Never desert a friend in adversity]. The phrase "rebus in adversis" parallels the opening of *Disticha Catonis* 2.25,[14] but the message of Alcuin's sentence as a whole bears no relation to that of the distich, which advises the individual to retain hope in difficult times.

Other related *sententiae* reflect the same temporal continuation as in passage V by averring that old friends are the best friends,[15] or that friends of old should not be forgotten or abandoned.[16] It should be noted that the proverbial opinion of friendship is not consistently high, as a significant number of *sententiae* warn against false friends in prosperity who may disappear when one's fortune turns.[17] However, this possibility is not expressed sententially in *Beowulf* (although it could be related to various scenes of ungrateful retainers), so we may go on to survey the more admirable attitude of the "friend in need."

The proverbial tradition describing the loyalty of a true friend in times of adversity is vast, both temporally and geographically, so it may help to divide the sentences into two groups: "calamity proves a friend" and "a friend helps in need." The Latin history of the first group begins with Ennius, as he was cited by Cicero: "Amicus certus

---

[13] Alcuin, *Monastica*, ed. Ernest Dümmler, MGH *Poetae Latini Aevi Carolini* (Berlin: Weidmannos, 1881), line 155 (1.280); Walther, no. 26387. See also Augustine, *Epistulae*, ed. Goldbacher, part 3: Epist. 124–184A, CSEL 44, epist. 130 (p. 54): "itemque amicitia non angustis finibus terminanda est."

[14] "Rebus in adversis animum submittere noli; spem retine: spes una hominem nec morte reliriquit" (*Dist. Cat.* 2.25 [Boas, p. 132]); the parallel is noted by Dümmler, in a note to Alcuin's *Monastica*, line 155 (MGH *Poet.* 1.280).

[15] Walther, no. 23376 (Plautus). See also *Die Sprichwörter und sprichwörtlichen Redensarten der Römer*, ed. A. Otto (Leipzig, 1890; repr. Hildesheim: Georg Olms, 1962), p. 23 (amicus 12), and Archer Taylor, "An Old Friend is the Best Friend," *Romance Philology* 9 (1955–56): 201–5; Taylor does not address variants of the proverb appearing before the late Middle Ages.

[16] Walther, nos. 17580.a, 4911 (*Dist. Cat.* 4.41), and 17347 (Egbert of Liège, *Fec. rat.* 1.190); *Hávamál*, st. 44 and 119; *Grímnismál*, st. 17; Zingerle, p. 41 (*Kaiserchronik*); Defensor, *Lib. scin.*, 64.15 (Ecclus. 9.14 [CCSL 117.199]); cf. Singer, 1.115.

[17] Walther, nos. 4164 (Hildebert), 4165 (Ovid, Odo of Cheriton), 6277 and 6535 (Ovid), 8083 (Ovid), 17691, and 31228 (*Proverbia communia*); Freidank, 96.5; Whiting, *Proverbs ... before 1500*, P418 (*Everyman*); Zingerle, 39. See also Ecclus. 6.10, cited by Defensor (*Lib. scin.* 64.12) and Sedulius Scottus (*Coll. misc.* 66.7).

in re incerta cernitur"[18] [A certain friend is discovered in an uncertain time]. Publilius Syrus provides "Amicum an nomen habeas, aperit calamitas"[19] [Though you may be called a friend, calamity shows it].

If this *sententia* did not enter medieval parlance from classical sources, it may have had a biblical origin in Ecclus. 12.8 ("Non agnoscetur in bonis amicus") [A friend will not be recognized in good times] or Prov. 17.17 ("Omni tempore diligit qui amicus est, et frater in angustiis conprobatur") [A friend shows love at all times, and a brother is proven in difficulties].[20] In any case, some version of it was well-established in the ninth century, as evidenced by Paschasius Radbertus, abbot of Corbie—"iuxta illud antiquum proverbium, quando amicus et medicus in necessitate probantur" [according to that old proverb, when a friend and a doctor are proved in necessity]—and still in the twelfth—"unde illud vulgare: In necessitate probatur amicus"[21] [whence that is commonly said: A friend is proved in necessity]. The same proverb is translated in the Durham Proverbs as "Æt þearfe man sceal freonda cunnian"[22] [A man must know his friends in need]. This "probare" version of the sentence does not seem to appear in English letters between the eleventh and fourteenth centuries, perhaps as a result of competition from the "friend in need" version, but it does reappear in Robert Mannyng's *Handlyng Synne* ("At nede shul men prove here frendys") and in the romance *Sir Ferumbras* ("Ne schal no man bet prove is frende bot a-say hem on his nede").[23]

---

[18] Cicero, *De amicitia* 17.64 (cited from Walther, no. 960); for the use of this and other *sententiae* by Ennius, see *The Tragedies of Ennius: The fragments edited with an introduction and commentary*, ed. H. D. Jocelyn, Cambridge Classical Texts and Commentaries 10 (Cambridge: Cambridge Univ. Press, 1969), 306.

[19] *Sententiae*, A41 (Bickford-Smith, 3).

[20] Prov. 17.17 appears in Defensor's *Lib. scin.*, 3.13 (CCSL 117.13). The eleventh-century English gloss is too literal to shed any light on the *Beowulf* passage: "on eallum timan lufað se þe freond ys [and] broðer on angnyssum byð afandud"; see *Defensor's Liber Scintillarum, with an Interlinear Anglo-Saxon Version made early in the Eleventh Century*, ed. E. W. Rhodes, EETS o.s. 93 (London: EETS, 1889).

[21] Both cited from "Dialogus de Pontificatu sanctae Romanae ecclesiae," in MGH Libelli de Lite III, p. 546 and note (for Paschasius). "Amicus necessitate probatur" was also used by Bernard of Clairvaux (see Steiner, "The Vernacular Proverb in Mediaeval Latin Prose," no. 4 [p. 49]).

[22] Olof Arngart, "The Durham Proverbs," *Speculum* 56 (1981): 291 (no. 3); Whiting, *Proverbs ... before 1500*, F634. For medieval Irish versions, primarily glosses or translations of Latin, see O'Rahilly, *Miscellany of Irish Proverbs*, no. 274 (pp. 80–81).

[23] Both cited from Whiting, *Proverbs ... before 1500*, F634.

The "friend in need" version of the sentence enjoyed no less distinguished a history, beginning with the *Epidicus* of Plautus: "Is est amicus, qui in re dubia re iuvat, si re est opus"[24] [He is a friend who aids a doubtful case with deeds, if there is need of deeds]. Petronius is more concise: "In angustiis amici apparent"[25] [Friends are seen in difficulties]. Germanic vernacular variants occur in Old Norse —"Skal vinar í þörf neyta"[26] [One in need must make use of a friend]—and in Middle High German:

> Wan daz dicke geschiht,
> daz friunt friunde gestât:
> er ist sêlic, der in hât,
> sô ez im gât an die nôt[27]

[For it often happens, that a friend helps a friend: he is blessed who has a friend in need].

Middle English uses of the proverb are copious, as these thirteenth- and fourteenth-century citations indicate:

A sug fere the his help in nod   (*Proverbs of Alfred*)

In nede than sal thai find us freind   (*Cursor mundi*)

And hit ys also worldes honur,
At nede ther frendes for to socour
                                           (Robert Mannyng, *Chronicle*)

Vor ate niede me yzizth huet vrend is
                                           (*Ayenbite of Inwit*)

For a frende that fyndeth hym failled hym nevere at nede
                                           (*Piers Plowman*)

Beter leche knowe I non
Then trewe frend is at neode   (Vernon Cato)

For Catoun seith: "If thou hast nede of help, axe it of
          thy freendes
                                           (Chaucer, *Tale of Melibee*)

---

[24] Plautus, *Epidicus* 1.2.10 (cited from Walther, no. 12955).
[25] Petronius, *Satyricon* 61 (cited from Walther, no. 11664).
[26] *Heiðarvíga saga*, chap. 21 (cited from *Íslenzkir Málshættir*, 357).
[27] *Biterolf*, line 1253 (cited from Zingerle, 39).

And soghten frendes ate nede
                    (Gower, *Confessio Amantis*)

Thus hiere I many a man compleigne,
That nou on daies thou schalt finde
At nede fewe frendes kinde   (ibid.).[28]

In light of the temporal and geographic distribution of these proverbs on friendship, it would be strange indeed if the *Beowulf*-poet knew
no variant of the sentence linking loyal fellowship to adversity. Although the "probare" and "friend in need" versions enjoyed the
greatest currency, I would still commend as the poet's "source" a
variant similar to that from Publilius and Sedulius, or perhaps even that
very sentence, as "He who grants favors in safety has help in adversity"
describes the situation of passage V as closely as one might like. Still, I
have shown that other proverbial models were available.

It is possible, perhaps, to raise an objection to these models on the
grounds that they describe an attitude of mutual friendship, rather than
the lord/retainer relationship to which passage V probably refers.
Sententiae advising proper princely behavior do, of course, exist, but I
have found none that parallels passage V, except perhaps for these lines
of *Maxims II*:

Geongne æðeling sceolan   gode gesiðas
byldan to beaduwe   and to beahgife.[29]

[Good companions should encourage a young prince to
battle and the bestowing of treasure.]

The similarities to *Beowulf* 20–25 are tantalizing—a young prince, a
group of *gesiðas*, the suggestions of battle and gift-giving—but the
relationships among the terms are entirely different in the two passages.
In *Beowulf* passage V, the poet describes a causal relationship between
the bestowal of treasure and military support that is lacking in *Maxims
II*, and the very subjects of the *sententiae* differ, from the young man
himself in *Beowulf*, to his companions in the gnomic poem. The connotation of the *Maxims* sentence seems to be that good companions (be
they friends, retainers, or even guardians) should instruct a young
prince in appropriate royal behavior, but their actions are not appar-

---

[28] All cited from Whiting, *Proverbs ... before 1500*, F634.
[29] *Maxims II*, lines 14–15 (ASPR 6.56).

ently conditioned or influenced by his. One might also note that the expected, but unprovoked *wig* of passage V more closely resembles the unavoidable misfortunes of the friendship proverbs than the *beaduwe* to which the prince of *Maxims II* is exhorted. I do not mean to imply that the *sententia* of passage V bears no connection to the generous lord/faithful retainer relationship so well-known from Old English poetry (and *Beowulf* not least), but rather, that the *Beowulf*-poet has here created a synthesis between the proverbial description of friendship and the behavior expected of heroic princes by using the former to describe the activities of Scyld's son Beowulf. The link between proverbial *amicitia* and the Germanic form of *comitas* should have been easy for the poet to make, considering that Old English *wine* (like Old Norse *vinr*) bears the connotations of both "friend" and "lord."

W. (lines 287b–89):

> Æghwæþres sceal
> scearp scyldwiga   gescad witan,
> worda ond worca,   se þe wel þenceð.

> [A keen warrior, he who thinks rightly, must know how to distinguish between words and works.]

Both the speaker and the connotation of this sentence have provided the matter of some dispute, as early editors of the poem declined to attribute it to the coastal warden,[30] and the meaning of the phrase "gescad witan" is not immediately transparent. Klaeber settled the first issue in his edition, where he noted that

> although the insertion of some descriptive and explanatory matter between the announcement and the beginning of a speech is quite customary ..., the intercalated statement never takes the form of an abstract maxim ... On the other hand, a maxim is placed at the beginning of a speech, 3077f. [passage BB, below].[31]

Klaeber's assessment corresponds to the findings of this study, in that we have seen *sententiae* included in speeches, or providing transitions

---

[30] See Moritz Heyne, *Beowulf. Mit ausführlichem Glossar*, 15th ed. rev. Else von Schaubert, 3 pts. (Paderborn, 1940), 2.36, and Dobbie, ASPR 4.131, note to lines 287b–89.

[31] Klaeber, *Beowulf*, note to lines 287b–89.

between narrative description and direct speech, but the latter function is here performed by the introductory "Weard maþelode" (286a) [The warden spoke] and unlikely to be duplicated by a maxim.

The second problem, the difficulty of *gescad witan* and its implications for the connotation of the sentence in context, is less easily resolved. W. S. Mackie and E. V. K. Dobbie gloss the phrase as "to know how to distinguish," but they follow that gloss with another, "to understand."[32] The semantic distinction was brought into focus by a scholarly disagreement between Robert Kaske and Stanley Greenfield, as the former interpreted "worda ond worcum" as the dual object of the coastguard's attention, while Greenfield perceived an intended distinction between the terms.[33] Most recent translators have favored the latter interpretation, providing "know the distinction between,"[34] "be skilled to discriminate,"[35] and "know how to distinguish the worth of."[36] Although elsewhere in the poem (1100a, 1833a) the formulaic collocation of words and works presents the terms as complementary elements, and although an intentional distinction between words and works on the part of the coastguard would result in a *lectio difficilior*, just such a division in this passage is strongly supported by the substantial number of proverbial analogues.

Sententiae pointing out the potential for discrepancy between one's words and works are not as easily classified as the friendship proverbs discussed above, but they consistently contrast the two activities, and invariably assign greater value to works. An interesting example from Seneca's *Epistulae ad Lucilium* links the doublet, as does the coastguard's speech, to the possession of wisdom: "Maximum hoc est et officium sapientiae et indicium, ut verbis opere concordent"[37] [This is

---

[32] W. S. Mackie, "Notes upon the Text and the Interpretation of 'Beowulf'," *Modern Language Review* 34 (1939): 517; Dobbie, ASPR 4.131, note to line 288.

[33] For the core of the argument, see Stanley B. Greenfield, "Of Words and Deeds: The Coastguard's Maxim Once More," in *The Wisdom of Poetry: Essays in Early English Literature in Honor of Morton W. Bloomfield*, ed. Larry D. Benson and Siegfried Wenzel (Kalamazoo: Medieval Institute Publications, 1982), 45–51; and R. E. Kaske, "The Coastwarden's Maxim in *Beowulf*: A Clarification," *Notes and Queries* 31 (March 1984): 16–18. See further Peter Baker, "Beowulf the Orator," *Journal of English Linguistics* 21 (1988): 3–23.

[34] Chickering, *Beowulf*, p. 65.

[35] Alexander, *Beowulf*, p. 60.

[36] *Beowulf: A Verse Translation into Modern English*, trans. Edwin Morgan (Berkeley: Univ. of California Press, 1952), p. 8.

[37] *L. Annaei Senecae ad Lvcilivm Epistvlae Morales*, ed. L. D. Reynolds, 2 vols.

the greatest duty and proof of wisdom, that words should accord with works]. Jerome builds an admonitory sentence around the contrast— "Nihil prodest habere te uerba, habere te scientiam, si non habueris operis"[38] [It avails you nothing to have words, to have knowledge, if you will not have had works]—while Augustine merely alludes to it— "ita nec facile illi credimus, nisi factis uerba confirmet"[39] [thus we do not easily believe him, unless he confirms his speech with deeds]. For Gregory the Great, works surpass words as indicators of understanding: "Et quasi per singulos gradus suos librum pronuntiat, qui percepisse se eius scientiam non per uerba tantummodo, sed etiam per opera demonstrat"[40] [And as if by single steps he renders his book, who shows himself to have grasped knowledge not so much through words but through works]. In a sentence cited by Defensor, Gregory employs the contrast in defining true faithfulness: "Tunc enim ueraciter fideles sumus, si quod uerbis promittimus, operibus adimplemus"[41] [For then we are truly faithful, if we fulfill in deeds what we promise with words]. Less optimistically, Sedulius Scottus couches the contrast in potentially insulting terms: "Quidam magni uiri sunt in loquendo, sed minimi sunt in operando"[42] [Some are great men in speaking, but least in doing]. As befitted his pedagogical purpose, Otloh included two sentences stressing the importance of works, the first of which also appears in the *Proverbiorum liber* of pseudo-Bede:

Doctrinae uerba paucis prosunt sine factis

[Words of doctrine avail little without deeds]

(Oxford: Clarendon Press, 1965), Epist. 20 (1.53); Walther, no. 33122.c, and Wander, *DS-L*, Mann 730. The *Florilegium Frisingense* includes an Isidoran sentence linking the possession of wisdom to the ability to make distinctions, but between good and evil rather than words and deeds: "Sapiens prudenter omnia aexaminat; inter bonum et malum sapiens intellegendo deiudicat; summum bonum est scire, quod caueas" (*Synonyma* 2.66, in *Flor. Fris.*, no. 392, CCSL 108D.33; see also no. 91 [p. 11]).

[38] *Tractatus in Marci euangelium*, in *S. Hieronymi presbyteri Opera*, part 2: Opera homiletica, ed. D. Germanus Morin, 2nd ed., CCSL 78 (Turnhout: Brepols, 1958), sermon 7 (p. 485).

[39] *Sancti Aureli Augustini Opera*, sect. 2, part 6: Epistolae ex duobus codicibus nuper in lucem prolatae, ed. Johannes Divjak, CSEL 88 (Vienna: Hoelder-Pichler-Tempsky, 1981), epist. 23 (p. 121).

[40] *S. Gregorii Magni Moralia in Iob*, ed. Marcus Adriaen, CCSL 143, 143A, and 143B (Turnhout: Brepols, 1979–85), bk. 22, par. 20 (CCSL 143A.1130).

[41] Defensor, *Lib. scin.*, 64.43 (CCSL 117.201).

[42] Sedulius Scottus, *Coll. misc.* 13.31.23 (CCCM 67.10; no source is given).

Nil prodest didicisse, nisi feceris illud[43]

[It does not help to have said something, if you will not
have performed it].

The phrase "doctrinae uerba" makes the contrast closer to, but not
identical with, the related theological pairing of faith and works, but
the "faith" element of that doublet is never denigrated to the extent
experienced by "words" in our examples.

The proverbial contrast between words and works was well-established in Latin by the twelfth century, although its expression continued to vary. The comedy *Pamphilus* includes the succinct "Non factis
sequimur omnia, que loquimur"[44] [We do not follow everything that
we say with deeds], while the variant found in the *Ysengrimus* is somewhat more detailed:

Materiam si vis laudari, fac opus et dic:
Absque operum titulis irrita verba volant[45]

[If you wish the matter to be praised, do a deed and
say: Words fly about idly without the glory of deeds].

Peter Abelard's version of the sentence resembles that of Seneca:

Factis non verbis sapientia se profitetur,
Solis concessa est gratia tanta bonis[46]

[Wisdom shows itself in deeds, not in words; only in
good deeds has such grace been granted].

Finally, a twelfth-century manuscript now in Paris preserves the
sententia "Non que verba iacent, sed mihi facta placent"[47] [To me are
pleasing not words, which do nothing, but deeds].

The varied diction of these Latin *sententiae* is evident in vernacular
examples as well, and may in fact indicate vernacular dissemination of

---

[43] Otloh, *Lib. prov.* D70 (Korfmacher, 20), and pseudo-Bede, *Prov. lib.*, in
Migne, *PL* 90.1095; Otloh, N85 (p. 53; Korfmacher notes the similarity of this
sentence to pseudo-Publilius 9: "Nihil prodest didicisse, bene facere si cesses");
Walther, no. 6202.

[44] *Pamphilus*, line 526 (cited from Walther, no. 17780).

[45] *Ysengrimus: Text with translation, commentary and introduction*, ed. and trans.
Jill Mann, Mittellateinische Studien und Texte 12 (Leiden: E. J. Brill, 1987), 4.1009–
10 (p. 416); Walther, no. 14478.

[46] Abelard, *Monita ad Astralabium*, lines 43–44, in Migne, *PL* 178.1760.

[47] Walther, no. 18319.

the contrast, which never assumed a standard Latin translation. The topos of comparison or contrast between speech and action appears frequently in Old English, and in some cases assumes sentential form. Ælfric offers two variants: "Se bið swiþe wis, se þe mid weorcum spricð" [He is very wise who speaks through works] and "Weorc sprecað swiþor þonne þa nacodan word, þe nabbað nane fremminge"[48] [Works speak louder than those bare words that have no performance]. Another is found in *Guthlac A*:

> Sume him þæs hades   hlisan willað
> wegan on wordum   ond þa weorc ne doð.[49]

> [Some desire to bear the glory of this estate in words,
> and they do not perform the works.]

Both Vercelli Homily 22—"Ac ðonne ðu hine cigst on þinum wordum, ne wiðsac ðu hine on þinum weorcum"[50] [But when you invoke him with your words, do not forsake him in your works]—and the Durham Proverbs—"Gyf þu well sprece wyrc æfter swa"[51] [If you speak well, work afterwards the same way]—directly admonish their audiences to correlate works with words.

The collocation of words and works in a sentential context occurs at least twice in the Old Saxon *Heliand*; in the first instance (lines 2607–12) they function as a unit, as Christ reminds his listeners that on the day of judgment they will be called to account for their words and their deeds. In the second example, the poet explicates the parable of the vineyard by equating the worker who arrives in the evening to a person who pursued a course of folly in his youth, but mends his ways when he reaches a more mature age:

> fâhit im te beteron than
> uuordon endi uuercon,   lêdit im is uuerold mid thiu,
> is aldar ant thena endi: cumit im alles lôn
> an godes rîkie,   gôdaro uuerko.[52]

---

[48] Both cited from Whiting, *Proverbs ... before 1500*, W642.

[49] *Guthlac A*, lines 60–61 (ASPR 3.51).

[50] Cited from Whiting, *Proverbs ... before 1500*, W642.

[51] Arngart, "The Durham Proverbs," no. 20 (p. 292); Whiting, *Proverbs ... before 1500*, S574.

[52] *Heliand* (ed. Behaghel/Taeger), fitt 42, lines 3472b–75. For a discussion of these and other *sententiae* in the *Heliand*, see Carroll E. Reed, "Gnomic Verse in the Old Saxon *Heliand*," *Philological Quarterly* 30 (1951): 403–10.

[Then he begins to improve his words and works, and
thus lead his life, his old age, up to the end: reward for
all his good works comes to him in the kingdom of
God.]

In this passage, which acquires its sentential status from its opening "sô
duot doloro filo" (3466b) [so does many a fool], words and works
initially appear together, but it is his works for which the latecomer is
eventually rewarded.

Perhaps the most compelling evidence for the *Beowulf*-poet's familiarity with the proverbial words/works contrast appears in the poem
itself. After the reclining Beowulf watches Grendel's horrendous
rending of his companion, he is himself seized by the monster. The
hero's rise to his feet and engagement in battle is prefaced by the phrase
"Gemunde þa se goda, mæg Higelaces, æfenspræce" (758–59a) [Then
the good one, the kinsman of Hygelac, remembered his evening
speech]. By *æfenspræce* the poet clearly refers to Beowulf's earlier boasts
that he will cleanse Heorot, but his choice of this term is probably
conditioned by the proverbial contrast between "evening song" and
"morning song." The most famous example appears in Chaucer's
"General Prologue" as "If even-song and morwe-song accorde,"[53] but
proverbial variants have also been found in two fifteenth-century
manuscripts:

Euen songe and morn songe beth not both on.[54]

Hef song and moro hys nat hall hone.[55]

More interesting in relation to *Beowulf* is a variant from the thirteenth-
century *Proverbia Ysengrimi* (excerpted from the twelfth-century
Ysengrimus), which establishes the proverb as a words/works comparison: "Verbula nocturna raro sunt facta diurna"[56] [The words of the
night rarely match the deeds of the day]. The connotation of the
proverb, as it must have been understood by the *Beowulf*-poet, is essen-

---

[53] *Canterbury Tales*, A.830, in *The Riverside Chaucer*, ed. Benson, 36; Whiting,
Proverbs ... before 1500, E160; *Oxford Dict. of Engl. Pbs.*, 3rd ed., p. 227. For a
discussion of the interplay among will, intent, words, and works in Chaucer, see P.
B. Taylor, "Chaucer's *Cosyn to the Dede*," *Speculum* 57 (1982): 315–27.

[54] *Oxford Dict. of Engl. Pbs.*, 3rd ed., p. 227.

[55] Whiting, *Proverbs ... before 1500*, E160.

[56] *Proverbia Ysengrimi*, line 420, ed. J. F. Willems, in *Belgisch Museum voor de
Nederduitsche Tael- und Letterkunde* 9 (1845): 242. On "words and works" in the
Ysengrimus, see Mann's introduction to her edition, pp. 58–77.

tially the same as that of passage W, that words and works ought to accord.

Once again, Middle English literature provides an embarrassment of riches, illustrating clearly the wide dissemination of the contrast:

> Ah schulen the wordes beon ischawet efter the werkes
> (*Ancrene Riwle*)

> Ac nim the to a stable mon
> That word and dede bi-sette con   (*Proverbs of Alfred*)

> Ower dede ne may be no wors than ower word is
> (Robert of Gloucester, *Metrical Chronicle*)

> That word and deed, as in conclusioun,
> Ben nothing lyk   (Chaucer, *Lak of Stedfastnesse*)

> Betwen the word and that thei werche
> Then is a full gret difference
> (Gower, *Confessio Amantis*).[57]

The persistence of this proverbial contrast suggests that passage W of *Beowulf*, the opening of the coastal warden's speech, would have been understood by its audience as implying some sort of distinction between words and works. The question, then, is whose words and what works? If the *sententia* does in fact form part of the warden's speech, it must refer to the words and works of Beowulf, who has just finished announcing his errand. While Klaeber's interpretation of the coastguard's meaning as "it was my duty to scrutinize your words and your conduct"[58] remains plausible on the grounds that Beowulf's "works"—his armed approach—must be weighed against his subsequent, friendlier words, the proverbial analogues argue against the valuation of speech over action. It seems more likely that the guard is continuing the cautious attitude he displayed in his first speech, but softening his criticism somewhat through the use of an impersonal *sententia*; he now accepts Beowulf's intentions at face value, but implies that the hero should back up his promising words with the appropriate action. In fact, the coastguard himself explicates the sentence in his next

---

[57] All cited from Whiting, *Proverbs ... before 1500*, W642.

[58] Klaeber, *Beowulf*, note to 287b–89. For a sympathetic reading of the exchange between Beowulf and the warden, see Margaret W. Pepperdene, "Beowulf and the Coast Guard," *English Studies* 47 (1966): 409–19.

two statements, which begin "Ic ... gehyre" [I hear] (the words component) and "Gewitaþ forð" [Go forth] (an exhortation to action). In
essence, the guard offers the same admonition as the Durham Proverb
cited above: "Gyf þu well sprece wyrc æfter swa."

X. (lines 1059–60a):

> Forðan bið andgit   æghwær selest,
> ferhðes foreþanc.

> [Therefore wisdom is always best, prudence of the spirit.]

The sentential form of this statement is established by the consuetudinal verb, *bið*, by the generality of *æghwær*, and by the superlative
modifier *selest*. Furthermore, the sentence holds the central position in
a six-line passage encompassing three *sententiae*.[59] The "selest" of
passage X relates it to an established tradition of proverbs and *sententiae*
on the value of wisdom, which typically take the form "Wisdom is
better than ...," but may also state unequivocably that wisdom and
prudence are the best of all things.

In the proverbial corpus, wisdom compares favorably to many items
and attributes, but its most frequent association is with wealth. The
Book of Proverbs probably represents the point of entry for such
sentences into medieval Latin literature, as at least two variants of the
proverb appear there; I cite from Defensor's collection, as representing
one popular version in which the verses circulated:

> Melior est enim sapiencia cunctis preciosisimis, et omne desidera-
> bile ei non potest conparari   (Prov. 8.11)

> [For wisdom is better than all the most precious goods, and all
> that men may desire most cannot be compared to it]

> Posside sapienciam, qui aurum melior est, et adquire prudenciam
> quia preciosior est argento   (Prov. 16.16)

> [Possess wisdom, which is better than gold, and acquire pru-
> dence, because it is more precious than silver].[60]

Egbert of Liège provides one variant—"Nam summi pretii melior sapientia

---

[59] The other *sententiae* have been discussed in chap. 2 and 3, above.

[60] *Lib. scin.* 18.14 and 18.28 (CCSL 117.81, 82). Prov. 8.11 also appears in the
Florilegium Frisingense, no. 390 (CCSL 108D.32).

gemmis"[61] [For wisdom is of greater value than the most precious gems]—and Alcuin another—"Omnibus est mundi melior sapientia gazis"[62] [Wisdom is better than all the riches of the world]. Alcuin's version was the more durable of the two, as it appears also in two twelfth-century manuscripts.[63] A longer variant offered by pseudo-Bede and Sedulius Scottus appears to be a pastiche of the phrases found elsewhere: "Melior sapientia auro et consilium preciosius argento et prudentia prelatior est omni lapide precioso et disciplina preminentior omni uestitu gemmato"[64] [Wisdom is better than gold, and good counsel is more precious than silver, and prudence is preferred to all precious stones, and learning is more excellent than all bejeweled vestments].

The sentential comparison of wisdom to wealth was less common in vernacular than Latin literature, but *Hávamál* provides an interesting parallel to *Beowulf* passage X:

> Byrði betri   berrat maðr brauto at,
>   enn sé manvit mikit;
> auði betra   þiccir þat í ókunnum stað,
>   slíct er válaðs vera.[65]

[No better burden does a man bear on the road than great wisdom; this is more valuable than riches in a strange place; such is the wealth of the poor.]

The first two lines of this stanza are repeated at the outset of the next, but in the latter case, wisdom is contrasted to beer! The cited stanza, however, not only compares wisdom to riches, but describes *manvit* as the best burden to bear on the road. The significance of this metaphor for passage X relates to the connotation of *æghwær*, which can mean either "always" or "everywhere." The context of the *Beowulf* passage provides no clue to the appropriate translation, unless one wished to invoke the temporal continuation implicit in the *sententiae* preceding and following it, but comparison with *Hávamál* stanzas 10 and 11 allows the meaning "everywhere."

---

[61] *Fec. rat.* 1.430 (Voigt, 92); Walther, no. 15868.

[62] *Monastica*, line 10 (MGH *Poet.* 1.275); Walther, no. 20121.

[63] See Walther, no. 20121.

[64] Sedulius, *Coll. misc.*, 5.1 (CCCM 67.20); pseudo-Bede, *Collectanea* (PL 94.542). The first two phrases seem drawn from Prov. 16.16, although Simpson notes that pseudo-Bede attributes the sentence to one "Gelflidius" (CCCM 67.19).

[65] *Hávamál*, st. 10 (*Edda*, ed. Neckel/Kuhn, 18).

One final example of a wisdom/wealth sentence, from the thirteenth-century *Proverbs of Hendyng*, does not compare the two elements, but unites them in a metaphor: "Wit and wisdom is god wareisun."[66] I would suggest, although tentatively, that the similarity of elements between this variant and the others—wisdom, wealth, the adjective "good"—indicates its derivation from the "wisdom is better ..." version.

Another proverbial coupling with biblical sanction is that of wisdom and strength: "Melior est sapientia quam vires, et vir prudens quam fortis" (Sapientia 6.1) [Wisdom is better than strength, and the wise man better than the strong]; (cf. Eccles. 9.16, 18). Robert Kaske's seminal article explicates the *sapientia et fortitudo* topos in *Beowulf* as a whole,[67] but most immediately relevant to passage X are sentential linkings of these attributes in the "melior est" form. Sedulius and Defensor present Sap. 6.1 in their collections,[68] and Alcuin includes several variants in his *Monastica*:

> Corporis exsuperat vires prudentia mentis
>
> [Prudence of the mind surpasses strength of the body]
>
> Vir prudens animo est melior, quam fortis in armis.
> Corporis excellit vires sapientia mentis[69]
>
> [The man who is prudent in his soul is better than the
> one strong in arms. Wisdom in the mind surpasses
> strength in the body].

Wipo, on the other hand, extols wisdom to the detriment of worldly power: "Melior est sapientia quam secularis potentia"[70] [Wisdom is better than worldly power]. The poet of *Hávamál* implies that wisdom surpasses even friendship:

---

[66] Cited from Whiting, *Proverbs ... before 1500*, W417.

[67] Robert E. Kaske, "*Sapientia et Fortitudo* as the Controlling Theme of *Beowulf*," *Studies in Philology* 55 (1958): 423–57; repr. in Nicholson, *Anthology of Beowulf Criticism*, 269–310.

[68] Sedulius, *Coll. misc.*, 65.9 (CCCM 67.264); Defensor, *Lib. scin.*, 18.92 (CCSL 117.87).

[69] *Monastica*, line 9 (MGH *Poet.* 1.275), and 117–18 (1.279); Walther, no. 3524.

[70] Wipo, *Prov.* 7 (in *Wiponis Opera*, ed. Harry Bresslau, 3rd ed. [Hannover and Leipzig: Hahnsche Buchhandlung, 1915], 66); Walther, no. 14591.

þvíat óbrigðra vin   fær maðr aldregi
enn manvit mikit[71]

[A man never travels with a more faithful friend than
great wisdom].

Perhaps the most forceful expression of the value of wisdom is found
in Isidore's *Synonyma*, in a sentence that subsequently became a favorite
in eighth- and ninth-century *florilegia*; it is repeated by Defensor,
Peregrinus, and Sedulius Scottus: "Nihil sapientia melius; nihil prudentia dultius; nihil scientia suauius; nihil stulcia peius"[72] [Nothing is
better than wisdom; nothing sweeter than prudence; nothing more
pleasant than knowledge; nothing worse than ignorance]. Centuries
before Isidore, the proverbial sentiment that "nothing is better than
wisdom" appears underlying a proof used by Augustine. In his *De
libero arbitrio*, Augustine argues against the proposition that the agent
of understanding is always superior to the thing understood: "Hoc
enim falsum est, quia homo intellegit sapientiam et non est melior
quam ipsa sapientia"[73] [This is false, because man understands wisdom
but is not better than wisdom itself]. His argument is cogent only if
one accepts that wisdom is better than all things, man included. Peregrinus, at least, thought that the sentiment had classical authority, as he
ascribes two variants of a related sentence to Virgil:

Nullius rei sub caelo dignitas sapientis potest minimi ne conparari

[The worth of nothing under heaven can be compared to the
least wisdom]

Totus mundus, caelum et terra, dico, sapientiae conparari non
potest[74]

[All the world, heaven and earth, I say, cannot be compared to
wisdom].

---

[71] *Hávamál*, st. 6.5–6 (*Edda*, ed. Neckel/Kuhn, 18).

[72] *Synonyma* 2.65, cited from Sedulius, *Coll. misc.* 7.5 (CCCM 67.26). The final
phrase on ignorance is omitted by Defensor (*Lib. scin.*, 18.108 [CCSL 117.88]) and
the *Flor. Fris.* (no. 90 [CCSL 108D.11]; see also no. 391 [p. 32]).

[73] *De libero arbitrio libri tres*, ed. W. M. Green, in *Aurelii Augustini Opera*, part
2.2, CCSL 29 (Turnhout: Brepols, 1970), bk. 2, chap. 5 (p. 245).

[74] *Flor. Fris.*, nos. 213 (CCSL 108D.20) and 218 (p. 21); the latter is repeated,
without attribution, as no. 442 (p. 37).

Albert Lehner, the editor of the *Florilegium Frisingense*, has not located these *sententiae* in the Virgilian corpus, and it is possible that Peregrinus's attribution simply reflects the method by which the names of influential authors or sages attracted anonymous sayings; Bede and King Alfred elsewhere received the same compliment.

I have already discussed (chapters 2 and 3, above) the manner in which lines 1057–62 of *Beowulf* create a transition between Hrothgar's bestowal of gifts and the resumption of the feast in Heorot. Apart from this function, the meaning of passage X in context is difficult to establish. The *forþan* that begins the sentence could indicate some relation between it and that which precedes it ("Metod eallum weold gumena cynnes, swa he nu git deð" [1057b–58]), but it is also possible that *forþan* is syntactically "neutral" here, like the "enim" found in many Latin *sententiae*, and indicates no causal or concessive relationship to the preceding sentence.[75] The distinction is not really important in this case, as the primary contextual function of passage X is to contribute to the theme of "rational trust in the governance of the Almighty"[76] developed by the entire series of three *sententiae*.

Y. (lines 1384b–85):

> Selre bið æghwæm,
> þæt he his freond wrece, þonne he fela murne.

> [It is better for every man to avenge his friend than to mourn greatly.]

This sentence attains sentential form through familiar features—the comparative construction "selre ... þonne ...," the consuetudinal *bið*, the generalized *æghwæm*—but proverbial analogues endorsing the taking of vengeance are scarce, and none offers a precise parallel. In Old Norse we find "Þræll einn þegar hefnisk, en argr aldri"[77] [Only a slave takes vengeance at once, and a coward, never], and "Goðin hefna eigi alls þegar"[78] [The gods do not avenge everything at once], but these say-

---

[75] The possibility of a "colorless" or "neutral" *forþan* has been discussed mostly with respect to the *Seafarer*; for a recent review of work on this subject, see Mitchell, *Old English Syntax*, 1.560–61, ¶3082.

[76] Klaeber, *Beowulf*, note to lines 1056–62.

[77] *Grettis saga Ásmundarsonar*, ed. Guðni Jónsson, Íslenzk Fornrit 7 (Reykjavík: Íslenzka Fornritafélag, 1936), chap. 15, p. 44.

[78] *Brennu-Njáls saga*, ed. Einar Ól. Sveinsson, Íslenzk Fornrit 12 (Reykjavík: Íslenzka Fornritafélag, 1954), chap. 88, p. 215.

ings focus on the proper *time* for vengeance, and do not include the elements of friendship or mourning. Publilius Syrus appears to approve of fitting vengeance, but with a reasoning not evident in the *Beowulf* passage: "Nisi vindices delicta, improbitatem adiuves"[79] [Unless you avenge a crime, you abet wickedness]. The closest parallel to passage Y occurs in Ovid—"Minuet vindicta dolorem"[80] [Vengeance will lessen sorrow]—but Walther records no early- or even high-medieval uses of the sentence, and I would hesitate to consider the *Beowulf*-poet as directly dependent on the *Amores*.

The paucity of medieval proverbs enjoining vengeance seems rather surprising considering the prominence of the theme in Germanic heroic literature, but two explanations may be adduced. The first is the influence of the church, which preferred to leave judgment and retribution in divine hands (based on such texts as Deut. 32.35). As Christian collectors and scribes are responsible for the transmission and preservation of most medieval proverbs, a certain amount of censorship is inevitable. The second explanation, perhaps related to the first, is the portrayal of feuds in medieval literature. A feud frequently results from the exchange and escalation of acts of revenge, which more often than not conclude in mutual disaster for the parties involved.[81] *Njáls saga*, the Sigurd legend, and the Finnsburh episode in *Beowulf* itself provide vivid illustrations of this process. A "clean" revenge can occasionally be obtained, as in *Völundarkviða*, but such is not the norm. The strict preservation of honor may require retribution in blood rather than money, but the very institutions of *wergild* and legal settlement suggest cultural ambiguity on this issue. Mixed feelings do not create successful proverbs.

Passage Y is the first of three *sententiae* spoken by Beowulf in his response to Hrothgar's long announcement of Æschere's murder. I have discussed the entire sentential passage in chapter 4, above, but will add two points here. The first is a simple explication of passage Y in its context: Beowulf uses the sentence to express his willingness to take up Hrothgar's complaint against Grendel's dam without appearing merce-

---

[79] Publilius Syrus, *Sent.*, N18 (Bickford-Smith, p. 25); Walther, no. 16946.

[80] *Amores* 1.7.63 (cited from Walther, no. 14890.c).

[81] For a different view of feuding and blood revenge, see Jesse L. Byock, *Feud in the Icelandic Saga* (Berkeley: Univ. of California Press, 1982). Byock's thesis of feuding as a "socially stabilizing process" in Iceland (p. 2 *et passim*) leads him to characterize blood vengeance as a form of "direct resolution" of conflicts (p. 99).

nary. Hrothgar has offered to Beowulf "feo" [riches], "ealdgestreo-num" [ancient treasures], and "wundnum golde" [gold rings] for his continued assistance, but it would not befit this *lofgeornost* [most eager for fame] hero to appear to respond to such a monetary enticement. Instead, the *sententia* allows the poet to couch Beowulf's agreement in more ethical terms, implying that he intends to behave as time-honored wisdom enjoins.

Secondly, Beowulf's triply sentential response to Hrothgar's speech displays the same sort of polite social grace as in his parting speech to the old king (see passage Z, below). Here, Hrothgar has not asked for advice or consolation, but those are exactly what Beowulf offers, so the indirect expression of the *sententiae* serves to illustrate the young warrior's undiminished respect for the clearly distraught ruler.

Z. (lines 1838b–39):

> Feorcyþðe beoð
> selran gesohte   þæm þe him selfa deah.

[Faraway places are best sought by him who is strong himself.]

The sentential elements of this sentence—*beoð, selran, þæm þe*—are by now familiar. The closest proverbial parallel is found in *Hávamál*:

> Vitz er þörf,   þeim er víða ratar,
>   dælt er heima hvat;
> at augabragði verðr,   sá er ecci kann
>   oc með snotrom sitr.[82]

[He who travels widely needs sharp wits, everything is easy at home; he who knows nothing but sits among the wise is easily found out.]

In their commentary, Sijmons and Gering point out much later English and Danish analogues on the order of "at home anything will do,"[83] which, combined with other parallel passages, suggest that this stanza of *Hávamál* records what were at some time three different *sententiae*. The first of these, "He who travels needs intelligence," is paralleled, of

---

[82] *Hávamál*, st. 5 (*Edda*, ed. Neckel/Kuhn, 17–18).
[83] *Die Lieder der Edda*, ed. B. Sijmons and H. Gering, 3 vols. (6 parts), German-istische Handbibliothek 7 (Halle: Buchhandlung des Waisenhauses, 1888–1927), Band 3.1: Götterlieder, 84.

course, by *Beowulf* passage Z. The second, "It's easy to be smart at home," is the proverb pointed out by Sijmons and Gering. The third distinct *sententia* in this stanza, "A fool will be found out among the wise," reflects a theme expressed in several other stanzas of *Hávamál* itself, but most straightforwardly in these:

> Ósnotr maðr   þicciz alt vita,
>   ef hann á sér í vá vero;
> hitki hann veit,   hvat hann scal við qveða,
>   ef hans freista firar.
>
> Ósnotr,   er með aldir kömr,
>   þat er bazt, at hann þegi;
> engi þat veit,   at hann ecci kann,
>   nema hann mæli til mart;
> veita maðr,   hinn er vætki veit,
>   þótt hann mæli til mart.[84]

[The stupid man thinks he knows all, if he is by himself at home; he does not know what he should answer if his ignorance is tested.

It is best for the stupid man to be quiet when he comes among others; it will not be plain that he knows nothing unless he speaks too much; the man is safe with others who know nothing, even if he speaks too much.]

The three proverbs of *Hávamál* stanza 5 combine easily, but must also have circulated separately.

The only other relevant analogue I have found to passage Z appears in the *South English Legendary* as "Ech londe is ... owe contreie to the stronge."[85] However, this sentence differs from passage Z in its emphasis, as it *assumes* ability on the part of the traveler, rather than recommending it.

An understanding of the full connotation of passage Z is complicated by the comparative *selran*. In any other *Beowulf*ian *sententia* using a form of *selra*,[86] the modified statement is followed by a "þonne ..." clause, which is lacking here. Dobbie interprets the sentence as if it

---

[84] *Hávamál*, st. 26–27 (*Edda*, ed. Neckel/Kuhn, 21).
[85] Cited from Whiting, *Proverbs ... before 1500*, L58.
[86] See lines 1384–85 and 2891–92.

implied a missing second half: "one who is worthy (such as Hrethric) will be better treated in a foreign country than one who is not worthy."[87] Hoops, on the other hand, decides that the comparative *selran* has here a simply positive sense: "der Besuch ferner Länder ist gut für den, der [selber tüchtig ist]."[88] The combined *sententiae* we have seen in *Hávamál* stanza 5 would support Dobbie's version, except for the fact that we would then need to assume that the *Beowulf*-poet, wishing only to include the first clause, omitted the second without correcting the grammar of the first. The skillful reworking and integration of *sententiae* elsewhere in *Beowulf* precludes this possibility.[89] Furthermore, Hoops's reading of the sentence as "foreign travel is good for the capable man" also finds support in *Hávamál*, which includes a stanza on the educational benefits of touring:

> Sá einn veit,   er víða ratar
>   oc hefir fiöld um farið,
> hverio geði   stýrir gumna hverr,
>   sá er vitandi er vitz.[90]

> [He alone knows, who travels widely and has journeyed about the earth, how each man's mind works, only he who is wise in thought.]

In sum, Beowulf's use of the sentence is intended to provide closure to his speech, to reinforce his invitation of Hreþric "to hofum Geata" [to the homes of the Geats], and subtly to compliment Hrothgar through praise of his son.

AA. (lines 2764b–66):

> Sinc eaðe mæg,
> gold on grunde   gumcynnes gehwone
> oferhigian,   hyde se ðe wille.

> [Treasure, gold in the ground, can easily overpower any man, hide it who will.]

---

[87] ASPR 4.209, note to lines 1838b–39.

[88] Hoops, *Kommentar*, 199.

[89] Klaeber (*Beowulf*, p. xcii) is among the scholars who have supported the appearance of the comparative absolute in *Beowulf* and elsewhere in Old English, but Mitchell (*Old English Syntax*, 1.81–83, ¶183–86) disagrees.

[90] *Hávamál*, st. 18 (*Edda*, ed. Neckel/Kuhn, 19).

The sentential form of this passage derives from the present tense of *mæg*, the indefinite *gumcynnes gehwone*, and the *se ðe* construction of the final clause. Perhaps because the literal meaning of these lines has proven elusive (*oferhigian* is otherwise unattested), editors of *Beowulf* have not looked kindly upon the sentence: Klaeber characterizes it as "[a]n apparently uncalled-for ethical reflection"[91] and Dobbie, "a general and irrelevant comment of the moral sort."[92] In any case, current opinion has settled on a translation resembling that given above, although some scholars still adhere to the translation of *hyde* as "heed."[93]

Proverbial analogues to passage AA support the consensus opinion of *oferhigian* as "overcome" or "overpower." In the first quarter of the twelfth century, the Peterborough Chronicle used the sentence to explain imperial history: "Ac þet ofer com Rome þet ofer cumeð eall weoruld, þet is gold and seolvre."[94] At the close of the century, Lagamon individualized the peril:

> Ware his nou the ilke man
> That ne may mid mede beo over-come?[95]

Three centuries later, Alexander Barclay wrote, "Money over man is like a conqueror."[96]

However, the closest parallel to passage AA, and the one with the most interesting implications for the purpose of the sentence, appears in Ecclus. 8.3: "Multos enim perdidit aurum et argentum, et usque ad cor regum extendit et convertit" [For gold and silver have ruined many, and they reach into and pervert the very heart of kings]. If some version of this sentence served as the model for passage AA, then the views of those critics who have questioned the wisdom of Beowulf's engagement with the dragon would be vindicated.[97] By his reference

---

[91] Klaeber, *Beowulf*, note to 2764b–66.

[92] ASPR 4.258, note to line 2766.

[93] Chickering, for example, translates 2766b twice, as "hide it who will— heed it who can!" (*Beowulf*, 215); for a discussion of the merits of the two interpretations, see Hoops, *Kommentar*, 291, and Dobbie, ASPR 4.258, note to line 2766.

[94] Cited from Whiting, *Proverbs . . . before 1500*, G296.

[95] Cited from Whiting, *Proverbs . . . before 1500*, M322.

[96] Cited from Whiting, *Proverbs . . . before 1500*, M624.

[97] See, for example, John Leyerle, "Beowulf the Hero and the King," *Medium Ævum* 34 (1965): 89–102. Leyerle condemns Beowulf not on the grounds of greed, but for excessive pride in his own strength and glory.

to the biblical *sententia*, the poet would imply that Beowulf the king had succumbed to the insidious influence of wealth, thus destroying himself and his people. If that assessment seems somewhat too harsh, a less drastic possibility remains, in that the entire verse of Ecclus. 8.3 is rather long to have enjoyed circulation as a proverb or sentence. The examples from the Chronicle and *Brut* show that the essence of the first half of the verse—"Multos enim perdidit aurum et argentum"—did enjoy some currency, so it may have been this less pointed sentence that the *Beowulf*-poet had in mind. Of course, none of these *sententiae* refer specifically to *buried* treasure, but I would offer that the localization of the hoard is simply a successful attempt by the *Beowulf*-poet to integrate a traditional sentence into the context of his narrative, and does not reflect any special maleficence associated with interred as opposed to openly displayed gold. In fact, the sentential analogues to passage AA suggest that a more appropriate reading of the lines might be "Although a man may hide gold in the ground, still it can overcome anyone."

BB. (lines 3077–78a):

> Oft sceall eorl monig   anes willan
> wræc adreogan.

> [Often many men must suffer misery for the will of one.]

Although the sentiment of this sentence is not paralleled in other surviving proverbs, it bears every hallmark of a traditional *sententia*: its generalization of time (*oft*) and of person (*eorl monig, anes*) combine with the modal verb *sceall* to endow the lines with proverbial form. Furthermore, the juxtapositioning of *manig* and *an* in this passage may perhaps be viewed as a variant of the *eal/an* collocation appearing frequently in *Beowulf*. Although the form of this collocation never achieves sufficient regularity to enable one to characterize it as formulaic or proverbial, it does represent a figure of speech or thought that the poet found useful for describing various types of circumstances. Two occurrences in close proximity combine to highlight the hero against the background of the assembled Danes and Geats anticipating Grendel's approach:

> ... þæt hie feond heora
> ðurh anes cræft   ealle ofercomon,
> selfes mihtum   (698b–700a)

[So that they all overcame their enemy through the skill of one, through his might alone]

... Sceotend swæfon,
þa þæt hornreced   healdan scoldon,
ealle buton anum   (703b–5a)

[The shooters slept, those who ought to guard the hall, all except one].

Much later in the poem, two more instances of the collocation frame the "Lament of the Last Survivor":

... Ealle hie deað fornam
ærran mælum,   ond se an þa gen
leoda duguðe,   se ðær lengst hwearf,
weard winegeomor,   wende þæs ylcan   (2236b–39)

[Death took them all at an earlier time, and the one who then remained from the host of people, he who moved longest there, who dwelt in mourning, expected the same]

Swa giomormod   giohðo mænde
an æfter eallum   (2267–68a)

[So the sad one complained of his sorrow, one alone after them all].

Thus, a contrast between the individual and the group appears as somewhat of a topos in the poem.

Equally important for the potential proverbiality of passage BB is the perception that the idea it expresses is simple enough to prove useful in varied situations, as a proverb must. In fact, the sentence is sufficiently ambiguous to allow its interpretation as an indictment of Beowulf's ill-fated attack, were it not for the counterinfluence of Wiglaf's unstinting praise of his fallen leader. Wiglaf directs the audience to the intended interpretation of the proverb by immediately referring to Beowulf as "leofne þeoden" (3079b) [beloved chief] and blaming the king's eagerness on powers beyond his control: "wæs þæt gifeðe to swið" (3085b) [that fate was too strong].

Sentential analogues to passage BB are less generous in their assessment of the relationship of the individual to the group. Beowulf could hardly be characterized as an *iniquus* or *pravus* king, but the second ele-

ment of this dual sentence, recorded from four fourteenth- and fifteenth-century manuscripts, otherwise corresponds to Wiglaf's warning:

> Mundo peior inimicus
> Non est quam princeps iniquus.
> Sepe perdit sua bona
> Gens sub prava stans persona[98]

> [There is no worse enemy in the world than an unjust
> prince. Often, a people ruled by a perverse person loses
> its goods].

W. F. Bolton has noted a potential parallel to passage BB in Alcuin's
Commentaria super Ecclesiasten,[99] a parallel that we might examine in
greater detail than Bolton affords it. Alcuin's text is Eccles. 9.18, part of
which we have already examined as a basis for the proverbial formula
"wisdom is better than X." The full verse reads: "Melior est sapientia
quam arma bellica, et qui in uno peccaverit, multa bona perdet" [Wis-
dom is better than the arms of war, and who will sin in one thing will
lose many good things]. Alcuin explains:

> Nunc quoque sapientiam præfert fortitudini, et dicit eam plus
> valere in præliis quam arma pugnantium; et crebro evenit, quod
> per unius insipientiam opes magnæ atque divitiæ pereunt.[100]

> [Now anyone prefers wisdom to strength, and declares it more
> valuable in battles than the weapons of war; and it often happens
> that through the foolishness of one, wealth and great riches perish.]

Alcuin begins to introduce proverbial, or at least formulaic, language
by recasting the initial contrast in the terms of the familiar *sapien-
tia/fortitudo* topos; he then prefaces his explanatory rewriting of the
second half of the verse with the phrase, "et crebro evenit." The
understanding that something "often happens" is, of course, a prerequi-
site for any proverbial truth, one that is made explicit by Alcuin and in
Beowulf passage BB ("Oft"). The remainder of Alcuin's explication
moves further away from passage BB, as Wiglaf refers not to the loss of

---

[98] Walther, no. 15629.

[99] W. F. Bolton, *Alcuin and 'Beowulf': An Eighth-Century View* (New Brunswick, N.J.: Rutgers Univ. Press, 1978), 138.

[100] Alcuin, *Commentaria super Ecclesiasten*, in *Opera omnia*, ed. Migne, *PL*
100.667–722 (707A).

"great wealth" (although this does occur), but to the more generalized misery that will be suffered by the Geats. Still, it appears that Alcuin and the *Beowulf*-poet may have been employing the same principles of composition along proverbial lines.

Middle English proverbs reverse the connotation of passage BB; rather than "many must suffer because of one," they imply that it is better for one person to suffer than many:

> Betere hit were that o man deyde,
> Than al volk were y-lore.
> . . . .
> For better is oo man dede, then tow.[101]

Unfortunately for the Geats, such a trade-off is not available in their dilemma.

Like the Danish coastguard, Wiglaf uses the sentence to initiate a formal message. His sentential introduction indicates the official nature of his communication and provides it with a measure of authority. Further, the *sententia* re-establishes the theme of imminent disaster prophesied earlier by Wiglaf and the unnamed messenger, after a lengthy description of the dead dragon and glittering hoard. In fact, the progress of the poem from Wiglaf's speech to the cowardly retainers to the final lament over Beowulf reflects the same interaction between individual and communal fate as does the sentence. Wiglaf's first speech and then that of the messenger alternate the two elements, both first describing the death of the king, then the anticipated troubles; passage BB refers to Beowulf and the Geatish people in short, and the remainder of Wiglaf's speech, along with the bulk of the funeral scene, concentrates on Beowulf. The female mourner takes up the thread of Geatish doom, and finally, the poem ends with praise of the hero. The function of passage BB within this structure is to provide a clear, directing exposition of the intertwined elements, and to focus a theme that extends over three hundred lines of poetry.

CC. (lines 2029b–31):

> Oft seldan hwær
> æfter leodhryre   lytle hwile
> bongar bugeð,   þeah seo bryd duge.

---

[101] *Cayphas* and *Ipomadon*, cited from Whiting, *Proverbs ... before 1500*, M49.

[Often, the deadly spear rests only for a short time
after the death of a prince, though the bride be good.]

These lines are not among the most carefully crafted of the poem,
but a certain amount of their awkwardness can be explained by the
poet's attempt to give sentential form to a non-proverbial statement. By
defining the passage as non-proverbial, I mean that it does not represent
a variant within an established proverbial corpus.

The greatest interpretative difficulty presented by passage CC
revolves around the adverbial progression "oft seldan hwær," but the
exact connotation of "lytle hwile" is unclear as well.[102] Klaeber and
Dobbie rightly follow Kock in their gloss of "as a rule" for *oft* in the
first phrase,[103] but no critic has explained the process by which such
an undeniably clumsy juxtaposition as "oft seldan" entered the poem
in the first place.[104] The answer lies in the poet's understanding of
sentential form, but lack of a proverbial model.

As I have pointed out in connection with many other passages of
Beowulf, a consistent element of proverbial form is the generalization of
place, person, and especially time; *oft* and *a* are used in many cases, and
æghwær in one (line 1059b, passage X, above). If we remove those
elements from passage CC, we are left with the core idea of the sentence: "æfter leodhryre lytle hwile bongar bugeð, þeah seo bryd duge"
("after the fall of a prince, the spear rests [only] for a little while,
though the bride be good"). To this potentially sentential, but non-
traditional core, the poet added elements of spatial and temporal
generalization in order to increase the perceived authority of his statement. The addition of *hwær* does not substantially affect the translation
I have offered above, but *seldan* interacts with *lytle hwile* to create
"Seldom anywhere does the spear rest *even* for a short time after the
death of a prince...."[105] The addition of *oft* caps the construction by
providing its most immediately recognizable sentential element. The

---

[102] Dobbie (ASPR 4.221, note to line 2029) suggests "[even] for a little while,"
but Klaeber (*Beowulf*, note to 2029–31) gives "only for a short time."

[103] Dobbie, ASPR 4.221; Klaeber, *Beowulf*, note to 2029–31.

[104] Although, the structure of this passage is treated briefly by Ommo Wilts,
Formprobleme Germanischer Spruchdichtung (Ph.D. diss., Christian-Albrechts-
Universität zu Kiel, 1968), 19.

[105] Such is the essence of Dobbie's translation (see n. 102, above). Alternatively,
seldan could have been included in the poet's "core" idea.

strength of *oft* as a proverbial marker must have prompted the poet to add it to his sentence, even at the risk of incoherence.

This hypothesized reconstruction of the creative process relies on the assumption that the core idea of passage CC was not otherwise available in sentential form. That assumption is supported not only by the circumstance that I have failed to locate any analogue to the passage, but also by the impression that the core of the sentence is too specific to have circulated proverbially.[106] In other words, the situation described by the poet would occur too infrequently to provide the material for a useful proverb.

Finally, we must consider why the *Beowulf*-poet created a sentence for insertion at this point of the narrative. Passage CC appears in Beowulf's report to Hygelac, between the announcement of Freawaru's betrothal to Ingeld and the detailed prediction of renewed hostilities between the Danes and Heathobards. The sentence, awkward as it is, provides a skillful transition between Beowulf's formal report and the inset narrative of Ingeld, in that it makes his prophecy of these well-known developments more believable—he seems simply to elaborate on an established pattern—and reduces the superfluity of the Ingeld "digression" by introducing it along the exemplum/proverb lines we have seen elsewhere.

DD. (lines 2166b–69a):

> Swa sceal mæg don,
> nealles inwitnet   oðrum bregdon
> dyrnum cræfte,   deað renian
> hondgesteallan.

[So should a kinsman do, he should not weave nets of intrigue for another with secret cunning, nor prepare death for his companion.]

EE. (lines 2600b–2601):

> Sibb' æfre ne mæg
> wiht onwendan   þam ðe wel þenceð.

[Nothing will alter kinship for him who thinks rightly.]

---

[106] In a letter, Alcuin mentions that "mors regum miseriae signum est," but his sentence contains fewer details than passage CC, as he specifies neither the cause of the king's death, nor the nature of the *miseria*; cited by Leyerle, "Beowulf the Hero and the King," 98.

With these passages, we continue our examination of lines which assume sentential form, but are not themselves proverbial. Passage DD takes advantage of the proverbial introduction "Swa sceal man don,"[107] but the repetition within the passage—"inwitnet ... bregdon; deað ... renian"—its specificity ("dyrnum cræfte"), and its placement disclose it as a moral judgment by the poet, cloaked in the garb of a traditional sentence. Similarly, passage EE employs familiar sentential elements (*æfre*, *mæg*, *þam ðe*) to authorize a value judgment.

Although proverbs do sometimes *describe* kinship bonds (e.g., "Blood is thicker than water"), such statements are few in number, and I have found only two *sententiae* offering direction for the behavior of kinsmen. The first of these, from *Sigrdrífumál*, is far more generalized than *Beowulf* DD:

> Þat ræð ec þér iþ fyrsta,   at þú við froendr þína
> vammalauss verir.[108]

> [I counsel you this first of all, that you be blameless toward your kinsmen.]

Lagamon's *Brut* offers the suggestion of a proverb, but I have not located other variants:

> The saeg wes itreouwe:
> Wa wurthe a thon brother,
> The biswiketh thene other.[109]

If Lagamon's "saw" is not popular and secular in origin, perhaps it reflects a reminiscence of the First Epistle of John, which repeatedly treats the responsibilities of brothers, or of Zach. 7.10: "et malum vir fratri suo non cogitet in corde suo" [And let a man not devise evil in his heart against his brother]. This surprising lack of familial prescriptions in the proverbial tradition can probably be attributed to the nearly universal valuation of kinship bonds: to prove useful, an advice-giving proverb should point out the better of two alternatives, but as the primacy of familial relationships can be taken for granted, *sententiae* supporting them would seem superfluous.

---

[107] For discussion of related formulas, see Archer Taylor, "The Proverbial Formula 'Man soll ... '," *Zeitschrift für Volkskunde*, n.s. 2 (1930): 152–56.

[108] *Sigrdrífumál*, st. 22.1–2 (*Edda*, ed. Neckel/Kuhn, 194).

[109] *Brut*, lines 4451–53; cited from Whiting, *Proverbs ... before 1500*, B570.

The primary purpose of passage DD is simple: it defines the significance of Beowulf's gift-giving, and characterizes the hero as a "shining example of fidelity."[110] By structuring the sentence in negative terms, the poet enhances Beowulf's position as counter-example; one recalls the "sella ... þonne ..." form of other *sententiae*, where two alternatives are presented, but only one endorsed. However, the artificiality of this *sententia* is highlighted by the contrast between "swa," which should introduce a prescriptive sentence, and "nealles," which instead begins a proscriptive pronouncement. Unlike an independently circulating proverb, this sentence compels the reader or listener to look outside the *sententia*, back to Beowulf's behavior, in order to grasp its meaning. The intended referent of *mæg* (2166b) is not clear, but neither is it important, as enough unfaithful kinsmen appear in the poem (Heoroweard, Hrothulf, Onela, etc.) that the sentence could refer to them collectively. The single reference can recall several episodes.[111]

The sentential form of passage EE serves primarily to effect a transition between the focus on Beowulf and that on Wiglaf. The sentence introduces Wiglaf as a kinsman of Beowulf (thus explaining the behavioral contrast between the Wægmunding and the other retainers), and immediately characterizes the younger hero as exemplary, one who "wel þenceð." Wiglaf goes on to become the most admirable figure in the remainder of the poem. Examined together, passages DD and EE illustrate the principle that a sentential construction is used by the *Beowulf*-poet to create a sort of exemplum from an episode or an instance of specific behavior, and that the sentence fulfilling this function may appear either at the beginning or the close of the intended example.

The title of this chapter portrays the *sententiae* discussed in it as "Warnings and Advice," but the passages themselves could in some cases be better characterized as *descriptions* of social behavior. They may provide examples of approved behavior, counter-examples to the same, or predictions based on communal past experience, but all of them partake, through their form, of sentential authority. To some degree, these passages are less easily applicable to the audience than are *sententiae* treating broader topics such as God or death. The situations described or assumed by *sententiae* in this chapter are often more

---

[110] Chickering, *Beowulf*, p. 355.

[111] For discussions of this ambiguity, see Klaeber, *Beowulf*, note to lines 2166f., and Chickering, *Beowulf*, p. 355; Chickering also addresses the matter of negative constructions in this passage, but with slightly different conclusions from mine.

specific—a young prince anticipating war, a bereaved people, a friend seeking revenge—and in these cases the function of the passage within the poem may assume greater importance than its message for the audience. Still, the poetic functions of these passages differ little from those we have seen in other groupings, in that they are used for purposes of characterization, of transition, and of thematic continuity.

The subject matter of these passages invites consideration of their role in the possible development of *Beowulf* as something like a "mirror for princes." It is perfectly fitting that the Fürstenspiegel, as an instructional genre, should include sentential wisdom,[112] and it is also true that most of the passages discussed in this chapter (i.e., V, Y–EE) are addressed or applied to present or future kings. The *sententiae* help to characterize these regnal characters, to support their function as (good or bad) examples, and to direct the audience's response to their described actions.

On the other hand, there exists somewhat of a productive tension between the specific status of the characters to whom the sentences are applied, and the generalized diction of the *sententiae* themselves. The inhabitants of the *Beowulf*ian world are almost exclusively aristocratic, but only passage CC refers to a prince or lord; the other passages are so worded as to be universally applicable. This generalized diction, and the exemplum/proverb model I have suggested in connection with several sentential passages, suggest that the intended audience of *Beowulf* is not automatically restricted to kings and princes, but includes any person who espouses the values developed in the poem. Hagiographic exempla are not directed towards saints, nor even necessarily towards anyone likely to achieve canonization, but towards an audience of the faithful who can use the lessons exemplified by the more spectacular experience of the saint as a guide (and support) for appropriate behavior in their more mundane existence. Likewise, folktales are frequently peopled with kings and princesses, even when the narratives are created by and for a much less exalted public. Thus, the generalized, sentential passages of *Beowulf*, which I have not found paralleled in texts designed specifically as *specula principum*, expand the range of possible "students" of the poem, from kings, queens, and princes such as it describes, to any member of Anglo-Saxon society.

---

[112] In fact, most of the medieval Irish gnomic corpus consists of instructions to princes; see P. L. Henry, *The Early English and Celtic Lyric* (London: George Allen & Unwin Ltd, 1966), 104–17.

6

Beowulf and the Uses of Proverbs

Although proverbs circulate primarily through oral channels, we can discuss medieval proverbs only with reference to the written record. Furthermore, no reliable method exists for determining the essential orality or literality of a given sentence, even when that sentence has become proverbial through the decontextualization of a quotation, or on the other hand, through the translation of vernacular material into a Latin context. We are prevented from examining the greater part of the medieval proverbial tradition, that is, its oral aspect, and must content ourselves with a consideration of the medieval use of proverbs in literary, or at least literate, sources. What follows will constitute not a complete study or survey of the uses of proverbs in early medieval writings, but perhaps a prolegomenon to such a study, in the form of a discussion of the types of writings that have provided analogues to the *sententiae* of *Beowulf*. These analogues have been drawn from gnomic, narrative, and lyric poetry; from deliberately compiled proverb collections and florilegia; from the Bible and liturgy; from homilies and sermons; from Christian Latin commentaries; and from Classical Latin drama, historiography, and philosophy.

The genre of gnomic or wisdom poetry is of primary importance for comprehending the proverbial tradition and its relationship to *Beowulf*. Not only do poems like *Maxims I*, *Maxims II*, and *Hávamál* provide a significant number of analogues to certain *sententiae* of *Beowulf*, but they also present vital information about the cultural conception and valuation of sentential pronouncements. With its sentential content far outstripping that of any other Old English narrative poem, *Beowulf* reflects an attitude towards sentential expression similar to that which must have motivated the redactor of *Hávamál*, or the Anglo-Saxon scribe who copied *Maxims II* in front of a version of the *Chronicle*. That attitude may be described in brief as a respect for and appreciation of the uses of traditional wisdom.

Although it has at times been called into question, there is no real reason to doubt the ancient origin of gnomic poetry in Germanic.[1] The existence of gnomic poems in both Old English and Old Norse, the embracing of sentential expression by the studiously antiquarian *Beowulf*-poet, and the near absence of such expressions in Old English Christian narrative poetry all argue for a pre-Christian flowering of the genre. Alternative arguments have most often been offered in connection with *Hávamál*, but these studies are flawed, from a paroemiological point of view, in mistakenly treating proverbs in the same way as sources: for Klaus von See, an analogue to the *Disticha Catonis* points to a Latin-learned origin for *Hávamál*, whereas for Roland Köhne, Middle High German analogues mean a late date and German origin.[2] These discussions fail to take into account the extraordinary mobility of proverbs, and indeed, of medieval texts. An analogue does not equal a source, nor even does an admitted source define the origin of a poem or genre. In an earlier chapter, I suggested that the deistic *sententiae* of *Beowulf* bore some relationship to, and may have been derived from, certain psalms, but that does not prove a Christian origin for Old English heroic poetry any more than Thomas Hill's discovery of Ecclus. 33.15 as the probable source for lines 50–57 of *Maxims II* indicates a Christian origin for that poem or any of its analogues.[3] A pre-existing generic frame may absorb material from any source, and in the case of proverbial material, sources are especially nebulous.

While West and North Germanic gnomic poems offer welcome evi-

---

[1] On gnomic poetry as a Common Germanic genre, see H. Munro Chadwick and N. Kershaw Chadwick, *The Growth of Literature*, vol. I: *The Ancient Literatures of Europe* (Cambridge: Cambridge Univ. Press, 1932), 386, 400; on *Hávamál* specifically, see the edition by David A. H. Evans, Viking Society for Northern Research Text Series, vol. 7 (London: Viking Society, 1986), 16–18.

[2] Klaus von See, "Disticha Catonis und Hávamál;" Köhne, Roland, "Zur Mittelalterlichkeit der eddischen Spruchdichtung," *Beiträge zur Geschichte der deutschen Sprache und Literatur* (Tübingen) 105 (1983): 380–417. For a more detailed defense of the native origin of *Hávamál*, see Joseph Harris, "Eddic Poetry," in *Old Norse-Icelandic Literature*, ed. Clover and Lindow, 107–11.

[3] See chap. 2, above, and pp. 150–51, below; and Thomas D. Hill, "Notes on the Old English 'Maxims' I and II," *Notes and Queries* 215 (1970): 445–47. It should be stressed that Hill does not make such an argument.

dence for the circulation of proverbs and sentences, they are of less value as encyclopedias of those proverbs. In the first place, the preserved corpus of vernacular *sententiae* is fairly small, so any correspondence between the gnomic poems and *Beowulf* depends primarily on chance, which is likely to favor only the most frequently repeated proverbs. Furthermore, the difference in thematic, structural, and aesthetic approaches between *Beowulf* and the gnomic poems limits the probability of overlap. Little is known, indeed few guesses are hazarded, about the compositional technique or intention of the *Maxims I* and *II* poets, but one may safely note that the statements they include are primarily descriptive, with a smattering of preceptual material; in this the poems resemble Welsh gnomic poetry more than the *sententiae* of *Beowulf*.[4] In the heroic poem, a high percentage of the *sententiae* are preceptual, and those that are descriptive treat not of the ways of nature, but of God, fate, and death; that is, of powers having a direct influence on human life. A gnomic poem may help the reader or listener to discern the order of creation by describing the inherent attributes of created things or beings and presenting them for consideration, but the concerns of most heroic poems are more immediate: human actions, their natural and supernatural causes, and their consequences. From this difference in focus arises the discrepancy in sentential form and content. The *sententiae* of *Beowulf* must relate somehow to the narrative, either by prescribing or describing a course of behavior, by reflecting or expressing the attitude of a character, or by simply explaining the action as an extension of the divine will. All but the last function are most effectively performed by preceptual sentences.

The structural and thematic principles governing *Hávamál*, the most famous representative of gnomic poetry in Old Norse, have occasioned even more controversy than those of *Maxims I* and *II*, if only by enjoying more frequent discussion. As it has been transmitted, *Hávamál* is a composite piece, although the exact divisions of the composition are not always agreed upon.[5] Unlike the Old English gnomic poems,

---

[4] On these aspects of Old English, Old Norse, and other gnomic traditions, see the discussion by Chadwick and Chadwick, chap. 12; the study by Blanche Colton Williams, *Gnomic Poetry in Anglo-Saxon*, is still valuable, as is that by T. A. Shippey, *Poems of Wisdom and Learning in Old English* (Cambridge: D. S. Brewer; Totowa, N.J.: Rowman and Littlefield, 1976). A more recent treatment is by Nicholas Howe, *The Old English Catalogue Poems*, Anglistica 23 (Copenhagen: Rosenkilde and Bagger, 1985).

[5] For a current discussion of the problems associated with *Hávamál*, see Evans, 9–23.

the bulk of *Hávamál* is made up of preceptual sentences, one or two to a stanza; some of these *sententiae* may represent pre-existing proverbs, but others probably do not.[6] Uncertainty regarding the origins and structure of *Hávamál* notwithstanding, we may yet note several points of interest with respect to *Beowulf* and its use of *sententiae*. First, of course, is the use of preceptual *sententiae* common to *Hávamál* and *Beowulf*. Although *Hávamál* is not particularly heroic in its outlook or advice, thus minimizing the probability of overlap between itself and *Beowulf*, it does offer a model for the adaptation and circulation of preceptual proverbs and sentences in poetic form.[7] Furthermore, *Hávamál* and *Sigrdrífumál* provide other instances, however poorly understood, of the combination of sentential and narrative matter within a single poem, but reversing the *Beowulf*ian proportions of the two constituents.[8] Finally, the composer of the gnomic verses of *Hávamál*, like the *Beowulf*-poet, ably manipulated proverbial form in creating non-traditional *sententiae* to suit his thematic or aesthetic ends. Such purposeful control of certain forms of syntax and diction argues for a well-established and widely practiced appreciation for the uses of *sententiae* in poetic expression.

The corpus of gnomic poetry surviving in Old English and Old Norse presents, despite its small size, a surprising variety of different *sententiae*. The poems' resemblance to each other resides primarily in their *mode* of expression—the sentential—rather than in their actual content. It seems as if these gnomic poems, like *Beowulf*, draw from a larger pool of available proverbs and *sententiae*, selecting and arranging their material towards individual ends. In the case of *Hávamál*, and to some extent *Sigrdrífumál*, the result is a poeticized series of instructions for the man who wishes to function safely and successfully in society. The Old English gnomic poems, with their combination of natural and human observations, and their frequently unclear thematic connections, more closely resemble riddles, in which constituents of the created world are related to each other in unexpected ways, thus compelling the listener to rethink his or her conceptions of cosmological order.

---

[6] Evans, 19–21. The adaptation of a single precept to a complete stanza is evident also in *Sigrdrífumál*.

[7] One thinks also of the Old English *Precepts*, but that poem seems too dependent on the Decalogue to be of much significance here.

[8] The relation of sentential and narrative material in Old English and Old Norse gnomic poetry is a topic of potential interest for literary history, one that I intend to investigate in a separate study.

The *sententiae* of *Beowulf* play both of these gnomic roles at various times, whether by addressing some aspect of eternal order ("Fate always proceeds as it must"), by asserting the influence of divine power in sublunary affairs ("He who has the favor of the Lord can successfully endure hardship"), or by offering sentential advice about strictly interpersonal relations ("A young man should give gifts to his companions, in order to have support when he is older"). Thus, the *Beowulf*-poet shares with those of the gnomic poems not only a profound understanding of proverbial structure, but a complex comprehension of proverbial function as well.

Another important form of wisdom literature, albeit one that is frequently overlooked because of its lack of aesthetic appeal, is the medieval proverb collection. I have located analogues to the *sententiae* of *Beowulf* in several of these collections, representing various periods and languages: in Old English the *Disticha Catonis* and Durham Proverbs; in Early Medieval Latin the *Disticha Catonis*, the *Liber proverbiorum* of pseudo-Bede, the collections by Otloh, Wipo, and Egbert of Liège; in High and Late Medieval Latin the *Proverbia Ysengrimi* and *Proverbia communia*; in Middle English, yet another translation of the *Disticha Catonis*, along with the so-called Proverbs of Alfred and Proverbs of Hendyng; and in Middle High German, Freidank's *Bescheidenheit*. Although less interesting as an artistic entity (indeed, nearly without interest in that regard), the proverb collection surpasses the gnomic poem as a record of the medieval proverbial corpus. In the first place, medieval proverb collections remain more numerous than gnomic poems, perhaps because of the greater skill required for the creation of the latter. Secondly, a proverb collection is almost always didactic in its intent, and often religiously didactic, but few other constrictions act upon it: proverbs and sentences may be presented in any order (or no apparent order at all), they may address any combination of topics, and they may be drawn from a great variety of sources, including the Bible, the Fathers, the classics, or oral tradition. In most cases, the proverb collection is free from whatever compulsions toward artistic or thematic unity and development might have affected the composition of a gnomic poem. As a result, medieval proverb collections as a group offer a larger and more varied cross-section of the medieval proverbial corpus.[9]

---

[9] We must bear in mind, however, that the "medieval" proverbial corpus was not monolithic and unchanging, although it was probably more stable than the modern corpus, however that is defined.

The interest of these proverb collections resides not only in their content, but also in their significance for the transmission of proverbs throughout the Middle Ages. Most of the collections are the products and instruments of the schools, the curricula of which often included the transcription and translation of proverbs and sentences. Early in the training of budding Latinists, a teacher could dictate proverbs in the vernacular, and students would translate them into Latin hexameters, pentameters, or any other required form. The teacher might then collect and copy the best of the student products, thus amassing the material for future exercises.[10] Proverb collections also served a morally didactic purpose, in that students were compelled to memorize various proverbs, through which practice they learned their Latin and absorbed ideas of virtue all at the same time.[11] These schoolroom activities assisted the dissemination of proverbs in several ways. First was the introduction of new proverbs to students, who would subsequently carry these proverbs with them when they left the site of their schooling. Second, as already mentioned, was the collection of proverbs from various sources into a curricular tool; in this process of collection, sentences from the Bible, Fathers, or writers of antiquity would be copied (sometimes in altered form) without attribution, an important step in the proverbialization of a quotation. Third, students would be inculcated with the idea of the proverb, in Latin and the vernacular, as a form of wisdom literature, and would continue to employ this form throughout their lives. Finally, the translation and transcription of proverbs in monastic schoolrooms effected cross-fertilization between the Latin and vernacular proverbial corpora, and between different national traditions.[12]

The movement of proverbs across boundaries of language and culture has ramifications for the study of analogues to *Beowulf*, and deserves more detailed consideration. In one sense, this free exchange inhibits precision in ascertaining the distribution of a medieval proverb, or even its language of origin. For example, an Anglo-Saxon vernacular proverb might form part of a dictation exercise in an English school, be entered into a proverb collection in its translated, Latin form, be

---

[10] On proverbs in the curriculum, see Friedrich Seiler, *Deutsche Sprichwörterkunde*, 77–79; Walther, 1.xiii; and Max Manitius, *Geschichte der lateinischen Literatur des Mittelalters*, 3 vols. (Munich: Beck, 1911–31), 1.255.

[11] Seiler, 77.

[12] See Manitius, 3.714, and Seiler, 80.

carried to Saxony as a curricular tool, and perhaps even be retranslated and enter the German proverbial repertoire. When we consider how often a scenario such as this might have been played out across medieval Europe, it becomes imperative to include sentences from Latin and various European vernaculars in our search for the proverbs that may have influenced the *Beowulf*-poet or any other author.

The type of proverb collection discussed above reflects an intellectual milieu which favored the learning and repetition of wise sentences, a practice that is frequently ascribed to oral, traditional cultures but which seems to have been exercised also by medieval purveyors of Latin learning. This same predeliction for organizing knowledge in small, easily-memorized, and repeatable chunks contributed to the proliferation of florilegia throughout the entire Middle Ages. Like proverb collections, from which they are sometimes barely distinguishable, florilegia played an important role in the creation and dissemination of proverbs and *sententiae*; they also constitute an indispensable resource for the reconstruction of the medieval proverbial corpus.

Florilegia differ from medieval proverb collections in only two basic aspects: they may contain passages longer than a single sentence, and these passages are more frequently, though not invariably, provided with source attributions. While individual florilegia may vary in their scope and purposes, certain principles of selection, as described by H.-M. Rochais, seem to apply universally: "ils recueillent avec prédilection les phrases bien frappés, les sentences paradoxales, les affirmations nettes, les mots à l'emporte-pièce, susceptibles de se graver profondément dans la memoire."[13] Memory served both the user and the compiler of a florilegium, for if the completed work assisted the reader in memorizing useful statements of doctrine, morals, and ethics, some of those statements themselves appeared in the work by virtue of having been previously memorized by the compiler. While most *flores* were excerpted and copied from one manuscript directly to another, some proportion of them underwent an intermediate stage in the memory of the compiler. Single sentences were most likely to move from the memory to the page in this way, and hence to be misremembered or misattributed. The roles of memory and felicitous wording in the compilation and use of florilegia highlight the close relationship of this genre to that of the medieval proverb collection, and even to the

---

[13] Henri-Marie Rochais, "Florilèges spirituels latins," in *Dictionnaire de Spiritualité, ascétique et mystique doctrine et histoire* (Paris: Beauchesne, 1964), vol. 5, col. 458.

process of proverb creation more generally. Once a sentence has been excerpted from a larger work, it has been decontextualized; when its source has been forgotten, the sentence (given appropriate form) becomes a *sententia*; with frequent repetition, it becomes a proverb. We need not be distracted by the circumstance that certain stages of this process, in fact, the only stages we can trace, took place in written, rather than oral communication.

Because florilegia provided a conduit through which excerpts from many different works, some rarely available in their entirety, reached a wider audience, they allow us to broaden our search for analogues to the *sententiae* of *Beowulf*. One would hesitate to ascribe to the *Beowulf*-poet a detailed knowledge of Seneca, Tacitus, and Virgil, or of the complete works of Augustine, but the transmission of *sententiae* from these and other authors through florilegia brings them within the possible range of influences on the poet.[14] However, there are limits to the potential usefulness of florilegia, limits (and advantages) which can be outlined through some general observations on the contents of these collections, and on their intended audiences.

The unmanageably large number of surviving (and lost) florilegia has precluded any comprehensive cataloguing of their contents, but certain trends may nonetheless be noted. In collections from the eighth and ninth centuries, including those of Defensor, Halitgar, Emmo, Hadoard, Sedulius Scottus, and Mico of St-Riquier, patristic authors appear most frequently, especially Augustine, Isidore, and Gregory the Great. Classical authors are led by Cicero, Horace, and Virgil, because many of their moral statements remained congenial to Christian compilers, but other excerpted writers include Macrobius, Seneca, and Valerius Maximus.[15] Pagan sentences might require an apologia or editorial adjustment,[16] but through the Carolingian Age and into the tenth

---

[14] Pierre Riché would attribute the ability of even such learned scholars as Aldhelm and Bede to cite ancient authors to the use of anthologies and florilegia; see *Éducation et culture*, 524.

[15] For brief descriptions of the florilegia considered here, see *Dictionnaire de spiritualité*, 5.440–43, 465, and *Florilegium Morale Oxoniense, Ms. Bodl. 633*, ed. C. H. Talbot, Analecta Mediaevalia Namurcensia 6 (Louvain: Édit. Nauwelaerts; Lille: Librairie Giard, 1956), 9–13.

[16] As noted by Rosamond McKitterick, *The Frankish Church and the Carolingian Reforms, 789–895*, Royal Historical Society Studies in History (London: Royal Historical Society, 1977), 163; see also Anders Gagnér, *Florilegium Gallicum: Untersuchungen und Texte zur Geschichte der mittellateinischen Florilegienliteratur* (Lund: Håkon Ohlsson, 1936), 24.

century, the compilers of florilegia continued to transmit classical *sententiae*. By the eleventh century, however, pedagogical favor had turned away from the classics and more exclusively towards Scripture as a source of moral pronouncements.[17] The period during which classical *sententiae* accompanied those from the Bible and Fathers in many florilegia—that is, the eighth through the tenth centuries—is also the period within which any acceptable dating of *Beowulf* must fall. Hence, it is reasonable to consider that the *Beowulf*-poet could have absorbed classical *sententiae* either from the florilegia themselves, or from the proverbs that such widely-used collections would inevitably spawn.

Two florilegia deserve special mention with relation to *Beowulf*: Defensor's *Liber scintillarum*, from the last years of the seventh century, and Sedulius Scottus' ninth-century *Collectaneum miscellaneum*. As indicated by the frequency with which I have had recourse to them in chapters two through five above, these two collections have provided the largest number of florilegial analogues to *Beowulf*. The content of the *Liber scintillarum*, which was certainly known in Anglo-Saxon England, as in nearly the entirety of Western Europe, is notable for its distribution of Scriptural material. Defensor makes unusually light use of the New Testament and Psalms, concentrating instead on *sententiae* from the books of Proverbs and Ecclesiasticus.[18] Such *Beowulf*ian *sententiae* as seem biblically based derive mainly from the psalter, but Ecclesiasticus also makes a strong showing; could the *Beowulf*-poet have been influenced by Defensor, or do the two authors perhaps display a shared appreciation for the sentential wisdom of *Iesus filius Sirach*? The question is probably unanswerable, but Defensor's popularity may tip the scales slightly in his favor.

The case of Sedulius is somewhat more complicated, and involves the transmission of classical as well as Christian *sententiae*. While it is tempting to look to Sedulius as a source of sentences from Seneca, Cicero, and Virgil, the possibility of direct influence on the *Beowulf*-poet is small, because of the *Collectaneum*'s ninth-century date and limited manuscript tradition. There is no firm evidence that Sedulius's *Collectaneum* was known to the Anglo-Saxons, but there is, on the

---

[17] This is the stance adopted by Egbert of Liège and Wipo; see also Talbot, *Flor. mor.*, 13–14.

[18] H.-M. Rochais, "Contribution à l'histoire des florilèges ascétiques du haut moyen age latin: le 'Liber scintillarum'," *Revue bénédictine* 63 (1953): 278–79.

other hand, some correspondence between his intellectual sources and theirs. Dean Simpson points out that "Many sections of the *Collectaneum* would seem to relate specifically to insular Latin scholarship," providing the examples that "Section LXXXIV contains material which parallels statements in the *De Locis Sanctis* of Bede and Adamnán, and the insular *De ordine Creaturarum* of Ps. Isidore. Section III . . . may be attributed to an Irish author on linguistic grounds."[19] Thus, the *Collectaneum miscellaneum* offers a fair example of the types of *sententiae* that would have circulated in an insular context, and becomes more valuable as a source of analogues to *Beowulf*. The influence of Irish scholarship on Anglo-Saxon thought needs no defense, although one might note here that Irish florilegia enjoyed frequent use by Anglo-Saxon homilists,[20] and that the circulation of the moral sentences they contained was thereby increased.

The use of florilegia in medieval schools was similar to, and as widespread as, the use of proverb collections. Patristic and biblical florilegia were valued primarily for their content, and while ethical considerations provided one principle of selection in creating classical florilegia,[21] quotations in the latter were often chosen based on their prosodic form. These prosodic florilegia were fairly common in the Carolingian period, and as B. Munk Olsen has pointed out, enjoyed an influence even more substantial than their numbers would indicate, because the student was supposed to learn them by heart.[22] Although the purpose of this memorization was to enhance the student's grasp of metrical forms, the content of the verses would of course be learned at the same time.

The schoolroom was not the only place in which florilegia were found useful, at least on the Continent. According to Rosamond McKitterick, ninth-century Frankish decrees and statutes recommended that each priest have a set of canons or *sententiae*, excerpted from the

---

[19] *Collectaneum Miscellaneum*, ed. Simpson, CCCM 67, pp. xxix-xxx.

[20] See Charles D. Wright, "The Irish 'Enumerative Style' in Old English Homiletic Literature, Especially Vercelli Homily IX," *Cambridge Medieval Celtic Studies* 18 (1989): 27–74, and Joan Turville-Petre, "Translations of a Lost Penitential Homily," *Traditio* 19 (1963): 62.

[21] McKitterick, *Frankish Church*, 161–62.

[22] Birger Munk Olsen, "Les florilèges d'auteurs classiques," in *Les genres littéraires dans les sources théologiques et philosophiques médiévales: définition, critique et exploitation*, Publications de l'institut d'études médiévales, 2nd series, vol. 5 (Louvain: Université catholique de Louvain, 1982), 157.

Fathers, in order to instruct himself and his flock about the virtues and vices.[23] Elsewhere, McKitterick argues strongly for widespread lay literacy in Carolingian Europe, and notes that the Christian florilegia of that period "were addressed, almost without exception, to laymen or laywomen and provided their addressees with definitions and expositions of the Christian ethic and the social behavior expected in accordance with it."[24] McKitterick's estimation of the extent of lay literacy on the Continent may be open to doubt, and the relevance of her findings to Anglo-Saxon England is certainly a question that needs to be considered, but the dedications of the florilegia she examines are a matter of record. If, as H.-M. Rochais infers, the eleventh-century glosses to Defensor's *Liber scintillarum* indicate the use of that text by a public unlearned in Latin,[25] we may assume some lay use of florilegia in England as well. In any case, it seems safe to conclude that at least the Christian florilegia served as a conduit for the transmission of *sententiae* from the milieux of the monasteries and schools to a wider public. The florilegium as a form may also have influenced ways of thinking about and employing expressions of received wisdom. As quoted above, McKitterick has described Carolingian florilegia as defining an ethic and prescribing the social behavior required by that ethic; the same could be said of the *sententiae* of *Beowulf*.

Medieval proverb collections and florilegia often contained, alongside other materials, quotations and adaptations of *sententiae* from the Bible. I have not hesitated to adduce biblical analogues to *Beowulf* where I thought they were relevant. If I were treating nearly any other Old English text, the relevance of these analogues could be taken for granted, but because the potential Christian influence on *Beowulf* has occasioned so much argument, it is perhaps necessary here to provide some overview of the Bible as a source of medieval proverbs and sentences. A complete survey of the transmission and influence of the Bible among the Anglo-Saxons is, of course, far beyond my scope and competence, so I will address only those questions that apply to the proverbialization of biblical *sententiae*: what biblical material was available (outside of the florilegia and collectanea, which I have already discussed above), to whom was it available, and what use was made of it?

---

[23] McKitterick, *Frankish Church*, 160–61.

[24] Rosamond McKitterick, *The Carolingians and the Written Word* (Cambridge: Cambridge Univ. Press, 1989), 266.

[25] Rochais, "Contribution," 270.

As Helmut Gneuss has demonstrated, Bibles represented the most important holdings of Anglo-Saxon libraries, even if complete texts were rare.[26] An examination of Michael Lapidge's edition of surviving Anglo-Saxon booklists reveals that the Book of Psalms appears most frequently in the thirteen lists (eleven times), outpacing even the Gospels (ten appearances). The proportions are reversed for the subjects of biblical commentaries, of which six treat the Book of Psalms (or some part thereof), and seven explicate one or more of the Gospels.[27] The prominence of the psalter in these lists reflects its importance in early-medieval education and worship, and supports my observation that the deistic *sententiae* of *Beowulf* may in some cases reflect circulating proverbs based on psalms. I have already described the ubiquity of the psalms in the medieval educational process,[28] but we might consider here who the recipients of that education were; in other words, whether there are grounds for assuming familiarity with the psalter by the laity as well as the clergy.

Little is known about private devotions among lay Anglo-Saxons, but the psalter seems likely to have figured prominently, as on the Continent.[29] Bede describes how even lay followers of St. Aidan were required to learn the Psalms or meditate on Scripture,[30] habits that would be inculcated more widely through the practice of educating the children of the lay nobility in monasteries rather than in private tutelage.[31] The Psalms also held a prominent place in the Divine Of-

---

[26] Helmut Gneuss, "Anglo-Saxon Libraries from the Conversion to the Benedictine Reform," in *Angli e Sassoni al di qua e al di là del mare*, Settimane di Studio del Centro Italiano di Studi sull'Alto Medioevo 32 (Spoleto: Centro Italiano, 1986), part 2, p. 662.

[27] Michael Lapidge, "Surviving booklists from Anglo-Saxon England," in *Learning and Literature in Anglo-Saxon England: Studies Presented to Peter Clemoes on the Occasion of his Sixty-Fifth Birthday*, ed. Michael Lapidge and Helmut Gneuss (Cambridge: Cambridge Univ. Press, 1985), 84–89; I have excluded from consideration those items listed only as commentaries or *questiones* on the Old and New Testaments, and items listed as *homiliae*. For descriptions of surviving psalters containing Old English, see Minnie Cate Morrell, *A Manual of Old English Biblical Materials* (Knoxville: Univ. of Tennessee Press, 1965), 45–153.

[28] Pages 36–37, above.

[29] See Thomas H. Bestul, "Continental Sources of Anglo-Saxon Devotional Writing," in *Sources of Anglo-Saxon Culture*, ed. Paul E. Szarmach with Virginia Darrow Oggins, Studies in Medieval Culture 20 (Kalamazoo: Medieval Institute Publications, 1986), 103–26.

[30] *Hist. Eccl.* 3.5; noted by Riché, *Éducation*, 365.

[31] Riché, *Éducation*, 370.

fice, and in fact, nearly all surviving Anglo-Saxon psalters are divided for liturgical use.[32] The exact form of the Divine Office used in Anglo-Saxon England remains uncertain, as does the extent to which the Office influenced lay worship, but, as Patricia Hollahan has pointed out, "Laymen ... would hear the psalms at least at Mass and in homilies, probably hearing at least some psalms often enough to recognize them."[33] Such exposure to the psalms required neither monastic education nor literacy.

Not only the availability of biblical text, but also attitudes towards that text affected the proverbialization of Scripture. The most accomplished scholars of the early Middle Ages might undertake textual and theological studies, but for the rest, and for the laity, the primary lessons of the Bible were moral.[34] As Walter Ullmann describes Frankish society, "The Bible was credited with the status of a textbook containing all the relevant maxims, axioms and norms relative to (private and) public life."[35] There is little reason to doubt that a similar view prevailed among the Anglo-Saxons, particularly during the early part of the period, when Frankish influence was substantial.[36] Under such circumstances, it would be surprising indeed if the Bible, a shared provider of Christian cultural values, did not also provide the material for the encapsulated expression of those values, that is, for proverbs. A poet such as that of *Beowulf* could employ those proverbs in perfect confidence that their burden would be accepted and endorsed by his audience, even if the exact source of the *sententiae* remained unrecognized.

Another convenient vehicle for the dissemination of ethical/moral *sententiae* would be, of course, the homily or sermon. However, as such texts have proven of small help in locating analogues to *Beowulf*, I will limit myself to a few general comments about them.[37] Through at

---

[32] Morrell, 46; for a list of 27 such psalters, see Helmut Gneuss, "Liturgical Books in Anglo-Saxon England and their Old English Terminology," in *Learning and Literature in Anglo-Saxon England*, ed. Lapidge and Gneuss, 114–16.

[33] Patricia Hollahan, *The Anglo-Saxon Use of the Psalms: Liturgical Background and Poetic Use* (Ph.D. diss., Univ. of Illinois, 1977), 32.

[34] Riché, *Éducation*, 527.

[35] Walter Ullmann, *The Carolingian Renaissance and the Idea of Kingship: The Birkbeck Lectures 1968–9* (London: Methuen, 1969), 18.

[36] On Frankish influence, see Riché, *Éducation*, 381, 415–17; Gneuss, "Anglo-Saxon Libraries," 659; and Patrick Sims-Williams, *Religion and Literature in Western England, 600–800*, Cambridge Studies in Anglo-Saxon England 3 (Cambridge: Cambridge Univ. Press, 1990), 110–13.

[37] My failure to locate significant, sentential analogues to *Beowulf* in Anglo-

least the eighth century, sermons concentrated on moral topics, and represented the most effective means of transmitting Christian doctrine and morality to a lay public.[38] At the same time, then, they would serve as conduits for the transmission of *sententiae* from a clerical to a wider public, and even for the translation of proverbs and sentences from Latin to the vernacular. Early-medieval preachers set great store by the effectiveness of sentential expressions, often favoring the sapiential books of the Bible[39] and making use of topically-arranged proverb collections.[40] Certainly, a comprehensive study of proverbs and *sententiae* in Anglo-Saxon sermons, and in their sources, remains a scholarly desideratum.

In rhetorical theory outside the sphere of preaching, *sententiae* enjoy only small significance. In his exposition of rhetorical terminology, Isidore of Seville mentions the *sententia* twice, defining it both times as a "dictum inpersonale" and distinguishing it from the *chria*, which is essentially a *sententia* with reference to specific persons added.[41] Isidore goes on to list more than twenty types of *sententiae* (e.g., indicative, comparative, interrogative, concessive), offering illustrative examples chiefly from Virgil, but he provides only very brief and infrequent instructions for the proper deployment of these types.[42] Isidore's primary interest is taxonomic.

The author of the *Rhetorica ad Herennium* offers a definition of the *sententia* that concentrates less on form, and more on origin and function: "Sententia est oratio sumpta de vita, quae aut quid sit aut quid esse oporteat in vita, breviter ostendit"[43] [A *sententia* is an expression taken from life, which briefly shows what happens or what ought to happen in life]. Several aspects of the pseudo-Ciceronian rhetorician's treatment of *sententiae* remind one of sentential statements

---

Saxon homiletic literature may result as much from the insufficiently indexed state of that corpus as from any real lack of correspondence.

[38] Ullmann, 36; Riché, *Éducation*, 541.

[39] Riché, *Éducation*, 541.

[40] Walther, 1.xv.

[41] *Isidori Hispalensis episcopi Etymologiarum sive originum*, ed. W. M. Lindsay, 2 vols. (Oxford: Clarendon Press, 1911), 2.11.1 and 2.21.4.

[42] E.g., "Aliae superlativae, quae cum aliquo motu animi et indignatione promuntur" (*Etym.* 2.21.16); for the complete list of *species sententiarum*, see *Etym.* 2.21.15–25.

[43] *Cornifici Rhetorica ad C. Herennium*, ed. Gualtiero Calboli, Edizioni e Saggi Universitari de Filologia Classica 11 (Bologna: Riccardo Pàtron, 1969), 4.16–24 (p. 170).

in *Beowulf*, from the inclusion of both descriptive and prescriptive *sententiae* in his definition, to the example texts he offers. Of the first five illustrative *sententiae*, three use the same demonstrative plus relative pronoun construction found so often in *Beowulf* (as "se þe"):

> Non solet *is* potissimum virtutes revereri, *qui* semper secunda fortuna sit usus

> [He is not wont to revere the virtues, who has always enjoyed the favors of fortune]

> Liber *is* est existimandus, *qui* nulli turpitudini servit

> [He is to be judged free, who serves no bad habit]

> Egens aeque est *is*, *qui* non satis habet, et *is*, *cui* satis nihil potest esse[44]

> [Equally poor are he who has not enough, and he to whom nothing can be enough].   (emphasis added)

I would hesitate to propose any influence of Latin syntax on that of *Beowulf*, particularly influence through a text like the *Rhetorica ad Herennium*, which was popular on the Continent but not necessarily known to the Anglo-Saxons; however, such syntactic congruence between Latin and vernacular *sententiae* would certainly facilitate the translation of proverbs and sentences from one language into the other, and may even mark those cases where translation has taken place.[45] Like Isidore, pseudo-Cicero offers little in the way of specific instructions for the deployment of *sententiae*, noting only that they may be prized for their brevity but should be used sparingly.[46] Quintilian discusses the issue at some length, condemning roundly the excessive use of *sententiae* and epigrams, but allowing their appearance, in moderation, as an effective ornament.[47] The major rhetoricians, then, provided little guidance for the proper use of *sententiae*, leaving the matter

---

[44] *Rhet. ad Her.* 4.16.24 (pp. 170–71; editorial brackets and italics have been removed).

[45] Although such syntactic evidence can be used only in addition to the location of close analogues.

[46] *Rhet. ad Her.* 4.16.24, 25 (p. 171).

[47] Quintilian *Institutio Oratoria*, ed. and trans. H. E. Butler, 4 vols., Loeb Classical Library (London: William Heinemann; New York: G. P. Putnam's Sons, 1921), 8.5.25–34 (vol. 3, pp. 294–99).

to the discretion of the writer or speaker;[48] thus, Latin rhetorical theory can hardly have affected the use of proverbs and *sententiae* in vernacular poetry.

Some years ago, Joseph Harris described *Beowulf* as a *summa litterarum*, an anthology of generic types in a work representing the culminating literary achievement of its age.[49] We may consider the *sententiae* of *Beowulf* as one component of this *summa*,[50] especially if we can postulate that the poet recognized the *sententia* as a discrete form and manipulated it consciously. I have offered internal evidence to support this view—viz., the poet's use of proverbial markers to transform non-proverbial utterances—but we might also look outside the poem to gain some idea about medieval perceptions of proverbial material in a narrative setting. The twelfth-century poem *Ysengrimus* provides an instructive parallel. Like *Beowulf*, the *Ysengrimus* is a long narrative poem based on a recognizable literary type (the animal tale *versus* the heroic legend), but which also draws from a large number of ancillary genres and sources. Again like *Beowulf*, the *Ysengrimus* incorporates a large number of proverbs and *sententiae*.[51] Differences between the two works abound, of course, even when we consider only those differences that impinge on the use of proverbial material: the *Ysengrimus* is Latin, learned, and satirical; *Beowulf* is none of these things. Nevertheless, we may perceive in the medieval reception of the *Ysengrimus* an appreciation of sentential matter that far outstrips any such sentiment I have postulated for the *Beowulf*-poet or his audience. Five *Ysengrimus* manuscripts (or parts of manuscripts) survive; all five of these are provided with marginal notations marking the locations of sentential utterances.[52] Furthermore, four medieval collections of

---

[48] This is also the conclusion reached by James J. Murphy, *Rhetoric in the Middle Ages: A History of Rhetorical Theory from Saint Augustine to the Renaissance* (Berkeley: Univ. of California Press, 1974), 233. Murphy does point out (234) that proverbs were recommended as epistolary exordia, but he is speaking of the high- to late-Middle Ages.

[49] Joseph Harris, "*Beowulf* in Literary History," *Pacific Coast Philology* 17 (1982): 16–23; repr. in *Interpretations of Beowulf: A Critical Anthology*, ed. R. D. Fulk (Bloomington: Indiana Univ. Press, 1991), 235–41.

[50] Harris himself mentions "gnomic verse" as one oral genre included in *Beowulf* ("*Beowulf* in Literary History," 236).

[51] These have been studied by Jill Mann, "Proverbial Wisdom in the *Ysengrimus*," *New Literary History* 16 (1984): 93–109; see also her edition of the poem.

[52] Mann, "Proverbial Wisdom," 96–97.

sententiae excerpted from the *Ysengrimus* also survive.[53] Obviously, some medieval readers at least valued this narrative poem as a source of proverbs and *sententiae*. The Latinity of the *Ysengrimus* makes it more likely than in the case of *Beowulf* that sentential recognition served some pedagogical function, but the scribal criteria for marking sentential passages in the Latin poem confirm, as far as is possible, my sense that both poets and audiences could recognize and respond to embedded *sententiae*. For, as Jill Mann has described, the annotaters and anthologizers of the *Ysengrimus* seem to have been affected more by the proverbial *form* of an utterance than by its content.[54] The authority (or lack of authority) of the speaker, the sense (or lack of sense) of the proverb make no difference at all to the excerpters, who mark passages, for whatever ultimate reason, based on their sentential, that is, generalized, form. The primacy of generalized expression in the medieval perception of proverbs is further supported by the wider practice of proverbializing a citation from a Latin author by replacing a specific term with a more general one.[55] In such excerpting and reworking of sentential or potentially sentential passages from the *Ysengrimus* and other narrative poems, we see the obverse of the *Beowulf*ian coin.

The thematic and structural uses of *sententiae* within a narrative work are more difficult to discuss from a comparative viewpoint, because each author will take an idiosyncratic approach to their deployment. It is perhaps best, then, to conclude with some general observations on the many and subtle uses to which the *Beowulf*-poet puts his *sententiae*. They can serve a simply explanatory or summary function, aid in characterization, create transitions between narrative episodes or between narrative and non-narrative passages (either in an introductory or closing role); they effect thematic continuity and structuring, and direct the response of the audience to the descriptions and actions related in the poem. The *sententiae* of *Beowulf* reflect both aspects of what Roger Abrahams has termed "active" and "passive" proverb use. In the former, proverbs refer to present events and suggest a strategy for responding to those events; an example of such use is Beowulf's answer to the news of Æschere's murder: "It is better to avenge a friend than to mourn him." Proverbs in passive use, on the other hand, refer to past events; they present an evaluation of these events or a

---

[53] Ibid.

[54] Mann, "Proverbial Wisdom," 104.

[55] See Walther, 1.xiv.

model for understanding them, and shape the hearer's "orientation toward similar events in the future."[56] This paradigm fairly describes what I have called the "exemplum/proverb" relationship in *Beowulf*, whereby a sentence is appended to a narrative episode in order to extrapolate a general lesson from that episode.

The relationship between an exemplum or fable and its attendant proverb has perhaps been described best by Roland Richter, who explains that the fable demonstrates the general assertion of the proverb in a specific, concrete action. This action, although fictitious, recalls a piece of real life, thereby becoming a symbolic representation of the reader's own experience. According to Richter, the difference between a proverb and fable is that the former provides the *result* of experience, whereas the latter shows an *example* of experience and may either draw a conclusion itself or allow the reader to do so.[57] In *Beowulf*, this fable (exemplum)/proverb dialectic may be employed mainly for the instruction of one character by another (as in Hrothgar's sermon), or by the poet for the edification of the audience.

This study has attempted to sketch the proverbial backgrounds to the *sententiae* of *Beowulf* in order to achieve a better understanding of the passages themselves, of their functions in the poem, and of the cultural background which might have influenced the *Beowulf*-poet. The most general conclusion that can be drawn is that nearly all of the sentential passages represent the reworking of known medieval proverbs and *sententiae*, and thus cannot be considered simply as self-indulgent or moralistic reflections on the part of the poet.

The analogues adduced in this study shed little or no light on the question of "learned" or "popular" origins for the *sententiae* of *Beowulf*. The deistic sentences of the poem seem mostly to derive from the Psalms, but no certain origin can be suggested for the other classes of *sententiae*. The very nature of the evidence renders the question moot, as medieval proverbs and sentences are preserved only in written, that is, learned, form, and mostly in Latin. Furthermore, some of the *sententiae* reflect such general ideas that they may represent independent creations along polygenetic lines. There is evidence, however, for

---

[56] This discussion of Abrahams' theory is taken from Fontaine, 53.

[57] Roland Richter, "Sprichwort und Fabel als dialektischer Denkvorgang," chap. 8 of his *Georg Rollenhagens Froschmeusler: Ein rhetorisches Meisterstück* (Bern and Frankfurt: Peter Lang, 1975), 113–26; repr. in *Proverbia in Fabula: Essays on the Relationship of the Proverb and the Fable*, ed. Pack Carnes, Sprichwörterforschung 10 (Bern: Peter Lang, 1988), 257. See also Fontaine, 9.

some proverbial crossover between the Latin and vernacular spheres.

Another issue is the relation between *Beowulf*ian *sententiae* and (oral) formulas. In general, the *sententiae* are too varied and of too great a length to serve any formulaic purpose in the construction of the verses, but they do themselves employ certain proverbial formulas (e.g., "swa sceal man don," "swa he nu git deð"). These formulas mark the passages as proverbial, even sometimes when they are not.

The thirty-odd passages of *Beowulf* that I have treated here are those which seem to me most likely to be themselves proverbial, or to be strongly influenced by proverbial structures and themes; the reader may judge the aptness of this perception by assessing my argument in each case. Furthermore, individual readers may think that I have omitted mention of some potentially proverbial passages of *Beowulf*; I hope to have demonstrated at least the possibility of amassing evidence for the proverbiality of such passages, and the productiveness of doing so. Finally, I hope also to have shown that proverbs performed an important function in the composition and thematic development of *Beowulf*, and constituted a significant part of the cultural discourse the poet shared with his audience. Although the modern literary aesthetic does not favor proverbs in this way, we should not overlook their role in literary production and reception among the Anglo-Saxons.

Bibliography

Abbreviations

CCCM   Corpus Christianorum, Continuatio Mediaeualis
CCSL   Corpus Christianorum, Series Latina
CSEL   Corpus Scriptorum Ecclesiasticorum Latinorum
EETS   Early English Text Society
MGH   Monumenta Germaniae Historica
PL   Patrologiae Cursus Completus, Series Latina, ed. by J.-P. Migne, 221 vols. (Paris, 1844–64)

Primary Sources

Abelard, Peter. *Monita ad Astralabium*. Edited by J.-P. Migne. PL 178, cols. 1759–62.

Albert von Stade. *Troilus*. Edited by Th. Merzdorf. Bibliotheca Scriptorum Medii Aevi Teubneriana. Leipzig: B. G. Teubner, 1875.

Alcuin. *Carmina*. In MGH *Poetae latini aevi carolini*, edited by Ernest Dümmler, 1:169–351. Berlin: Weidmannos, 1881.

——. *Commentaria super Ecclesiasten*. In *Opera omnia*, edited by J.-P. Migne. PL 100, cols. 667–722.

——. *Monastica*. In MGH *Poetae latini aevi carolini*, edited by Ernest Dümmler, 1:275–81. Berlin: Weidmannos, 1881.

Aldhelm. *Aenigmata*. Edited by Maria De Marco. In *Tatvini Opera omnia; Variae collectiones Aenigmatum merovingicae aetatis; Anon-*

ymus De dubiis nominibus. CCSL 133, pp. 359–540. Turnhout: Brepols, 1968.

———. *The Riddles of Aldhelm: Text and Verse Translation with Notes*. Edited and translated by James Hall Pitman. Yale Studies in English, 67. New Haven: Yale University Press, 1925.

Alfred the Great. *King Alfred's Version of St. Augustine's 'Soliloquies'*. Edited by Thomas A. Carnicelli. Cambridge, Mass.: Harvard University Press, 1969.

Altercatio Hadriani Augusti et Epicteti Philosophi. Edited by Lloyd William Daly and Walther Suchier. Illinois Studies in Language and Literature, vol. 24, nos. 1–2. Urbana: University of Illinois Press, 1939.

Anglo-Saxon Poetic Records. Edited by George Philip Krapp and Eliott van Kirk Dobbie. 6 vols. New York: Columbia University Press, 1931–53.

Audacht Morainn. Edited by Fergus Kelly. Dublin: Institute for Advanced Studies, 1976.

Augustine of Hippo. *De libero arbitrio libri tres*. Edited by W. M. Green. In *Aurelii Augustini Opera*, part 2.2. CCSL 29, pp. 205–321. Turnhout: Brepols, 1970.

———. *De sancta uirginitate*. In *Sancti Aureli Augustini De fide et symbolo*, etc., edited by Iosephus Zycha. CSEL 41, pp. 233–302. Vienna: Tempsky, 1900.

———. *Enarrationes in Psalmos*. Edited by D. Eligius Dekkers, O.S.B., and Johannes Fraipont. CCSL 38, 39, 40. Turnhout: Brepols, 1956.

———. "Epistolae ex duobus codicibus nuper in lucem prolatae." Edited by Johannes Divjak. CSEL 88. Vienna: Hoelder-Pichler-Tempsky, 1981.

———. *Epistulae*. Edited by Al. Goldbacher. CSEL 44, 57. Vienna: Tempsky, 1904, 1911.

———. *Retractationum libri II*. Edited by Almut Mutzenbecher. CCSL 57. Turnhout: Brepols, 1984.

———. *Sermones*. Edited by J.-P. Migne. PL 38. Paris, 1841.

Ausonius. *Opuscula*. Edited by Carolus Schenkl. MGH Auctores 5.2. Berlin: Weidmannos, 1883.

Babrius and Phaedrus. Edited and translated by Ben Edwin Perry. Loeb Classical Library, 436. Cambridge, Mass.: Harvard University Press, 1965.

Bede. *Collectio Psalterii*. In *Bedae Venerabilis Opera*, part 4: Opera rhythmica, edited by J. Fraipont. CCSL 122, pp. 452–70. Turnhout: Brepols, 1955.

——. "Homeliarum euangelii libri ii." In *Bedae Venerabilis Opera*, part 3: Opera homiletica, edited by D. Hurst, O.S.B. CCSL 122, pp. 1–378. Turnhout: Brepols, 1955.

——. *In Lucas*. In *Bedae Venerabilis Opera*, part 2.3: Opera exegetica, edited by D. Hurst, O.S.B. CCSL 120, pp. 1–425. Turnhout: Brepols, 1960.

——. *In Proverbia*. In *Bedae Venerabilis Opera*, part 2.2B: Opera exegetica, edited by D. Hurst, O.S.B., and J. E. Hudson. CCSL 119B, pp. 21–163. Turnhout: Brepols, 1983.

Beowulf. Translated by Michael Alexander. New York: Penguin Books, 1973.

Beowulf: A Dual-Language Edition. Edited and translated by Howell D. Chickering, Jr. Garden City: Anchor Books, 1977.

Beowulf and the Fight at Finnsburg. Edited by Fr. Klaeber. 3rd ed. Boston: D. C. Heath & Co., 1950.

Beowulf and the Finnesburg Fragment. Translated by John R. Clark Hall. New ed. revised by C. L. Wrenn. London: George Allen & Unwin Ltd., 1950.

Beowulf: A Verse Translation into Modern English. Translated by Edwin Morgan. Berkeley: University of California Press, 1952.

Beowulf. Heyne-Schückings Beowulf. 3 parts. 15th ed. revised by Else von Schaubert. Paderborn, 1940.

Brennu-Njáls saga. Edited by Einar Ól. Sveinsson. Íslenzk Fornrit, 12. Reykjavík: Íslenzka Fornritafélag, 1954.

Caesarius of Arles. *Sermones*. Edited by D. Germanus Morin, O.S.B. CCSL 103, 104. Turnhout: Brepols, 1953.

Carmina Burana: die Gedichte des Codex Buranus lateinisch und deutsch. Edited and translated by Carl Fischer, Hugo Kuhn, and Günter Bernt. Zurich: Artemis Verlag, 1974.

Chaucer, Geoffrey. *The Riverside Chaucer*. Edited by Larry D. Benson. 3rd ed. Boston: Houghton Mifflin Co., 1987.

Cornelius Nepos. *Vitae excellentium imperatorum*. Edited by J. Fr. Fischer. London: A. J. Valpy, 1822.

Defensor. *Liber scintillarum*. Edited by D. Henricus M. Rochais, O.S.B. In *Defensoris Liber scintillarum; Desiderii Cadurcensis Epistulae; Epistulae austrasicae aliaeque*. CCSL 117, pp. 1–307. Turnhout: Brepols, 1957.

——. *Defensor's Liber Scintillarum, with an Interlinear Anglo-Saxon Version made early in the eleventh century*. Edited by E. W. Rhodes. EETS, o.s. 93. London: EETS, 1889.

Dielitz, J., ed. *Die Wahl- und Denksprüche, Feldgeschreie, Losungen, Schlacht- und Volksrufe besonders des Mittelalters und der Neuzeit.* Frankfurt: Wilhelm Rommel, 1884.

Disticha Catonis. Edited by Marcus Boas. Amsterdam: North-Holland Publ. Co., 1952.

Disticha Catonis (OE). "The Old English Dicts of Cato." Edited by R. S. Cox. *Anglia* 90 (1972): 1–32.

"Durham Proverbs." Edited by Olof Arngart. *Speculum* 56 (1981): 288–300.

Edda. *Die Lieder der Edda.* Edited by B. Sijmons and H. Gering. 3 vols. (6 parts). Germanistische Handbibliothek, 7. Halle: Buchhandlung des Waisenhauses, 1888–1927.

Edda: Die Lieder des Codex Regius nebst verwandten Denkmälern. Edited by Gustav Neckel. 4th ed. revised by Hans Kuhn. Germanische Bibliothek. Heidelberg: Carl Winter, 1962.

Egbert of Liège. *Fecunda ratis.* Edited by Ernst Voigt. Halle: Max Niemeyer, 1889.

Ennius. *The Tragedies of Ennius: The fragments edited with an introduction and commentary.* Edited by H. D. Jocelyn. Cambridge Classical Texts and Commentaries, 10. Cambridge: Cambridge University Press, 1969.

Eraclius: deutsches und französisches Gedicht des zwölften Jahrhunderts. Edited by H. F. Massmann. Bibliothek der gesammten deutschen National-Literatur, 6. Quedlinburg: Gottfr. Basse, 1842.

Eusebius 'Gallicanus'. *Sermones extravagantes.* Edited by Fr. Glorie. CCSL 101B. Turnhout: Brepols, 1971.

Flateyjarbók: En samling af Norske Konge-Sagaer. Edited by Guðbrandur Vigfússon and C. R. Unger. 2 vols. Oslo: P. T. Malling, 1860–68.

Florilegium Frisingense. See Peregrinus.

Florilegium Gallicum: Untersuchungen und Texte zur Geschichte der mittellateinischen Florilegienliteratur. Edited by Anders Gagnér. Lund: Håkon Ohlsson, 1936.

Florilegium Morale Oxoniense, Ms. Bodl. 633: Secunda pars, Flores Auctorum. Edited by C. H. Talbot. Analecta Mediaevalia Namurcensia, 6. Louvain: Édit. Nauwelaerts; Lille: Librairie Giard, 1956.

Freidank. *Bescheidenheit.* Edited and translated by Wolfgang Spiewok. Leipzig: Philipp Reclam, 1985.

Fulgentius of Ruspe. *Epistulae.* In *Sancti Fulgentii episcopi Ruspensis Opera*, edited by J. Fraipont. CCSL 91, 91A. Turnhout: Brepols, 1968.

Genesis A: A New Edition. Edited by A. N. Doane. Madison: University of Wisconsin Press, 1978.

Gisls þáttr Illugasonar. In *Íslendinga þættir*, edited by Guðni Jónsson. Reykjavík: Sigurðar Kristjanssonar, 1945.

Gregory the Great. *Moralia in Iob.* Edited by Marcus Adriaen. CCSL 143, 143A, 143B. Turnhout: Brepols, 1979–85.

Grettis saga Ásmundarsonar. Edited by Guðni Jónsson. Íslenzk Fornrit, 7. Reykjavík: Íslenzka Fornritafélag, 1936.

Hartmann von Aue. *Iwein.* Edited by G. F. Benecke and K. Lachmann. 6th ed. Berlin: Walter de Gruyter & Co., 1959.

Hávamál. Edited by David A. H. Evans. Viking Society for Northern Research Text Series, vol. 7. London: Viking Society for Northern Research, 1986.

Heliand und Genesis. Edited by Otto Behaghel. 9th ed. revised by Burkhard Taeger. Tübingen: Max Niemeyer, 1984.

Herhold, Ludwig. *Lateinischer Wort- und Gedankenschatz.* Hannover: Hahn'schen Buchhandlung, 1887.

Isidore of Seville. *Etymologiarum sive originum libri xx.* Edited by W. M. Lindsay. 2 vols. Oxford Classical Texts. Oxford: Clarendon Press, 1911.

Jerome. *Commentarii in Isaiam.* In *S. Hieronymi presbyteri Opera*, part 1: Opera exegetica, edited by M. Adriaen. CCSL 73, 73A. Turnhout: Brepols, 1963.

——. *In Marci evangelium.* Edited by D. Germanus Morin. In *S. Hieronymi presbyteri Opera*, part 2: Opera homiletica. 2nd ed. CCSL 78, pp. 449–500. Turnhout: Brepols, 1958.

——. *In Osee.* In *S. Hieronymi presbyteri Opera*, part 1: Opera exegetica; no. 6: Commentarii in prophetas minores, edited by M. Adriaen. CCSL 76, pp. 1–158. Turnhout: Brepols, 1969.

Jezebel: A Norman Latin Poem of the Early Eleventh Century. Edited by Jan M. Ziolkowski. Humana Civilitas, 10. New York: Peter Lang, 1989.

Juvenal. *The Satires: A Text with Brief Critical Notes.* Edited by E. Courtney. Rome: Edizioni dell' Ateneo, 1984.

Lehmann, Paul, ed. *Pseudo-antike Literatur des Mittelalters.* Studien der Bibliothek Warburg, 13. Leipzig: B. G. Teubner, 1927.

Liber Sacramentorum Augustodunensis. Edited by O. Heiming, O.S.B. CCSL 159B. Turnhout: Brepols, 1984.

Liber Sacramentorum Engolismensis: Manuscrit B. N. Lat. 816, Le Sacramentaire Gélasien d'Angoulême. Edited by Patrick Saint-Roch. CCSL 159C. Turnhout: Brepols, 1987.

Liber Sacramentorum Gellonensis. Edited by A. Dumas, O.S.B. CCSL 159. Turnhout: Brepols, 1981. Introduction, Tables, and Indices in CCSL 159A, edited by J. Deshusses, O.S.B. Turnhout, 1981.

Lucan. *De bello civili.* Edited by D. R. Shackleton Bailey. Bibliotheca scriptorum Graecorum et Romanorum Teubneriana. Stuttgart: B. Teubner, 1988.

Manilius. *Astronomicon.* Edited by Franciscus Semi. Scriptorum Romanorum quae extant omnia, 224–25. Pisa: Giardini, 1975.

Margalits, Eduardus. *Florilegium proverbiorum universae latinitatis.* Budapest: Ludovicus Kókai, 1895.

Njáls saga. See *Brennu-Njáls saga.*

Olafsson, Guðmundur. *Thesaurus adagiorum linguae septentrionalis anti-quae et modernae.* Edited by Gottfrid Kallstenius. Skrifter utgivna av Vetenskaps-Societete i Lund, 12. Lund: C. W. K. Gleerup, 1930.

O'Rahilly, Thomas F., ed. *A Miscellany of Irish Proverbs.* Dublin: The Talbot Press, 1922.

Otloh. *Libellus proverbiorum.* Edited by Gulielmus Carolus Korfmach-er. Chicago: Loyola University Press, 1936.

Otto, A., ed. *Die Sprichwörter und sprichwörtlichen Redensarten der Römer.* Leipzig, 1890; repr. Hildesheim: Georg Olms, 1962.

Otto of Freising. *Ottonis et Rahewini Gesta Friderici I. Imperatoris.* Edited by G. Waitz. 2nd ed. Hannover: Hahn, 1884.

Ovid. *The Art of Love and Other Poems.* Edited and translated by J. H. Mozley. Loeb Classical Library. Cambridge, Mass.: Harvard University Press, 1947.

Peregrinus. *Florilegium Frisingense.* In *Florilegia,* edited by Albert Lehner. CCSL 108D, pp. 1–39. Turnhout: Brepols, 1987.

Plautus. *Plautus in Five Volumes.* Edited and translated by Paul Nixon. Loeb Classical Library. Cambridge, Mass.: Harvard University Press, 1966.

Proverbia communia. Edited by R. Jente. Indiana University Publications, Folklore Series, 4. Bloomington: University of Indiana Press, 1947.

Proverbia Ysengrimi. Edited by J. F. Willems. *Belgisch Museum voor de Nederduitsche Tael- und Letterkunde* 9 (1845): 238–42.

Publilius Syrus. *Sententiae.* Edited by R. A. H. Bickford-Smith. London: C. J. Clay & Sons, 1895.

Quintilian. *Institutio Oratoria.* Edited and translated by H. E. Butler. 4 vols. Loeb Classical Library. London: William Heinemann; New York: G. P. Putnam's Sons, 1921.

Rather of Verona. *Praeloquiorum libri VI*. Edited by Petrus L. D. Reid. CCCM 46A, pp. 1–196. Turnhout: Brepols, 1984.

Rhetorica ad Herennium. Cornifici Rhetorica ad C. Herennium. Edited by Gualtiero Calboli. Edizioni e Saggi Universitari de Filologia Classica, 11. Bologna: Riccardo Patron, 1969.

Saga Sverris konungs. Fornmanna sögur, 8. Copenhagen, 1834.

Saxo Grammaticus. *Gesta Danorum*. Edited by J. Olrik and H. Ræder. 3 vols. Copenhagen, 1931.

Schulze, Carl. *Die biblischen Sprichwörter der deutschen Sprache*. Göttingen, 1860. Repr. edited by Wolfgang Mieder. New York: Peter Lang, 1987.

Sedulius Scottus. *Collectaneum Miscellaneum*. Edited by Dean Simpson. CCCM 67. Turnhout: Brepols, 1988.

Seneca. *Ad Lucilium Epistulae Morales*. Edited by L. D. Reynolds. 2 vols. Oxford: Clarendon Press, 1965.

———. *Dialogorum libri duodecim*. Edited by R. D. Reynolds. Scriptorum Classicorum Bibliotheca Oxoniensis. Oxford: Clarendon Press, 1977.

———. *Tragoediae*. Edited by Otto Zwierlein. Scriptorum Classicorum Bibliotheca Oxoniensis. Oxford: Clarendon Press, 1986.

Skeat, Walter W. *Early English Proverbs: Chiefly of the Thirteenth and Fourteenth Centuries*. Oxford: Clarendon Press, 1910.

Solomon and Saturn (poetic). *The Poetical Dialogues of Solomon and Saturn*. Edited by Robert J. Menner. MLA Monograph Series, 13. New York: Modern Language Association of America; London: Oxford University Press, 1941; repr. New York, 1973.

Solomon and Saturn (prose). *The 'Prose Solomon and Saturn' and 'Adrian and Ritheus'*. Edited by James E. Cross and Thomas D. Hill. McMaster Old English Studies and Texts, 1. Toronto: University of Toronto Press, 1982.

Sutphen, Morris C. "A Further Collection of Latin Proverbs." *American Journal of Philology* 22 (1901): 241–60.

Tacitus. *Agricola*. Edited and translated by Maurice Hutton. Loeb Classical Library. Cambridge, Mass.: Harvard University Press, 1946.

Tibullus. *The Elegies of Albius Tibullus: The Corpus Tibullianum edited with introduction and notes on Books I, II, and IV, 2–14*. Edited by Kirby Flower Smith. Darmstadt: Wissenschaftliche Buchgesellschaft, 1971.

Vatnsdæla saga. Edited by Einar Ól. Sveinsson. Íslenzk Fornrit, 8. Reykjavík, 1939.

Vilhjálmsson, Bjarni, and Halldórsson, Óskar, eds. *Íslenzkir Málshættir.* Reykjavík: Almenna Bókafélagið, 1966.

Vincent of Beauvais. *De eruditione filiorum nobilium.* Edited by Arpad Steiner. Medieval Academy of America, publ. no. 32. Cambridge, Mass.: Medieval Academy of America, 1938.

Virgil. *The Works of Virgil.* Edited by John Conington, revised by Henry Nettleship. 3 vols. Hildesheim: Georg Olms, 1979.

Vitalis of Blois. *Geta.* Edited by Ferruccio Bertini. In *Commedie Latine del XII e XIII secolo.* 5 vols. Genoa: Istituto di Filologia Classica e Medievale, 1976–86.

Völsungasaga. Edited by Wilhelm Ranisch. Berlin: Mayer & Müller, 1891.

Walter of Châtillon. *Alexandreis.* Edited by Marvin L. Colker. Thesaurus Mundi: Bibliotheca scriptorum latinorum mediae et recentioris aetatis, 17. Padova: Antenore, 1978.

———. *Moralisch-satirisch Gedichte Walters von Châtillon aus deutschen, englischen, französischen und italienischen Handschriften.* Edited by Karl Strecker. Heidelberg: Carl Winter, 1929.

Walther, Hans. *Proverbia sententiaeque latinitatis medii aevi,* completed by Paul Gerhard Schmidt. Carmina Medii Aevi Posterioris Latina, part 2. Göttingen: Vandenhoeck & Ruprecht, 1963–69.

Wander, Karl Friedrich Wilhelm. *Deutsches Sprichwörter-Lexikon: Ein Hausschatz für das deutsche Volk.* 5 vols. Darmstadt: Wissenschaftliche Buchgesellschaft, 1964.

Werner, Jakob. *Lateinische Sprichwörter und Sinnsprüche des Mittelalters aus Handschriften gesammelt.* Heidelberg: Carl Winter, 1912.

Whiting, Bartlett Jere. *Modern Proverbs and Proverbial Sayings.* Cambridge, Mass.: Harvard University Press, 1989.

———, with Whiting, Helen W. *Proverbs, Sentences, and Proverbial Phrases from English Writings Mainly before 1500.* Cambridge, Mass.: Harvard University Press, 1968.

William of Tyre. *Chronicon.* Edited by R. B. C. Huygens, with H. E. Mayer and G. Rösch. CCCM 63, 63A. Turnhout: Brepols, 1986.

Wilson, F. P., ed. *The Oxford Dictionary of English Proverbs.* 3rd ed. Oxford: Clarendon Press, 1970.

Wipo. *Opera.* Edited by Harry Bresslau. 3rd ed. Leipzig: Hahnsche Buchhandlung, 1915.

Wireker, Nigel. *Speculum stultorum.* In *The Anglo-Latin Satirical Poets and Epigrammatists of the Twelfth Century,* edited by Thomas Wright. 2 vols. London, 1872.

Ysengrimus: Text with translation, commentary and introduction. Edited and translated by Jill Mann. Mittellateinische Studien und Texte, 12. Leiden: E. J. Brill, 1987.

Zingerle, Ignaz v. *Die deutschen Sprichwörter im Mittelalter.* Vienna: Wilhelm Braumüller, 1864.

Secondary Sources

Andersson, Theodore M. *Early Epic Scenery: Homer, Virgil, and the Medieval Legacy.* Ithaca: Cornell University Press, 1976.

——. "Tradition and Design in *Beowulf.*" In *Old English Literature in Context: Ten Essays,* edited by John D. Niles, 90–106. Cambridge: D. S. Brewer; Totowa, N.J.: Rowman & Littlefield, 1980.

Arora, Shirley L. "The Perception of Proverbiality." *Proverbium* 1 (1984): 1–38.

Baker, Peter. "Beowulf the Orator." *Journal of English Linguistics* 21 (1988): 3–23.

Barley, Nigel. "A Structural Approach to the Proverb and Maxim with Specific Reference to the Anglo-Saxon Corpus." *Proverbium* 20 (1972): 737–50.

Benson, Larry D. "The Pagan Coloring of *Beowulf.*" In *Old English Poetry: Fifteen Essays,* edited by R. P. Creed, 192–213. Providence: Brown University Press, 1967.

Bessinger, Jess B. *A Concordance to the Anglo-Saxon Poetic Records,* programmed by Philip H. Smith. Ithaca: Cornell University Press, 1978.

Bestul, Thomas H. "Continental Sources of Anglo-Saxon Devotional Writing." In *Sources of Anglo-Saxon Culture,* edited by Paul E. Szarmach with Virginia Darrow Oggins, 103–26. Studies in Medieval Culture, 20. Kalamazoo: Medieval Institute Publications, 1986.

Biggs, Frederick M., and Sandra McEntire. "Spiritual Blindness in the Old English *Maxims I,* Part I." *N&Q* n.s. 35 (1988): 11.

Blackburn, F. A. "The Christian Coloring in the *Beowulf.*" *PMLA* 12 (1897): 205–25. Repr. in *An Anthology of Beowulf Criticism,* edited by Lewis E. Nicholson, 1–21. Notre Dame: University of Notre Dame Press, 1963.

Blaise, Albert. *Le vocabulaire Latin des principaux thèmes liturgiques,* revised by Antoine Dumas, O.S.B. Turnhout: Brepols, 1966.

Bloomfield, Morton W. "Understanding Old English Poetry." *Annuale*

Mediaevale 9 (1968): 5–25. Repr. in his *Essays and Explorations: Studies in Ideas, Language, and Literature*, 58–80. Cambridge, Mass.: Harvard University Press, 1970.

Bolton, W. F. *Alcuin and 'Beowulf': An Eighth-Century View*. New Brunswick, N.J.: Rutgers University Press, 1978.

Brandl, Alois. "Beowulf-Epos und Aeneis in systematischer Vergleichung." *Archiv für das Studium der neueren Sprachen und Literaturen* 171 (1937): 161–73.

Brodeur, Arthur Gilchrist. *The Art of Beowulf*. Berkeley: University of California Press, 1959.

Burlin, Robert. "Gnomic Indirection in *Beowulf*." In *Anglo-Saxon Poetry* (John C. McGalliard festschrift), edited by L. E. Nicholson and D. W. Frese, 41–49. Notre Dame: University of Notre Dame Press, 1975.

Byock, Jesse. *Feud in the Icelandic Saga*. Berkeley: University of California Press, 1982.

Cavill, Paul. "Notes on Maxims in Old English Narrative." *N&Q*, n.s. 33 (1986): 145–48.

Chadwick, H. Munro, and N. Kershaw Chadwick. *The Growth of Literature*. Vol. 1, *The Ancient Literatures of Europe*. Cambridge: Cambridge University Press, 1932.

Comparetti, Domenico. *Vergil in the Middle Ages*. Translated by E. F. M. Benecke. London: Swan Sonnenschein & Co., 1895.

Cox, Betty S. *Cruces of Beowulf*. The Hague: Mouton, 1971.

Curtius, Ernst Robert. *European Literature and the Latin Middle Ages*. Translated by Willard R. Trask. Bollingen Series, 36. Princeton: Princeton University Press, 1973.

Durant, Jack. "The Function of Joy in *Beowulf*." *Tennessee Studies in Literature* 7 (1962): 61–69.

Fontaine, Carol R. *Traditional Sayings in the Old Testament: A Contextual Study*. Bible and Literature Series, 5. Sheffield: The Almond Press, 1982.

Frakes, Jerold C. *The Fate of Fortune in the Early Middle Ages: The Boethian Tradition*. Studien und Texte zur Geistesgeschichte des Mittelalters, 23. Leiden: E. J. Brill, 1988.

Frank, Grace. "Proverbs in Medieval Literature." *Modern Language Notes* 58 (1943): 508–15.

Glauche, Günter. *Schullektüre im Mittelalter: Entstehung und Wandlungen des Lektürekanons bis 1200 nach den Quellen dargestellt*. Münchener Beiträge zur Mediävistik und Renaissance-Forschung, 5. Munich: Arbeo-Gesellschaft, 1970.

Gneuss, Helmut. "Anglo-Saxon Libraries from the Conversion to the Benedictine Reform." In *Angli e Sassoni al di qua e al di là del mare*, part 2, 643–88. Settimane di Studio del Centro Italiano di Studi sull'Alto Medioevo, 32. Spoleto: Centro Italiano, 1986.

———. "Liturgical Books in Anglo-Saxon England and their Old English Terminology." In *Learning and Literature in Anglo-Saxon England: Studies Presented to Peter Clemoes on the Occasion of his Sixty-fifth Birthday*, edited by Michael Lapidge and Helmut Gneuss, 91–141. Cambridge: Cambridge University Press, 1985.

Goldsmith, Margaret E. *The Mode and Meaning of 'Beowulf'*. London: The Athlone Press, 1970.

Greenfield, Stanley B. "The Authenticating Voice in *Beowulf*." *Anglo-Saxon England* 5 (1976): 51–72. Repr. in *Hero and Exile: The Art of Old English Poetry*, edited by George H. Brown, 43–54. London: The Hambledon Press, 1989.

———. "Of Words and Deeds: The Coastguard's Maxim Once More." In *The Wisdom of Poetry: Essays in Early English Literature in Honor of Morton W. Bloomfield*, edited by Larry D. Benson and Siegfried Wenzel, 45–51. Kalamazoo: Medieval Institute Publications, 1982.

Haber, Tom Burns. *A Comparative Study of the Beowulf and the Aeneid*. Princeton: Princeton University Press, 1931.

Hagenlocher, Albrecht. *Schicksal im Heliand: Verwendung und Bedeutung der nominalen Bezeichnungen*. Niederdeutsche Studien, 21. Cologne: Böhlau Verlag, 1975.

Hamilton, Marie P. "The Religious Principle in *Beowulf*." *PMLA* 61 (1946): 309–31. Repr. in *An Anthology of Beowulf Criticism*, edited by Lewis E. Nicholson, 105–35. Notre Dame: University of Notre Dame Press, 1963.

Hansen, Elaine Tuttle. "*Precepts*: An Old English Instruction." *Speculum* 56 (1981): 1–16.

———. *The Solomon Complex: Reading Wisdom in Old English Poetry*. McMaster Old English Studies and Texts, 5. Toronto: University of Toronto Press, 1988.

Harris, Joseph. "*Beowulf* in Literary History." *Pacific Coast Philology* 17 (1982): 16–23. Repr. in *Interpretations of Beowulf: A Critical Anthology*, edited by R. D. Fulk, 235–41. Bloomington: Indiana University Press, 1991.

———. "'Deor' and its Refrain: Preliminaries to an Interpretation." *Traditio* 43 (1987): 23–53.

———. "Eddic Poetry." In *Old Norse-Icelandic Literature: A Critical*

Guide, edited by Carol J. Clover and John Lindow, 68–156. Islandica, 45. Ithaca: Cornell University Press, 1985.

———. "Elegy in Old English and Old Norse: A Problem in Literary History." In *The Vikings*, edited by R. T. Farrell, 157–64. London: Phillimore & Co., Ltd, 1982.

———. "Hadubrand's Lament: On the Origin and Age of Elegy in Germanic." In *Heldensage und Heldendichtung im Germanischen*, edited by Heinrich Beck, 81–114. Berlin: Walter de Gruyter, 1988.

Harris, Leslie. "The Vatic Mode in *Beowulf*." *Neophilologus* 74 (1990): 591–600.

Henry, P. L. *The Early English and Celtic Lyric*. London: George Allen & Unwin Ltd, 1966.

Heusler, Andreas. "Sprichwörter in den eddischen Sittengedichten." *Zeitschrift des Vereins für Volkskunde* 25 (1915): 108–15; 26 (1915): 42–57. Repr. in *Kleine Schriften, II*, 292–313. Berlin: de Gruyter, 1969.

Hill, Thomas D. "Notes on the Old English 'Maxims' I and II." *Notes and Queries* 215 (1970): 445–47.

Hollahan, Patricia. "The Anglo-Saxon Use of the Psalms: Liturgical Background and Poetic Use." Ph.D. diss., University of Illinois, 1977.

Hoops, Johannes. *Kommentar zum Beowulf*. Heidelberg: Carl Winter, 1932.

Howe, Nicholas. *The Old English Catalogue Poems*. Anglistica, 23. Copenhagen: Rosenkilde and Bagger, 1985.

Hunter Blair, Peter. "From Bede to Alcuin." In *Famulus Christi: Essays in Commemoration of the Thirteenth Centenary of the Birth of the Venerable Bede*, edited by Gerald Bonner, 239–60. London: S.P.C.K., 1976.

Karkov, Catherine, and Robert Farrell. "The Gnomic Passages of *Beowulf*." *Neuphilologische Mitteilungen* 91 (1990): 295–310.

Kaske, Robert E. "The Coastwarden's Maxim in *Beowulf*: A Clarification." *N&Q* n.s. 31 (1984): 16–18.

———. "*Sapientia et Fortitudo* as the Controlling Theme of *Beowulf*." *Studies in Philology* 55 (1958): 423–57. Repr. in *An Anthology of Beowulf Criticism*, edited by Lewis E. Nicholson, 269–310. Notre Dame: University of Notre Dame Press, 1963.

Klaeber, Fr. "Aeneis und Beowulf." *Archiv für das Studium der neueren Sprachen und Literaturen* 126 (1911): 40–48, 339–59.

———. "Die christliche Elemente im *Beowulf*." *Anglia* 35 (1911–12): 111–36, 249–70, 453–82; 36 (1912): 169–99.

Köhne, Roland. "Zur Mittelalterlichkeit der eddischen Spruchdichtung." *Beiträge zur Geschichte der deutschen Sprache und Literatur*
(Tübingen) 105 (1983): 380–417.

Krikmann, Arvo. "On Denotative Indefiniteness of Proverbs." *Proverbium* 1 (1984): 47–91.

Lapidge, Michael. "Surviving booklists from Anglo-Saxon England." In
*Learning and Literature in Anglo-Saxon England: Studies Presented to
Peter Clemoes on the Occasion of his Sixty-Fifth Birthday*, edited by
Michael Lapidge and Helmut Gneuss, 33–89. Cambridge: Cambridge
University Press, 1985.

Larrington, Carolyne. "*Hávamál* and Sources outside Scandinavia."
Saga-Book of the Viking Society for Northern Research 23 (1992): 141–
57.

Leyerle, John. "Beowulf the Hero and the King." *Medium Ævum* 34
(1965): 89–102.

Mackie, W. S. "Notes upon the Text and the Interpretation of 'Beowulf'." *Modern Language Review* 34 (1939): 515–24.

Malone, Kemp. "Beowulf." *English Studies* 29 (1948): 161–72. Repr. in
An Anthology of Beowulf Criticism, edited by Lewis E. Nicholson,
137–54. Notre Dame: University of Notre Dame Press, 1963.

———. "Words of Wisdom in *Beowulf*." In *Humaniora: Essays in Literature, Folklore, Bibliography, honoring Archer Taylor*, 180–94. Locust
Valley, N.Y.: J. J. Augustin, 1960.

Manitius, Max. *Geschichte der lateinischen Literatur des Mittelalters*. 3
vols. Munich: Beck, 1911–31.

Mann, Jill. "Proverbial Wisdom in the *Ysengrimus*." *New Literary
History* 16 (1984): 93–109.

McKitterick, Rosamond. *The Carolingians and the Written Word*.
Cambridge: Cambridge University Press, 1989.

———. *The Frankish Church and the Carolingian Reforms, 789–895*. Royal
Historical Society Studies in History. London: Royal Historical
Society, 1977.

Mitchell, Bruce. *Old English Syntax*. 2 vols. Oxford: Clarendon Press,
1985.

———. *On Old English: Selected Papers*. Oxford: Basil Blackwell, 1988.

Morrell, Minnie Cate. *A Manual of Old English Biblical Materials*.
Knoxville: University of Tennessee Press, 1965.

Murphy, James J. *Rhetoric in the Middle Ages: A History of Rhetorical
Theory from Saint Augustine to the Renaissance*. Berkeley: University
of California Press, 1974.

Ogilvy, J. D. A. *Books Known to the English, 597–1066*. Medieval Academy of America, publ. no. 76. Cambridge, Mass.: Medieval Academy of America, 1967.

Olsen, Birger Munk. "Les florilèges d'auteurs classiques." In *Les genres littéraires dans les sources théologiques et philosophiques médiévales: définition, critique et exploitation*, 151–64. Publications de l'institut d'études médiévales, 2nd series, vol. 5. Louvain: Université catholique de Louvain, 1982.

Pepperdene, Margaret W. "Beowulf and the Coast Guard." *English Studies* 47 (1966): 409–19.

Pipping, Rolf. "Hávamál 21 och ett par ställen hos Seneca." *Acta Philologica Scandinavica* 20 (1949): 371–75.

Reed, Carroll E. "Gnomic Verse in the Old Saxon *Heliand*." *Philological Quarterly* 30 (1951): 403–10.

Reichert, Heinrich G. *Lateinische Sentenzen: Essays*. Wiesbaden: Dieterich, 1948.

Reynolds, L. D., ed. *Texts and Transmission: A Survey of the Latin Classics*. Oxford: Clarendon Press, 1983.

Riché, Pierre. *Éducation et culture dans l'Occident barbare, VIe–VIIIe siècles*. 3rd ed. Patristica Sorbonensia, 4. Paris: Éditions du Seuil, 1962.

——. "Le Livre Psautier, livre de lecture mérovingien." *Etudes mérovingiennes, Actes des Journées de Poitiers, 1952*. Paris, 1953.

Richter, Roland. "Sprichwort und Fabel als dialektischer Denkvorgang." Chap. 8 in his *Georg Rollenhagens Froschmeusler: Ein rhetorisches Meisterstück*, 113–26. Bern: Peter Lang, 1975. Repr. in *Proverbia in Fabula: Essays on the Relationship of the Proverb and the Fable*, edited by Pack Carnes, 255–75. Bern: Peter Lang, 1988.

Rochais, Henri-Marie. "Contribution à l'histoire des florilèges ascétiques du haut moyen age latin: le 'Liber scintillarvm'." *Revue bénédictine* 63 (1953): 246–91.

——. "Florilèges spirituels latins." In *Dictionnaire de Spiritualité, ascétique et mystique doctrine et histoire*, vol. 5, cols. 435–60. Paris: Beauchesne, 1964.

Schaefer, Ursula. *Vokalität: Altenglische Dichtung zwischen Mündlichkeit und Schriftlichkeit*. ScriptOralia, 39. Tübingen: Gunter Narr Verlag, 1992.

Schrader, Richard J. "Beowulf's Obsequies and the Roman Epic." *Comparative Literature* 24 (1972): 237–59.

See, Klaus von. "Disticha Catonis und Hávamál." *Beiträge zur Ge-*

schichte der deutschen Sprache und Literatur (Tübingen), 94 (1972): 1–18.

Seiler, Friedrich. *Deutsche Sprichwörterkunde*. Munich: Beck, 1967.

Shippey, T. A. "Maxims in Old English Narrative: Literary Art or Traditional Wisdom?" In *Oral Tradition/Literary Tradition: A Symposium*, edited by Hans Bekker-Nielsen, 28–46. Odense: Odense University Press, 1977.

———. *Poems of Wisdom and Learning in Old English*. Cambridge: D. S. Brewer; Totowa, N.J.: Rowman and Littlefield, 1976.

Sims-Williams, Patrick. *Religion and Literature in Western England, 600–800*. Cambridge Studies in Anglo-Saxon England, 3. Cambridge: Cambridge University Press, 1990.

Singer, Samuel. *Sprichwörter des Mittelalters*. 3 parts. Bern: Lang, 1944–47.

Smith, Charles G. *Shakespeare's Proverb Lore: His Use of the Sententiae of Leonard Culman and Publilius Syrus*. Cambridge, Mass.: Harvard University Press, 1963.

Steiner, Arpad. "The Vernacular Proverb in Mediaeval Latin Prose." *American Journal of Philology* 65 (1944): 37–68.

Sühnel, Rudolf. "Vergil in England." In *Festschrift für Walter Hübner*, edited by Dieter Riesner and Helmut Gneuss, 122–38. Berlin: Erich Schmidt, 1964.

Tausin, Henri. *Dictionnaire des devises ecclésiastiques*. Paris: Lechevalier, 1907.

Taylor, Archer. "An Old Friend is the Best Friend." *Romance Philology* 9 (1955–56): 201–5.

———. *The Proverb*. Cambridge, Mass.: Harvard University Press, 1931.

———. "The Proverbial Formula 'Man soll ...'" *Zeitschrift für Volkskunde*, n.s. 2 (1930): 152–56.

———. "The Wisdom of Many and the Wit of One." *Swarthmore College Bulletin* 54 (1962): 4–7. Repr. in *The Wisdom of Many: Essays on the Proverb*, edited by Wolfgang Mieder and Alan Dundes, 1–6. Garland Folklore Casebooks, 1. New York: Garland Publishing, Inc., 1981.

Taylor, P. B. "Chaucer's *Cosyn to the Dede*." *Speculum* 57 (1982): 315–27.

Turville-Petre, Joan. "Translations of a Lost Penitential Homily." *Traditio* 19 (1963): 51–78.

Ullmann, Walter. *The Carolingian Renaissance and the Idea of Kingship: The Birkbeck Lectures 1968–9*. London: Methuen, 1969.

Wessén, Elias. *Hávamál: Några stilfråger*. Filologiskt arkiv, 8. Stockholm: Almqvist & Wiksell, 1959.

———. "Ordspråk och lärodikt: Några stilformer i Hávamál." In *Septentrionalia et Orientalia: Studia Bernardo Karlgren ... dedicata*, 455–73. Kungl. Vitterhets Historie och Antikvetets Akademiens handlingar, 91. Stockholm, 1959.

Whitelock, Dorothy. *The Audience of Beowulf*. 2nd ed. Oxford: Clarendon Press, 1958.

Whiting, Bartlett Jere. "The Nature of the Proverb." *Harvard Studies and Notes in Philology and Literature* 14 (1932): 273–307.

———. "The Origin of Proverb." *Harvard Studies and Notes in Philology and Literature* 13 (1931): 47–80.

———. *Proverbs in the Earlier English Drama, with Illustrations from Contemporary French Plays*. Harvard Studies in Comparative Literature, 14. Cambridge, Mass.: Harvard University Press, 1938.

Williams, Blanche Colton, ed. *Gnomic Poetry in Anglo-Saxon*. New York: Columbia University Press, 1914; repr. New York: AMS Press, 1966.

Willis, G. G. *Further Essays in Early Roman Liturgy*. Alcuin Club Collections, no. 50. London: S. P. C. K., 1968.

Wilts, Ommo. *Formprobleme Germanischer Spruchdichtung*. Ph. D. diss., Christian-Albrechts-Universität zu Kiel, 1968.

Wright, Charles D. "The Irish 'Enumerative Style' in Old English Homiletic Literature, Especially Vercelli Homily IX." *Cambridge Medieval Celtic Studies* 18 (1989): 27–74.

Wright, Herbert G. "Good and Evil; Light and Darkness; Joy and Sorrow in *Beowulf*." *Review of English Studies* 8 (1957): 1–11. Repr. in *An Anthology of Beowulf Criticism*, edited by Lewis E. Nicholson, 257–67. Notre Dame: University of Notre Dame Press, 1963.

Zappert, Georg. *Virgils Fortleben im Mittelalter*. Vienna, 1851.

Ziolkowski, Jan. "Cultural Diglossia and the Nature of Medieval Latin Literature." In *The Ballad and Oral Literature*, edited by Joseph Harris, 193–213. Harvard Studies in English, 17. Cambridge, Mass.: Harvard University Press, 1991.

Indices

A. Index to lines of Beowulf

B. *General Index*

Beowulf **and the Medieval Proverb Tradition** is a study of the sentential passages of *Beowulf*: their form, their functions in the poem, and their place within the larger corpus of medieval proverbs. The body of the book examines the *Beowulf*ian *sententiae* in context, but also, and for the first time, presents the results of an exhaustive search for analogues in Old English, Old Norse, Old Saxon, Old Irish, Middle High German, and Medieval Latin texts. These analogues (for which translations are provided) connect the *Beowulf*-poet to his contemporaries in their common use of proverbs. The book closes with a substantial bibliography and indices. *"Beowulf" and the Medieval Proverb Tradition* should prove interesting and useful to serious students of *Beowulf*, of Anglo-Saxon literary culture, and of the proverb in any period.

Susan E. Deskis is Assistant Professor of English at Northern Illinois University. She has published numerous essays on the proverbial tradition in literature.